HEALTH CARE COVERAGE
DETERMINATIONS

STATE OF HEALTH SERIES

Edited by Chris Ham, Professor of Health Policy and Management at the University of Birmingham.

Current and forthcoming titles

Noel Boaden: *Primary Care: Making Connections*
Angela Coulter and Chris Ham (eds): *The Global Challenge of Health Care Rationing*
Angela Coulter and Helen Magee (eds): *The European Patient of the Future*
Chris Ham (ed.): *Health Care Reform*
Chris Ham and Glenn Robert (eds): *Reasonable Rationing: International Experience of Priority Setting in Health Care*
Rudolf Klein, Patricia Day and Sharon Redmayne: *Managing Scarcity*
Nicholas Mays, Sally Wyke, Gill Malbon and Nick Goodwin (eds): *The Purchasing of Health Care by Primary Care Organizations*
Ruth McDonald: *Using Health Economics in Health Services*
Martin A. Powell: *Evaluating the National Health Service*
Ray Robinson and Andrea Steiner: *Managed Health Care: US Evidence and Lessons for the NHS*
Anne Rogers, Karen Hassell and Gerry Nicolaas: *Demanding Patients? Analysing the Use of Primary Care*
Marilynn M. Rosenthal: *The Incompetent Doctor: Behind Closed Doors*
Richard B. Saltman and Casten von Otter: *Planned Markets and Public Competition: Strategic Reform in Northern European Health Systems*
Richard B. Saltman and Casten von Otter: *Implementing Planned Markets in Health Care: Balancing Social and Economic Responsibility*
Richard B. Saltman, Josep Figueras and Constantino Sakellarides (eds): *Critical Challenges for Health Care Reform in Europe*
Claudia Scott: *Public and Private Roles in Health Care Systems*
Ellie Scrivens: *Accreditation: Protecting the Professional or the Consumer?*
Peter C. Smith (ed.): *Reforming Markets in Health Care: An Economic Perspective*
Kieran Walshe: *Regulating Health Care: A Prescription for Improvement*
Peter A. West: *Understanding the NHS Reforms: The Creation of Incentives?*
Charlotte Williamson: *Whose Standards? Consumer and Professional Standards in Health Care*
Bruce Wood: *Patient Power? The Politics of Patients' Associations in Britain and America*
Robin Gauld (ed.): *Comparative Health Policy in the Asia-Pacific*
Russell Mannion, Huw T.O. Davies and Martin N. Marshall (eds): *Cultures for Performance in Health Care*
Peter C. Smith, Laura Ginnelly and Mark Sculpher (eds): *Health Policy and Economics: Opportunities and Challenges*

HEALTH CARE COVERAGE DETERMINATIONS:
An International Comparative Study

Edited by
Timothy Stoltzfus Jost

Open University Press

Open University Press
McGraw-Hill Education
McGraw-Hill House
Shoppenhangers Road
Maidenhead
Berkshire
England
SL6 2QL

email: enquiries@openup.co.uk
world wide web: www.openup.co.uk

and

Two Penn Plaza, New York, NY 10121–2289, USA

First published 2005

A catalogue record of this book is available from the British Library

ISBN 0 335 21495 9 (pb) 0 335 21496 7 (hb)

Library of Congress Cataloging-in-Publication Data
CIP data applied for

Typeset by YHT Ltd, London
Printed in Great Britain by Bell & Bain Ltd, Glasgow

Dedicated to Robert L. and Crystal Willett

CONTENTS

CONTRIBUTORS

Liliana Bulfone, MBA, is a senior research fellow at the Centre for Health Economics, Monash University. She was formerly employed as an evaluator in the Commonwealth government and now has a major responsibility within the group at Monash University in the preparation of commentaries on submissions to the Pharmaceutical Benefits Advisory Committee (PBAC).

Tanisha Carino, PhD, was a recent Fulbright Scholar to the Netherlands where she was affiliated with the Institute for Technology Assessment and Department of Health Policy and Management at Erasmus University in Rotterdam. Prior to her fellowship, she served as a policy analyst for the Coverage Analysis Group in the Centers for Medicare and Medicaid Services while completing a doctorate in health policy from Johns Hopkins University.

Peter C. Coyte, PhD, is a Professor of Health Economics, the CHSRF/CIHR Health Services Chair, and the Co-Director of the Home and Community Care Evaluation and Research Centre of the Department of Health Policy, Management, and Evaluation at the University of Toronto, and the President of the Canadian Association for Health Services and Policy Research.

Colleen M. Flood, SJD, LLM, is a Canada Research Chair in Health Law and Policy, and is an Associate Professor at the Faculty of Law, University of Toronto, and at the Department of Health, Policy, Management and Evaluation, University of Toronto.

Anna García-Altés MSc, MPH, is located at the Fundación Instituto de Investigación en Servicios de Salud, and Agència de Salut Pública de Barcelona. She worked formerly at the Catalan Agency for Health Technology Assessment, at the Department of Health and Mental Hygiene of New York City, and as a consultant for the World Bank.

Stefan Greß, PhD, is an Assistant Professor at the Institute for Health Care Management at the School of Business and Economics of the University of Duisburg-Essen, Germany.

Felix Gurtner, MD, MSc, is a Scientific Collaborator at the Accident and Sickness Insurance Unit of the Swiss Federal Office of Public Health (FOPH).

Anthony Harris, MA, MSc, is an Associate Professor in Economics at the Centre for Health Economics, Monash University. He is a former member of the Economics sub-Committee of the Pharmaceutical Benefits Advisory Committee (PBAC) and manages a group at Monash that evaluate the clinical and cost effectiveness of medical technologies under contract to the Commonwealth government.

Timothy Stoltzfus Jost, JD, is the Robert Willett Family Professor of Law at the Washington and Lee University School of Law.

Eric Nauenberg, PhD, is an associate professor of health economics in the Department of Health Policy, Management, and Evaluation at the University of Toronto. He has worked in health technology assessment in Ontario and has published in health technology assessment (HTA) particularly related to cardiothoracic surgery.

Christopher Newdick, LLM, Barrister, is a reader of law at the Law School of the University of Reading, UK and a member of the Berkshire Priorities Committee.

Dea Niebuhr is PhD student at the Institute for Health Care Management at The School of Business and Economics of the University of Duisburg-Essen, Germany.

Guillaume Roduit, Lic. phil., Lic. iur., is a Scientific Collaborator at the Institute of Health Law, University of Neuchâtel.

Heinz Rothgang, PhD, is an Assistant Professor at the Centre for Social Policy Research at the University of Bremen, Germany.

Frans F.H. Rutten, PhD is Professor of Health Economics at the Erasmus University Rotterdam, where he founded the Associated Institute for Medical Technology Assessment in 1988 and was managing director in 1988–2000. He is also chairman of the Institute of Health Policy and Management. He was President of the International Health Economics Association (IHEA) in 2001/2002.

Dominique Sprumont, Lic. iur., Dr iur., is Associate Professor at the Faculties of Law of the Universities of Fribourg and Neuchâtel, Deputy Director of the Institute of Health Law, University of Neuchâtel; and a Member of the Federal Commission on the Basic Principles in the Sickness Insurance.

Jürgen Wasem, PhD, is Director of the Institute for Health Care Management at the School of Business and Economics of the University of Duisburg-Essen, Germany.

FOREWORD

The World Health Organization Report of 2000 ranked the performance of the United States health system number 37 in the world, sandwiched between Costa Rica and Slovenia. For a country whose citizens like to exclaim whenever possible, 'We're number 1,' this ranking should have caused some consternation. Yet, the WHO ranking, which used a very controversial methodology to score country performances, caused barely a ripple of interest, even among health policy analysts, much less the public at large.

Health care systems reflect country-specific political values, economic choices, culture, and tradition so why even attempt to rank or compare them? There are many possible answers to this question, but one of the simplest is that all health systems, however configured, face common challenges at an operational level. The topic of this book, medical technology, is a prime example. The potential of amazing, new technology to both improve population health and drive up health care costs is not limited by boundaries.

A number of recent studies have reaffirmed that health technology, whether pharmaceuticals, devices, implants or innovative clinical procedures, improves health, is cost-effective in aggregate, but at the same time is perhaps the leading driver of inflationary health care cost spending – in the United States and in the rest of the developed world. Surely each country has unique financial and organizational arrangements that affect its ability to decide which technologies should be approved and paid for. But all countries trying to improve the health of their population at an acceptable cost confront similar challenges in making coverage determinations about what technologies should be supported.

Tim Jost and the group of distinguished international experts who made contributions to this book have provided a valuable and ground breaking set of case studies about how coverage decisions are made in eight countries that represent a range of financing and organizational arrangements. One of the most important lessons of this comparative analysis is that what happens on the ground in the countries examined often bears little relation to *a priori* expectations based on health system stereotypes. So, for example, the United Kingdom and Canada, which together have become for many the epitome of government controlled, impersonal care, should presumably display systems of top-down, uniform coverage determinations? Actually, we learn that both countries feature devolution of decision-making on which technologies patients actually receive to regional and local authorities and, sometimes, to physicians at the bedside. In contrast, Switzerland and Germany, with social health insurance programs featuring competition among sickness funds, seek more uniform application of policies across the population, limiting local variations.

These findings do more than caution us not to make assumptions based on caricature about how complex health systems actually operate. In addition, the international case studies help inform current debates taking place in all countries grappling with the technology challenge. In recent years, in the Medicare program, the proper place for local vs. national coverage decisions has become a very contentious issue. With publication of *Health Care Coverage Determinations: An International Comparative Study*, we learn that the United States is not alone in grappling with this and many other difficult issues involved with the introduction of new technology.

We also learn how health systems review clinical evidence of effectiveness of new technology, the role of costs in coverage decisions, and how transparent to stakeholders and the public the coverage-making process is. The book is loaded with useful information on an increasingly important topic. And it provides a perfect demonstration that for increasingly challenging issues in health policy, we need all the help we can get, even if that involves learning from the experience of other countries.

Robert A. Berenson, M.D.

Senior Fellow at the Urban Institute, Washington D.C. and former Director of the Center for Health Plans and Providers of the United States Medicare program.

SERIES EDITOR'S INTRODUCTION

Health services in many developed countries have come under critical scrutiny in recent years. In part this is because of increasing expenditure, much of it funded from public sources, and the pressure this has put on governments seeking to control public spending. Also important has been the perception that resources allocated to health services are not always deployed in an optimal fashion. Thus at a time when the scope for increasing expenditure is extremely limited, there is a need to search for ways of using existing budgets more efficiently. A further concern has been the desire to ensure access to health care of various groups on an equitable basis. In some countries this has been linked to a wish to enhance patient choice and to make service providers more responsive to patients as 'consumers'.

Underlying these specific concerns are a number of more fundamental developments which have a significant bearing on the performance of health services. Three are worth highlighting. First, there are demographic changes, including the ageing population and the decline in the proportion of the population of working age. These changes will both increase the demand for health care and at the same time limit the ability of health services to respond to this demand.

Second, advances in medical science will also give rise to new demands within the health services. These advances cover a range of possibilities, including innovations in surgery, drug therapy, screening and diagnosis. The pace of innovation quickened as the end of the twentieth century approached, with significant implications for the funding and provision of services.

Third, public expectations of health services are rising as those who use services demand higher standards of care. In part, this is stimulated by developments within the health service, including the availability of new technology. More fundamentally, it stems from the emergence of a more educated and informed population, in which people are accustomed to being treated as consumers rather consumers rather than patients.

Against this background, policy makers in a number of countries are reviewing the future of health services. Those countries which have traditionally relied on a market in health care are making greater use of regulation and planning. Equally, those countries which have traditionally relied on regulation and planning are moving towards a more competitive approach. In no country is there complete satisfaction with existing methods of financing and delivery, and everywhere there is a search for new policy instruments.

The aim of this series is to contribute to debate about the future of health services through an analysis of major issues in health policy. These issues have been chosen because they are both of current interest and of enduring importance. The series is intended to be accessible to students and informed lay readers as well as to specialists working in this field. The aim is to go beyond a textbook approach to health policy analysis and to encourage authors to move debate about their issues forward. In this sense, each book presents a summary of current research and thinking, and an exploration of future policy directions.

Professor Chris Ham
Professor of Health Policy and Management at the University of Birmingham

1

METHODOLOGICAL INTRODUCTION

NEW HEALTH CARE TECHNOLOGIES: THE PRIMARY DRIVER OF HEALTH CARE COST GROWTH

All of the world's developed nations are currently struggling with the high and continually rising cost of health care.[1] This struggle manifests itself in different ways in different nations depending on how these countries structure health care financing. In the United States, which relies heavily on private insurance, it is seen in growing private health insurance premiums, higher cost-sharing for insured individuals, cutbacks in public programmes, and growth in the number of uninsured as insured individuals and families give up trying to pay unaffordable health insurance premiums. In Germany, a country with social health insurance, it is seen in proposals to restructure relationships between the payers and providers as the social insurance funds endeavour to hold the line on provider budgets, and in debate about how to allocate the burden of financing health care between employers, employees, and the state. In the United Kingdom, Canada, and other countries with tax-financed national health insurance systems it reveals itself in growing frustration with constraints on rapid access to the most modern health care and proposals to increase private expenditures on health care.

There are many reasons why the cost of health care is growing, and these vary somewhat from country to country. Most experts who have examined the problem agree, however, that the leading contributor to increases in health care costs in developed countries is the constant introduction of new health care technologies.[2]

Throughout the world, new drugs, devices, and medical procedures – 'health care technology' as we use that term in this book – are continually being developed and coming into use. Some treat conditions for which there was previously no effective treatment; some provide new options for patients who were resistant to treatment using earlier technologies; some make chronic and incurable conditions more tolerable; some improve the accuracy of diagnosis; others are simply more effective, convenient, or safe than prior technologies; while yet others are not necessarily cheaper or better, but just new.

New technologies increase health care costs for various reasons. Some technologies, like organ transplants, add to the cost of the health care system because they allow treatment of previously untreatable conditions.[3] Other technologies replace existing technologies, but cost more than those that they replace, sometimes dramatically more.[4] A classic example is low-osmolar contrast agents for radiology, which cost ten to twenty times as much as high-osmolar agents, but have a lower rate of adverse reactions and are thus more safe and comfortable to use.[5] Other new technologies may cost the same as, or perhaps even less than, previously existing technologies, but are used much more and for wider indications than the technologies they replace because they cause less pain, require shorter recuperation times, or are easier to use, or perhaps simply because they are cheaper than the earlier technology.[6] Even when the price that must be paid for diagnosing or treating a particular condition goes down when a new technology comes on line, if the condition is diagnosed or treated more often, the total cost of that condition to the health care system may increase.

New technologies also contribute to health care cost inflation indirectly as well as directly. High-tech equipment that is cost-effective when used appropriately, may nonetheless drive up costs if institutions paid on a fee-for-service basis use the equipment excessively and inappropriately in an attempt to recover their capital investment in the equipment.[7] New technologies also contribute to expanded utilization of existing health care services that are needed to support the application of the new technology.[8] When a new surgery becomes available, for example, the health care system must not only absorb the cost of the particular surgery, but also the cost of the hospitalization necessary for the surgery and of conventional pre- and post-surgical care. Finally, the development of ever more effective (but often very expensive) diagnostic and screening technologies facilitates the discovery of conditions that previously would have gone undetected, but which now must be must be treated at additional expense.[9]

Mark Pauly, an eminent American health care economist, claims that if we could simply freeze health care technology in its present state, the United States could absorb other factors that increase health care costs through general economic productivity growth, thus covering growth in the cost of public programmes without needing to raise taxes.[10] It is unlikely, however, that we would ever choose to do this. As already noted, improvements in health care technology make our lives longer, more comfortable, and more productive.[11, 12] On the other hand, we cannot indefinitely and uncontrollably increase our expenditures on health care at the cost of all of the other things in life that we need and desire.

We are, of course, accustomed to allocating our resources among the various goods and services we want. Every day we make choices to purchase some products while foregoing others, trying to maximize our utility. How much we purchase depends on our wealth (or perhaps our credit), and once that is exhausted we must stop purchasing. But health care is different. For reasons that have long been well understood, we do not, as individuals or as societies, subject health care to the normal disciplines of the market.[13] Health care is too important, and too costly, and, perhaps most importantly, too skewed in the distribution of its costs, to simply leave it up to individual purchases.[14] All developed countries, therefore, use health insurance to pool health care risk. All developed countries also have either social insurance programmes, usually funded through payroll taxes or wage-related premiums, or national health insurance, funded through general revenue taxes, to cover some populations or types of health care costs with respect to which private insurance markets fail. Most developed countries in fact cover their entire population with public health insurance, at least for some services.

Health insurance, however, be it public or private, brings with it the risk of moral hazard. It is always possible, indeed likely, that insured persons will use their insurance to purchase goods and services that they would not purchase if they had to pay for them out of pocket, even if they had the resources to do so.[15] This hazard is increased by the fact that purchasing decisions in health care are often made by health care professionals, who must prescribe or order services and must admit patients to hospital, but who often stand to profit in some way from the insured purchase.[16]

Insurers attempt to address the problem of moral hazard, and more generally attempt to control their risk and expenditures, by limiting access by insureds to health care products and services. When this is done by private insurers or managed care organizations, it is often accomplished through the use of provider incentives such as capitation or bonus or withhold arrangements; selective contracting with providers who adopt a conservative practice style; or case-by-case utilization review. Public insurers are more likely to limit access to goods and services by limiting budgets available to providers, thus slowing adoption of new technologies and forcing providers to engage in implicit rationing of scarce resources among various patients.[17]

TECHNOLOGY ASSESSMENT FOR COVERAGE POLICY: A SOLUTION TO THE COST ESCALATION PROBLEM?

Increasingly, however, both private and public insurers are seeking to limit their exposure for the costs of new health care technologies through the application of coverage policies developed through a process that relies on health technology assessment (HTA). One can trace the origins of HTA to the 1930s, when Bradford Hill laid down the principles for randomized controlled trials, or to 1972, in which year Archie Cochrane published his landmark book, *Effectiveness and Efficiency*, and the US Office of Technology Assessment (OTA) was established. Certainly its principles were well established by the mid-1970s, although the US Food and Drug Administration has been testing pharmaceuticals for efficacy using randomized controlled trials since the early 1960s.[18; 19]

HTA is used for many purposes. It is relied on, for example, to evaluate the safety and effectiveness of new health care technologies, to decide how to allocate health care research funds, and to make institutional purchasing decisions.[20] One thesis that will be explored in this book, however, is that HTA can be, and indeed is, increasingly being used in many countries to evaluate new technologies for public insurance coverage to control escalation in health care costs.

This development coincides with two other important trends in health care that have also emerged over the past two decades. The first involves attempts by public health insurance programmes to engage in priority setting.[21; 22] It has long been clear that public insurance programmes cannot provide all possible health care items and services for all of their insureds. A number of nations, including the Netherlands[23] and New Zealand,[24] have, therefore, attempted to identify 'core' service packages to cover through public insurance, leaving peripheral services to private insurance or for out-of-pocket payment. These exercises have usually involved a review of categories of services, but on occasion have focused on specific products or services. They have also tended to be sporadic rather than ongoing, and to founder when they encounter intractable technical and political difficulties.

The other development is evidence-based medicine. Beginning in the 1970s, health services research identified widely varying utilization rates for common medical procedures, not only internationally but also among various localities within countries.[25] This research reinforced our understanding that much of medicine is not based on hard scientific evidence, but rather on belief and on accumulated anecdotal experience.[26] Moreover, when clinical research has been undertaken to evaluate medical practice, it has not infrequently proved accepted medical practice to be largely ineffective.[27] This has resulted in attempts to base the adoption of new technologies, and even the continued use of existing technologies, on firmer scientific evidence – ideally on the basis of controlled clinical trials.

These trends come together in efforts to use evidence-based evaluations of new (or existing) health care technologies to decide whether those technologies are sufficiently effective (or cost-effective) to warrant coverage under public insurance programmes.[28] A number of countries have established institutions to perform such evaluations to decide whether or not to cover new health care technologies.[29] This book examines these programmes in eight countries.

CRITERIA FOR EVALUATING PUBLIC HEALTH INSURANCE COVERAGE DETERMINATIONS

Though coverage decisions are in theory (and to some extent in practice) evidence-based, they are also unavoidably political. In general, there is some pressure on institutions that make decisions affecting coverage policy to limit the growth and diffusion of new technologies. These institutions exist for this purpose. On the other hand, these bodies often face tremendous pressure from the proponents of new technologies to approve coverage for those technologies. The problem then becomes how to structure decision-making entities and processes so as to balance the power of the contending interests involved, thus making possible decisions that are in the public interest, that is, decisions that are:

1. scientifically based and technically accurate;[30]
2. efficient in their use of limited resources;
3. distributionally just.

The task of technology evaluation is in part technical – determining whether on the basis of the scientific evidence a technology is effective, or perhaps cost-effective. A simple review of whether a technology 'works', however, will generally be inadequate for determining whether it should be covered.[31] Any drug that is being evaluated for coverage has already been approved as safe and effective for at least some indications by a national or regional regulatory agency.[32] Medical devices are also evaluated by some countries for safety and effectiveness. Most technologies that reach the coverage review stage, therefore, are already known to be effective for some purposes.

In those situations where coverage of a technology is contested, however, the evidence will rarely be unequivocally in favour of coverage of the technology for all potential indications. In some instances the effectiveness of a technology will not have been clearly established by 'gold standard' double-blinded clinical trials (particularly if the technology is not a drug); or the clinical trials will have involved only a small subset of the insured population (excluding, for example, children, the elderly, pregnant women, minorities, or patients with complications or co-morbidities) or have lasted only a short duration (and thus not have detected long-term effects); or the trials will have been conducted against a placebo control rather than against a competing product, and thus will not have established the comparative cost effectiveness of the technology.[33]

Furthermore, even the best evidence-based information cannot decide how to prioritize the treatment of different medical problems or patient populations where resources are limited, as they always are in public health care programmes. Do we favour technologies that help the sickest or the most easily cured, the oldest or the youngest? What about technologies that simply improve quality of life without improving health? The 'technocratic wish'[34] that we can use science to solve what are essentially social, ethical, or, most often, political judgements, is often only a dream. Decisions for or against coverage must be made by humans through the procedures of institutions created for this purpose.

Institutions and procedures must be established, therefore, to evaluate equivocal evidence and to reach judgements as to whether the weight of the evidence favours coverage or not, or, as is more commonly the case, to determine when a technology is appropriate and when it is not. This book describes how eight nations have designed such institutions and procedures and how they are being used. It also evaluates how these institutions and procedures are performing.

In recent years, the most widely discussed proposal for ground rules for evaluating institutions and procedures for making coverage determinations is that of Norman Daniels and James Sabin.[35] This model suggests that decision-making bodies should be evaluated by how well they meet four criteria:

1. a publicity (transparency) condition: rationing decisions and their justifications must be accessible to the public;
2. a relevance condition: decision-making criteria should be reasonable, that is based on evidence, reasons, and principles that are accepted as relevant by 'fair-minded people';
3. a revision and appeals condition: decisions and policies must be subject to review and revision;
4. a regulative condition: either voluntary or public regulation must make certain the first three conditions are fulfilled.[36]

Though Daniels and Sabin designed this model for evaluating the decisions of private managed care organizations in the United States, it has also been applied to evaluating coverage determinations in public systems in other countries Daniels and Sabin themselves analyze the experience of other countries with rationing in light of their model.[37] *Reasonable Rationing*, a recent book in this State of Health series, applies this model for evaluating public coverage determinations in other countries.[38]

The Daniels and Sabin model is consistent with the last half-century of administrative law, which has stressed transparency of public agencies and processes, notice and comment rule making, and the right to a hearing in adjudicative processes.[39] It is thus not surprising that commentators would use this model for evaluating the work of public bodies. Nevertheless, Daniels and Sabin designed their model to evaluate decision-making by privately managed care organizations in the United States, and it works awkwardly for measuring public institutions that make generally applicable coverage decisions.[40]

The problem that Daniels and Sabin address is how to make sure that such entities do not deny their members effective (or perhaps cost-effective) treatments in their desire to make money. The transparency criteria assures that members know what decisions are being made and why. The relevance criterion assures that decisions are comprehensible and based on shared values. The appeal criterion provides individual insureds with a second look at a denial and the possibility of access to a neutral decision-maker. The regulation requirement assures that the private managed care organization (MCO) decision-maker is accountable to a public regulatory body, or at least to a credible form of self-regulation.[41]

In public health insurance systems, however, HTA for coverage policy is usually made ultimately by government agencies, though they may be advised by the corporate institutions of quasi-public social insurers or other expert bodies, which are accountable to their members, and to a certain extent to the public as well. Applying the Daniels and Sabin conditions to such agencies is problematic. The criterion of transparency and relevance would certainly apply, as they do to any public law bodies. It is less clear, however, exactly how the appeal criterion applies. Should any member of the public or of a social insurer be able to appeal a coverage decision of such a body? Should technology manufacturers or providers be able to appeal? Is an appeal to the courts sufficient, or should there also be some administrative body available for appeal? On the other hand, is a right to judicial review necessary, or is an administrative appeal sufficient? The regulation criterion fits public bodies even less comfortably. In what sense is a public agency subject to regulation, unless the meaning of regulation is contorted to include legislative or judicial oversight?

A more fundamental problem with the model, however, is that it was designed to address a setting in which an MCO is asked to cover a product but faces a financial incentive to deny that service. Private MCOs operate in a competitive market environment, trying to make a profit or to compete against MCOs that are profit-making. The private MCO in this setting faces strong financial incentives to limit access to expensive new technologies.[42] The Daniels and Sabin model mediates what is essentially a conflict of interest, subjecting the MCO to the discipline of public accountability in addition to the market discipline to which it is already subject.[43]

Public insurers also face an incentive to hold down their expenses, and thus to deny unnecessary or ineffective services, or perhaps even services that are not cost-effective. But they must also serve a plethora of public interests that go beyond the private interests of a MCO plan. A public insurer is certainly interested in controlling the costs of the total health care system, or of those particular segments of it for which the public insurer is responsible.[44] It must also attempt, however, to make appropriate technology available to those who can benefit from it. A third goal of public systems is to encourage technological innovation to improve health, while a fourth is to maintain the availability of health care services to those who are dependent on existing technologies, and who thus must compete for limited funds with those who desire new treatments. Other goals may include encouraging domestic medical technology innovation or production; expanding alternatively either public or private coverage of health care services; encouraging the creation and development of lower-cost technologies; protecting or expanding the income of providers who offer particular technologies; and providing health care professionals or providers with an expanded armamentarium of technology. Any complete understanding of the operation of public coverage determination processes must take into account all of these incentives and pressures.

PUBLIC CHOICE THEORY AND THE COVERAGE DETERMINATION PROCESS: THE ROLE OF INTEREST GROUPS

Much of the legal, economic, and political science scholarship examining public administrative agencies during the last three decades has focused on the problem of political regulatory decision-making in an environment of interest group pressure. The legal literature has been heavily influenced by the economic theory of 'public choice'.[45] Public choice theory treats regulatory institutions as markets in which regulatory 'goods' are supplied and demanded according to the same economic principles that govern the supply and demand of other goods.[46] These regulatory goods are supplied by the state – which has a monopoly over supplying them – to interest groups who stand to gain from them.[47]

The classic public choice story begins with the propositions that the primary goal of legislators is to retain their office, that to accomplish this goal they must raise campaign funds, and that to do this they must depend on interest groups.[48] Legislators, in return for interest group support, pass legislation that allows interest groups opportunities to gain 'rents' in the form of direct cash subsidies, market entry controls, price controls, and favourable contracts.[49] In the modern administrative state, the power to dispense many of these rent-seeking opportunities is often not directly under the control of the legislature, however, but rather delegated by legislatures to administrative agencies. It is obviously not possible for the legislature directly to administer complex regulatory programmes, and it is also often to the advantage of the legislature to avoid taking direct responsibility for dispensing rents to interest groups.[50] Indeed, it is sometimes advantageous for the legislature (or the government) to hive off responsibility on local or regional entities, and then itself to behave like an interest group in relationship to these entities.

Administrators, according to some versions of public choice theory, are motivated primarily by retaining their jobs and expanding their power and budgets.[51] Legislators are able to direct the actions of administrators to do their bidding – and thus to carry out the deals the legislature has made with interest groups – by controlling the budgets of agencies and their statutory jurisdiction and responsibilities, and by subjecting them to oversight hearings and to direct 'constituency casework'.[52] Interest groups also attempt to influence the behaviour of administrators directly by offering them the possibility of future post-civil service employment, and by 'wining and dining' them to the extent legally permissible.[53]

This description of legislative and administrative behaviour does not, of course, always square with reality. Indeed the public choice theory as a realistic explanation of regulatory behaviour, is subject to considerable controversy.[54; 55] Legislators are, in fact, often motivated by ideology, as well as by the desire to serve their constituencies, and many represent 'safe districts' where they do not have to worry excessively about raising money for re-election. Dependence on interest-group contributions also varies considerably among political systems. Administrators also are often ideologically committed to the mission of their agency and to the public interest, either as they view it themselves in a 'Burkian' sense, or as they understand the desires of the average voter.[56] One can easily think of many public-policy initiatives of the past half-century, including the rise of environmental regulation and the deregulation of a number of industries, that square very poorly with the public-choice understanding of regulatory agency behaviour.

On the other hand, the core understanding of public-choice economics seems to have undeniable truth, and squares with a half century of political science literature: interest groups do have a disproportionate influence on regulatory policy. In particular, one of the insights of Mancur Olson, one of the fathers of public-choice economics seems particularly helpful in describing the influence of interest groups.[57] Olson's book, *The Logic of Collective Action*, described the problem of motivating people to work together voluntarily to accomplish a common purpose, when each person as an individual could individually benefit from the collective action, but might well obtain the same benefit without getting involved, by 'free riding' on the actions of others. When each individual has an incentive to free ride, it is likely that the quantity of collective action will be suboptimal. Individuals or small groups that have a strongly concentrated interest in a particular issue, however, are more likely to take action to influence legislative or administrative action than large groups with small, diffuse interests in the action.[58] Thus a small group of agricultural producers who stand to make a large profit from a special tariff or farm subsidy will be more effective in dealing single-mindedly with the legislature or administrative agency that offers the tariff or subsidy, than will the immense group of consumers who consume the overpriced product or the taxpayers who pay for the subsidy, but who each individually pay pennies for the higher cost of the product or the subsidies, and who have many other things on their minds.

In most instances, interest groups get special consideration by supplying information, or perhaps simply by being a constant presence. Though it may not always be true, as Woody Allen supposedly said, that '85 per cent of success in life is just showing up', much of the success achieved before administrative agencies is. However much one assumes that administrators get up every morning intending to serve the public's interest, once they get to work they do not meet the general public, but rather the representatives of special-interest groups. When they send out proposed rules for comment, most of the comments come from special-interest groups.[59] When hearings are held on formal agency rules, most of the participants are special-interest group representatives.[60] When administrators meet informally with persons prior to the publication of proposed rules to gather information, those persons are likely to represent interest groups. When administrators receive phone calls from legislators inquiring about the status of a request of a constituent, or chastizing the administrator for treating a constituent unfairly, that constituent is likely to be an interest group. When, at the end of a long day of serving the public, the administrator goes home from work, most of the information the administrator will have absorbed during the day will have come from interest groups,[61] and most of the people with whom she will have interacted face to face, other than other agency staff, will have been interest-group representatives. It would be remarkable if the administrator did not ultimately come to see the world to a considerable extent through the eyes of interest groups.

Under some circumstances, of course, countervailing interest groups arise.[62] Environmental regulators must meet not only with the representatives of polluting industries, but also of environmental groups. Occupational Health and Safety regulators talk to unions as well as to manufacturers. One competitor may push approval of its product for approval by the agency, another competitor may oppose the approval of the competing product.

Under other circumstances, however, one side of the table may be empty. The administrator will receive information almost exclusively from interest groups on one side of an issue and hear only their arguments. In this situation, it is possible that the institutional culture in the agency may be strong enough to withstand interest-group pressure. If all of the information, all of the arguments, and all of the legislative constituent casework and oversight are pushing in one direction, however, it will be very difficult to stand against the tide.

This is often the situation that exists when public insurers make coverage determinations. Consider the interests affected by technology decisions. First, and most obvious, are the creators or manufacturers of the technology, who can be counted on to advocate its adoption vigorously. To the extent that product sponsors are major employers and contributors to local economies in legislative districts, they can count on the support of their legislative representatives in dealing with government agencies.[63] Professionals and providers, and in particular specialists and health care institutions, can usually be counted on to support the introduction of new technologies that can provide them with more options for diagnosis and treatment, as well as additional opportunities to provide income producing services.[64] Indeed, they may see denial of access to new technologies as unwarranted interference with their therapeutic freedom.[65] Health care professionals also often argue effectively that coverage denial will diminish the 'quality' of care, and can rally the public in their support when necessary. Disease-specific patient groups will almost invariably also favour the approval of new options for treatment. To the extent that a nation depends on the pharmaceutical and medical technology sector as an important segment of its economy or import earnings, there will also be political support for rapid adoption of the products of this market. Finally, there is in general strong public support in most countries (and particularly in the United States) for medical research and innovation in general.[66] All of these forces push powerfully for rapid, often largely uncritical, adoption of new technologies.

Aligned against the coverage of new technologies in public systems is a potentially much weaker array of interests. To the extent that health care budgets are subject to upward pressure, those who pay for health care services are most obviously negatively affected by the introduction of new technologies. Depending on the design of the health care system, payers might be taxpayers, employees, employers, or patients. The entity making coverage policy is in most countries at least nominally an agent of these payers, and thus should be attentive to this concern. But usually institutional payers are also attentive to the big picture. Approval of any single technology will often have a minuscule effect on total budgets, and payers are unlikely to devote significant resources to opposing approval of a new technology except in unusual circumstances where a potentially very costly technology is involved (though, as this book demonstrates, how coverage approval processes are structured can have an important effect on the influence of payers on coverage policy). And, as noted earlier, payers face conflicting obligations, because they, or their employees or members, want access to up-to-date technologies, even if it drives up cost.

Approval of new technologies may also be opposed by the producers of competing technologies, or providers who specialize in the use of existing technologies and who may lose market share if a new technology is introduced. Drug manufacturers, for example, do attempt to delay or forestall marketing approval of new competitors in the US.[67] Approval of a new drug for marketing, however, has a tremendous impact on existing single source drugs, which effectively lose a monopoly. There is great incentive, therefore, to fight for delay of approval. Approval of public insurance coverage has less of an effect, however, as the price paid for the existing product by a public programme does not necessarily change, and market share may not immediately be significantly affected. Companies with multiple products, moreover, may fear retaliation from competitors in the future. In any event, competitors rarely oppose coverage for new technologies.[68]

The real losers from decisions extending coverage of new technologies are often patients and providers who lose access to health care budgets as they are redirected toward covering new technologies. As noted in Newdick's chapter later in this book, English primary care trusts, which must cover all new drugs approved by the National Institute for Clinical Excellence (NICE), might need to cut back on other forms of care, such as nursing care, to pay for the new technologies. But the persons affected by these cutbacks, or by the lack of expanded expenditures for other purposes, are unlikely to identify the source of their plight as the coverage of new technologies, and it is almost inconceivable that they will react to their situation by opposing coverage of new technologies. Finally, organizations that represent programme beneficiaries are more likely to attend to their better organized and more vociferous members, who favour coverage of new technologies that might benefit them personally, than to their passive members who may be hurt by programme cutbacks driven by the cost of technology.

What we would expect to see, therefore, with respect to technology coverage determinations is a situation where interests are arrayed overwhelmingly in favour of coverage approval. Agencies may attempt to evaluate new technologies strictly on the scientific merits, and all claim to do so, but unless coverage determination agencies create or commission technology appraisals themselves, the vast majority of the information they will obtain will be from interests that favour approval. The arguments they hear day in and day out, the comments they get at public hearings, the calls they get from legislators, and the lectures they get at oversight hearings, will all urge them to approve new technologies, and to approve them more expeditiously.

If the Daniels and Sabin procedural criteria are applied under these circumstances, untoward results can result. If the only interests favouring approval are constantly monitoring information coming from the agency, transparency only strengthens their hand.[69] Any sign that the agency is leaning toward disapproval can be readily detected and met with vigorous opposition. If approval criteria must be based on consensus standards, but the only interests at the table to form a consensus are those that favour approval, the criteria will be stacked to favour approval. If appeals are available, but only from coverage denials, or only those denied technology approval are likely to appeal, the appeal criteria will always drive the agency toward approval. If those who monitor the agency want it to approve technologies rather than disapprove, again, the evidence base may get lost. Perhaps, therefore, we need to go beyond the Daniels and Sabin model when considering how we might improve public insurance coverage processes the better to assure that they serve the public interest.

One of the tasks of this book is to examine whether this hypothesized application of the public choice thesis to coverage policy is in fact born out by reality. The experience of each of our eight countries will be examined to see to what extent it accords with this thesis. To the extent that the experience of some of our countries does not seem to fit this mould, this will help us to address yet another question: how might we design institutions so that, in spite of the pressures that favour approval, technologies are nevertheless evaluated fairly, and to the extent possible are evaluated based on the scientific evidence? Are there, perhaps, even criteria that could improve on the Daniels and Sabin criteria for evaluating public insurance coverage determination processes to determine whether they will serve the public interest?

THE APPROACH OF THIS BOOK

We take two approaches to revealing the experience of our case study countries. First, and primarily, each chapter describes in detail how each country in fact makes public insurance coverage determinations. Each chapter begins by describing briefly how the public health insurance system of the studied country works. The chapters next discuss how the country conducts HTA, and how HTA feeds into coverage policy. Each chapter explains who makes public health insurance coverage determinations, the procedures they follow, and the opportunities the public is given to participate in those processes. Finally, each chapter describes how appeals can be taken from coverage determinations.

To get more directly at how coverage determinations are made, however, and also to examine comparatively how those determinations vary from country to country, we further analyse how each of our study countries has dealt with several specific technologies. To accomplish this end, we began by identifying technologies that had been assessed by more than one of our study countries. Because most countries have still explicitly assessed only a small number of technologies, we could find no single technology that all countries had evaluated, indeed there were few technologies other than pharmaceuticals that had been assessed by very many countries at all. A further problem was that our study countries vary as to the technologies they assess. Some countries' assessment programmes focus on pharmaceuticals, while other countries do not cover pharmaceuticals at all through their public health insurance system, and thus do not assess outpatient drugs.

In the end, we decided to focus on four technologies, two pharmaceutical and two non-pharmaceutical. One of these, positron emission tomography (PET) scanning, is primarily a diagnostic technology. The second, hyperbaric oxygen (HBO2) therapy is a technology used in treatment. The other two technologies are drugs, Glivec® (imatinib) for chronic myeloid leukaemia (CML), and the three drugs of zanamivir, oseltamivir, and amantadine for influenza. Coverage of other technologies is discussed in the context of particular countries, but not comparatively.

Although no one of these technologies has been assessed by all of our countries, each has been assessed by more than one. We discuss the coverage assessment process for each of these four technologies for each of the countries in which it has been assessed. The coverage determination process for PET scanning is examined for the US, Germany, Switzerland, Spain, Australia and Canada; hyperbaric oxygen therapy for the US, Germany, Switzerland and Australia; Glivec for the Netherlands, Switzerland, Australia, and England; and zanamivir, oseltamivir and amantadine for England, Switzerland and the Netherlands.

PET is described in a report from the International Network of Agencies for Health Technology Assessment as follows:

> PET is a minimally invasive imaging procedure that uses a radioactive tracer to assess perfusion and metabolic activity in various organ systems of the human body. The tracer decays by emitting a positively charged electron, called a positron, from the nucleus. The positron collides with a negatively charged electron resulting in two high energy ... photons travelling in opposite directions. The high energy photon is subject to less absorption or scatter by tissue.
>
> A positron camera (tomograph) arranged in a ring around the patient detects the two photons simultaneously (coincidence detection) to produce cross-sectional tomographic images.[70]

Though PET has been used for the study of basic physiology since the discovery of the positron in the 1930s, its development as a diagnostic tool has been limited by the fact that PET requires a charged-particle accelerator, usually a cyclotron, to produce tracers, and that this equipment has in most countries only been available in research centres.[71] PET is an expensive technology to purchase and maintain, and has not disseminated as quickly as alternative imaging technologies such as CT or MRI. The increasing availability of radiopharmacologic products commercially, however, makes the use of PET more economical, and has contributed to its diffusion.

Hyperbaric oxygen therapy (HBOT) treats various medical conditions by creating a pressurized environment in which patients breathe 100 per cent oxygen intermittently for periods lasting from one to two hours.[72] Though the process was initially developed (and is still used) for the treatment of decompression sickness, it is primarily used now for wound care. It serves four functions: increasing the concentration of oxygen in the blood, which enhances profusion; stimulating the formation of a collagen matrix to develop new blood vessels; releasing inert gasses in the bloodstream with oxygen, which is metabolized by the body; and killing bacteria.[73]

Glivec® is an orphan drug[74] offered by Novartis Europharm Ltd as a treatment for chronic myeloid leukemia (CML).[75] CML is a rare (approximately 1 per 100,000 persons/year) and life-threatening cancer occurring most commonly in patients aged from 55 to 60 and associated with a median overall survival from diagnosis of four to six years. Clinically, CML progresses through distinct phases from a relatively indolent initial phase (chronic phase) to acute leukemia (blast crisis phase) in a median of three to five years. This final stage is rapid and terminal. For 40 to 50 per cent of people diagnosed with CML, there is an intermediate phase (accelerated phase) that generally lasts about one year, but the cytogenetic and haematologic criteria to define this stage are lacking.

The only curative treatment of chronic phase CML is bone marrow transplant (BMT) but few patients (10–15 per cent) are eligible and there is a high rate of transplant mortality (20–30 per cent). Probability of long-term survival post-BMT when performed in the chronic phase is approximately 60 per cent. The first line treatments for CML patient ineligible for BMT include interferon-alpha (IFN) alone or in combination with cytosine-arabinoside (Ara-C). IFN is usually associated with a cytogenetic response of between 10 to 38 per cent compared with only 0 to 5 per cent with chemotherapy. This response has been shown to be associated with improved survival. Approximately 20 to 30 per cent of patients are forced to stop IFN treatment due to toxicity. Some do not respond and a vast majority develop resistance. For patients failing IFN, there is no generally accepted standard treatment.[76]

The active ingredient of Glivec® or Gleevac® is imatinib mesilate, a protein inhibitor which inhibits the development of CML. In early clinical trials, patients receiving imatinib showed complete or partial cytogenetic haematological responses. The main clinical efficacy data submitted for the original approval of Glivec for CML was based on early clinical evidence of its effect in three open-label non-randomized phase II studies with a total of 1027 adult patients with advanced stages of CML or in chronic phase after failure of IFN therapy. The chosen endpoints were overall haematologic and cytogenetic response rates. The results showed significant partial or complete response to therapy. However, there were no mature data from these trials that demonstrated a clear clinical benefit or increased survival.[77; 78; 79] This clinical evidence was submitted as the basis for the initial market approval for Glivec in the US and Europe.

Finally, zanamivir, amantadine, and oseltamivir are antiviral drugs that have been evaluated for the treatment of influenza. Zanamivir is a neuraminidase inhibitor licensed for the treatment of influenza A and B in people age 12 years and older if given within 48 hours of the onset of symptoms, when influenza is circulating. Influenza causes significant morbidity and increased mortality. Symptoms can range from asymptomatic infection through mild symptoms and respiratory illness to multi-system complications affecting the heart, lungs, brain, liver, kidneys and muscle. Influenza-associated death usually results from viral or bacterial pneumonia. In most people, influenza only causes mild symptoms though productivity costs may be substantial. High-risk groups include those with chronic respiratory disease, significant coronary heart disease (excluding those with only hypertension), chronic renal disease, diabetes mellitus, the immunocompromised, and those over the age of 65.

Based on clinical evidence, zanamivir decreases an individual's period of the illness by 1.5 days on average in healthy persons. In high-risk groups, zanamivir was shown to be potentially more effective in preventing or reducing complications resulting in a potentially substantial benefit. Amantadine inhibits the M2 membrane protein ion channel activity of the influenza A virus, but has no effect on influenza B. Zanamivir is a neuraminidase inhibitor licensed for treatment of influenza A and B, as is oseltamivir.[80] Clinical trials indicate that each of the drugs reduces the duration of influenza symptoms by about one day, though the drugs vary in their side effects and cost effectiveness.

The chapters that follow describe how each of the countries that we study has decided whether or not – or, more often, to what extent and under what circumstances – to cover one or more of these technologies under public insurance. It would seem that human physiology does not vary significantly from country to country, and that, for example, a diagnostic technology or pharmaceutical would have the same effect in one country as in the next. Nonetheless, and probably not surprisingly, different countries have reached different conclusions as to whether HTA does or does not support coverage under public insurance systems with respect to the same technologies. As we examine how our study countries make technology coverage decisions, we will focus in particular how their decision-making processes, and their decisions, have varied with respect to these technologies.

CONCLUSION

In sum, the chapters that follow examine whether and to what extent our study countries are using HTA for establishing coverage policy to control cost escalation in public health insurance systems, and the institutions and procedures they are using for this purpose. We will focus in particular on whether or not the predictions of public choice theory – that agencies that make coverage determinations will face pressure primarily to expand coverage – are borne out in reality. We will do this both by describing the institutions and processes through which each of our countries makes coverage policy, and also by examining the experience of each country with respect to our chosen case study technologies.

References

1 Between 1990 and 2000, average per capita annual spending growth on health care in OECD countries was 3.1%, compared to 1.9% in GDP growth per capita. In the countries this paper covers, health spending per capita exceeded GDP growth per capita 0.9% (Germany), 2.2% (Switzerland), 1.8% (UK), and 0.9% (US). G.F.

Anderson, et al. (2003), 'It's the Prices, Stupid: Why the United States Is So Different from Other Countries', *Health Affairs*, 89(3): 89–105.
2 P.E. Mohr, et al. (2001), *The Impact of Medical Technology on Future Health Care Costs: Final Report*. Bethesda: Project Hope.
3 B.A. Weisbrod (1994), 'The Nature of Technological Changes: Incentives Matter!', in A.C. Gelijns and H.V. Dawkins (eds.), *Adopting New Medical Technologies*. Washington: National Academies Press, 73–87.
4 Gelijns and Dawkins (1994), p. vi.
5 P.D. Jacobson and C.J. Rosenquist (1996), 'The Use of Low-Osmolar Contrast Agents: Technological Change and Defensive Medicine', *Journal of Health, Politics, Policy and Law*, 10: 243–66.
6 Mohr, et al. (2001), pp. 31–2.
7 Mohr, et al. (2001), p. 21.
8 Mohr, et al. (2001), p. 36.
9 Mohr, et al. (2001), p. 31.
10 M. Pauly (2004), 'What if Technology Never Stops Improving? Medicare's Future under Continuous Cost Increases', *Washington and Lee Law Review*, 60(4): 1233–50.
11 D.M. Cutler and M. McClellan (2001), 'Is Technological Change in Medicine Worth It?', *Health Affairs*, 20(5): 11–29.
12 F.R. Lichtenberg (2001), 'Are the Benefits of Newer Drugs Worth their Cost? Evidence from the 1996 MEPS', *Health Affairs*, 20(5): 241–51.
13 N. Daniels and J.E. Sabin (2002), *Setting Limits Fairly: Can We Learn to Share Medical Resources*. New York: Oxford University Press.
14 T.S. Jost (2003), *Disentitlement? The Threats Facing our Public Health-Care Programs and a Rights-Based Response*. New York: Oxford University Press.
15 See P. Zweifel and W.G. Manning (2000), 'Moral Hazard and Consumer Incentives in Health Care', in A.J. Culyer and J.P. Newhouse (eds.), *Handbook of Health Economics*. Amsterdam: Elsevier Science.
16 Whether or not physicians induce demand for health care has proved a very controversial question. If induced demand is defined to mean that physicians provide unnecessary medical services to their patients simply to make money, there is not much evidence that the practice is widespread. On the other hand, the need for medical care is often unclear, and there is a great deal of international evidence of the number of services provided by patients increasing when per-service payments decline. T.G. McGuire (2000), 'Physician agency', in A.J. Culyer and J.P. Newhouse, *Handbook of Health Economics*. Amsterdam: Elsevier, 462–536.
17 R. Klein, P. Day, and S. Redmayne (1996), *Managing Scarcity: Priority Setting and Rationing in the National Health Service*. Maidenhead: Open University Press.

18 D. Banta (2003), 'The Development of Health Technology Assessment', *Health Policy*, 63(2): 121–32.

19 H.D. Banta and B.R. Luce (1995), *Health Care Technology and its Assessment: An International Perspective*. Oxford: Oxford University Press.

20 M.S. Donaldson and H.C. Sox, Jr. (1992), *Setting Priorities for Health Technology Assessment*. Washington: National Academy Press.

21 C. Ham and G. Robert (2003), *Reasonable Rationing: International Experience of Priority Setting in Health Care*. Maidenhead: Open University Press.

22 A. Coulter and C. Ham (2000), *The Global Challenge of Health Care Rationing*. Maidenhead: Open University Press.

23 M. Berg and T. van der Grinten, 'The Netherlands', in Ham and Robert (2003), p. 122.

24 A. Bloomfield, 'New Zealand', in Ham and Robert (2003), p. 19.

25 J. Wennberg and A. Gittelsohn (1973), 'Small Area Variations in Health Care Delivery', *Science*, 182: 1102–9.

26 L. Noah (2002), 'Medicine's Epistemology: Mapping the Haphazard Diffusion of Knowledge in the Biomedical Community', *Arizona Law Review*, 44: 373–466.

27 Recent notorious examples include the use of post-menopausal hormone replacement therapy or of autologous bone marrow transplantation for breast cancer. J. Hays, et al. (2003), 'Effects of Estrogen Plus Progestin on Health-Related Quality of Life', *New England Journal of Medicine*, 348(19), 1839–54.

28 Technology assessment programmes, that is to say, may limit themselves to merely determining whether the technology in fact provides benefit to patients in actual practice, or attempt further to decide whether the technology provides benefit justifying its cost.

29 C. Wild and B. Gibis (2003), 'Evaluations of Health Interventions in Social Insurance-Based Countries: Germany, the Netherlands, and Austria', *Health Policy*, 63(2): 187–96.

30 It must be acknowledged, however, that some important services, such as 'caring' service or palliative care, are difficult to evaluate fully on the basis of scientific evidence.

31 S. Tanenbaum (1994), 'Knowing and Acting in Medical Practice: The Epistemological Politics of Outcomes Research', *Journal of Health Politics, Policy and Law*, 19(1): 27–44.

32 In the United States the agency would be the Food and Drug Information, which is charged by law with determining whether drugs are 'safe and effective'. 21 U.S.C. § 355(b)(1). In Europe, the European Agency for the Evaluation of Medicinal Products, approves medicinal products, though the European countries also maintain their own drug and/or device approval agencies. See < www.emea.eu.int >.

33 See Noah (2002), pp. 387–91.

34 G. Belkin (1997), 'The Technocratic Wish: Making Sense and Finding

Power in the Managed Medical Marketplace', *Journal of Health Politics, Policy and Law*, 22(2): 509–26.

35 Daniels and Sabin (2002).
36 Daniels and Sabin (2002), p. 45.
37 Daniels and Sabin (2002), pp. 149–68.
38 Coulter and Ham (2000).
39 E.D. Kinney (2002), *Protecting American Health Care Consumers*. Raleigh: Duke University Press.
40 Daniels and Sabin (2002), p. 8.
41 Daniels and Sabin (2002), pp. 43–65.
42 The incentives of MCO's in deciding whether or not to cover a new technology are in fact mixed. An MCO that routinely and openly denied state-of-the art treatment to its members would certainly face market resistance, and might face liability litigation as well. On the other hand, MCOs usually are selected by the employers of their members, and are only selected by the members themselves when multiple plans are available. Thus, MCOs often face relatively little direct market pressure from the consumers of their services. Compare, discussing the incentives of MCOs in making coverage decisions, *Farley* v. *Arkansas Blue Cross and Blue Shield Plan*, 147 F.3d 774 (8ᵗʰ Cir. 1998) (plans face market incentives to make decisions that are appropriate for members) with *Killian* v. *Healthsource Provident Administrators*, 152 F.3d 514 (7ᵗʰ Cir. 1998) (plans face incentives to deny treatment to save money).
43 Daniels and Sabin (2002), pp. 44–5.
44 Some insurers, for example, cover only hospital or physician care, and thus might not have the same interest in controlling long-term care costs.
45 C.R. Farina and J.J. Rachlinski (2002), 'Foreword: Post-Public Choice? Symposium: Getting beyond Cynicism: New Theories of the Regulatory State', *Cornell Law Review*, 87: 267–79 ('[Public choice theory] has dominated academic discussion of the regulatory state for nearly two decades; even legal scholars who do not consider themselves public choice practitioners work in its shadow.')
46 S.P. Croley (1998), 'Theories of Regulation Incorporating the Administrative Process', *Columbia Law Review*, 98: 1–168.
47 Croley (1998), p. 35.
48 G. Stigler (1971), 'The Theory of Economic Regulation', *Bell Journal of Economics*, 2(1): 3–21.
49 W.C. Mitchell and M.C. Munger (1991), 'Economic Models of Interest Groups: An Introductory Survey', *American Journal of Political Science*, 35: 512–46.
50 S.P. Croley (2000), 'Public Interested Regulation', *Florida State Law Review*, 28: 7–107.
51 W.A. Niskanen Jr. (1971), *Bureaucracy and Representative Government*. Chicago: Aldine, Atherton.

52 Croley (2000), pp. 11–13.
53 R.A. Posner (1969), 'The Federal Trade Commission', *University of Chicago Law Review*, 37: 47–89.
54 E.L. Rubin (2002), 'Public Choice, Phenomenology, and the Meaning of the Modern State: Keep the Bathwater, but Throw Out that Baby', *Cornell Law Review*, 87: 309–61.
55 M. Kelman (1988), 'Democracy-Bashing: A Sceptical Look at the Theoretical and "Empirical" Practice of the Public Choice Movement', *Virginia Law Review*, 74: 199–273.
56 M.E. Levine and J.L. Forrence (1990), 'Regulatory Capture, Public Interest, and the Public Agenda: Toward a Synthesis', *Journal of Law, Economics and Organization*, 6: 167–98.
57 M. Olson (1965), *The Logic of Collective Action: Public Goods and the Theory of Groups*. Cambridge: Harvard University Press.
58 Olson (1965), pp. 3, 48, 127–8.
59 See C. M. Kerwin (1994), *Rulemaking: How Government Agencies Write Law and Make Policy*. Washington: Congressional Quarterly Press.
60 Staff of Senate Comm. On Governmental Affairs, 95th Cong., 1st Sess. (1977) *Study on Federal Regulation, Vol. III*, Washington: U.S. Congress.
61 D.B. Spence and F. Cross (2000), 'A Public Choice Case for the Administrative State', *Georgetown Law Journal*, 89: 97–142.
62 The political science literature on interest-group pluralism, going back to the Federalist Papers, has long stressed the fact that interest groups compete with and counterbalance each other. The economist Gary Becker has provided an economic model for such a result. G.S. Becker (1983), 'A Theory of Competition among Pressure Groups for Political Influence', *Quarterly Journal of Economics*, 98(3): 371–400. There is empirical support for the influence of citizens' groups on administrative processes, and there are clearly instances where the positions of citizens' groups have triumphed over the desires of special interests.
63 B.C. Vladeck (1999), 'The Political Economy of Medicare', *Health Affairs* 18(1): 22–36.
64 See R.F. Ochs-Ross and T.A. Connaughton (2002), 'The Perspective of Providers', in E.D. Kinney (ed.), *Guide to Medicare Coverage Decision-Making and Appeals*. Chicago: ABA.
65 Ochs-Ross and Connaughton (2002).
66 M. Kim, R.J. Blendon, and J.M. Benson (2001), 'How Interested are Americans in new Medical Technologies? A Multicountry Comparison', *Health Affairs*, 20(5): 194–201.
67 E. Powell-Bullock (2002), 'Gaming the Hatch-Waxman System: How Pioneer Drug Makers Exploit the Law to Maintain Monopoly Power in the Prescription Drug Market', *Journal of Legislation*, 19: 21–50.
68 This may change as public coverage determinations become more prominent. It may be possible, moreover, for manufactures to recruit

specialty societies to represent them in opposing competing technologies, thus making their involvement less visible.

69   E. Garrett (2000), 'Interest Groups and Public Interested Regulation', *Florida State University Law Review*, 28: 137–54.
70   E. Adams, et al. (1999), *Positron Emission Tomography: Experience with PET and Synthesis of the Evidence*. Stockholm: International Network of Agencies for Health Technology Assessment.
71   Adams, et al. (1999), p. 2.
72   Department of Health and Human Services, Office of Inspector General (2000), *Hyperbaric Oxygen Therapy: Its Use and Appropriateness*. Washington: OIG.
73   DHHS, 01 – (2000) p. 1.
74   An orphan drug is a drug that treats a rare disease affecting a small number of people and is thus not commercially viable without government development assistance.
75   The following text describing CML and its treatment and Glivec®, as well as much of the text following describing the use of zanamivir, oseltamivir, and amatadine for the treatment of influenza, was provided by Tanisha Carino.
76   H.M. Kantarjian, F.J. Giles, et al. (1998), 'Clinical Course and Therapy of Chronic Myelogenous Leukemia with Interferon-Alpha and Chemotherapy', *Hematology/Oncology Clinics of North America*, 12(1): 31–80.
77   B.J. Druker, et al. (2001), 'Activity of a Specific Inhibitor of the BCR-ABL Tyrosine Kinase in the Blast Crisis of Chronic Myeloid Leukemia and Acute Lymphoblastic Leukemia with the Philadelphia Chromosome', *New England Journal of Medicine*, 344(14): 1038–42.
78   B.J. Druker, et al. (2001), 'Efficacy and Safety of a Specific Inhibitor of the BCR-ABL Tyrosine Kinase in Chronic Myeloid Leukemia', *New England Journal of Medicine*, 344(14): 1031–7.
79   The European Agency for the Evaluation of Medicinal Products (EMEA) (2001), *Committee for Proprietary Medicinal Products European Public Assessment Report (EPAR) on Glivec*. London: EMEA.
80   National Institute for Clinical Excellence (2003), *Guidance on the Use of Zanamivir, Oseltamivir and Amantadine for the Treatment of Influenza*. London: National Institute for Clinical Excellence.

2

GETTING VALUE FOR MONEY: THE AUSTRALIAN EXPERIENCE

Anthony Harris and Liliana Bulfone[1]

INTRODUCTION: HEALTH CARE FINANCE IN AUSTRALIA

Australia has a national system for the delivery of health care which generally covers all permanent residents of Australia. The system is financed by a mixture of universal public insurance for primary and hospital care and a parallel private insurance system that covers inpatient private hospital charges. Public health insurance is provided through Medicare, a tax financed reimbursement system. Duckett[2] provides a detailed description of the Australian health care system and its financing.

The Commonwealth of Australia government has a leadership role in policy formulation, particularly in areas such as public health, research, and national information management. It funds directly most non-hospital medical services, pharmaceuticals, and health research. With the states and territories, it jointly funds public hospitals, and home and community care for aged and disabled persons. Residential facilities for aged persons are funded by a number of sources, including the Commonwealth.

The states and territories are primarily responsible for the delivery and management of public health services and the regulation of health care providers. They deliver public hospital services and a wide range of community and public health services. For example, some state and territory government-funded organizations provide school dental care and dental care for low-income earners, with other dental care being delivered in the private sector without government funding. Local governments within states deliver most environmental health programmes.

Medicare provides access to free treatment as a public patient in a public hospital. Aside from those patients, health care is generally delivered by private practitioners on a fee-for-service basis to: 1. private patients in public hospitals; 2. patients in private hospitals; and 3. patients in the community. However, all Australians are automatically insured under Medicare for many services delivered by health care practitioners (doctors, including specialists, and participating optometrists). Fees for specific services are determined by the government and are listed in the Medicare Benefits Schedule (MBS). For professional services rendered to private patients in hospital, Medicare reimburses patients 75 per cent of the Schedule fee. Private hospital insurance covers the other 25 per cent of the MBS fee. For services delivered in the community, Medicare provides an automatic entitlement to reimbursements of fees equal to 85 per cent of the Schedule fee, with a maximum payment of AU$58.60 (indexed annually) by the patient for any one service where the Schedule fee is charged. The maximum cumulative 'gap' (defined as the difference between the Medicare rebate and Schedule fee) payable by a family group or an individual in any one calendar year is AU$319.70 (indexed annually from 1 January).[3] It is important to note that doctors in private hospitals and in the community are free to set their own fees. All excesses beyond the Schedule fee are borne by the patient and are not insurable. Private insurance is not permitted to cover charges in excess of the Medicare Schedule fee. Doctors may also accept the Medicare benefit (that is, 85 per cent of the MBS Schedule fee) as payment in full. Where a doctor is prepared to accept the Medicare benefit as payment in full, the doctor may send their patients' bills in bulk directly to the government. Thus, patients visiting doctors who 'bulk-bill' incur no out-of-pocket expenses at the point of service delivery. In the December quarter of 2003, 66.5 per cent of general practitioner consultations were bulk-billed.[4]

In Australia, the provision of a subsidy for pharmaceuticals is shared between the states or territories and the Commonwealth government. Pharmaceuticals provided by public hospitals operated by the states or territories are subsidized by the state or territory government assisted by Commonwealth grants. The Commonwealth government assumes direct responsibility for patients' pharmaceutical needs once a patient leaves hospital. Out-of-hospital prescription drugs are provided under the Pharmaceutical Benefits Scheme (PBS). The PBS is intended to cover patients in the community setting. From 1 January 2004, general patients are required to pay the first AU$23.70 per prescription while concession card holders (low-income, unemployed and the elderly) are required to pay a lower fixed copayment of AU$3.80 per item. These payments, commonly called patient contributions or patient copayments, are revised annually in line with the Consumer Price Index. Public hospitals provide medicines to inpatients free of charge. However, fees similar to those charged under the PBS are charged for medications supplied to outpatients of public hospitals. Safety net arrangements apply for those patients and their families who require a large number of prescriptions per year. Patient expenses for both PBS medicines and public hospital outpatient medicines contribute to a safety net threshold. After reaching the safety net threshold, further medicines are supplied at a reduced cost (or free) for the remainder of the calendar year. If a general patient reaches the current safety net threshold of AU$726.80 in the current calendar year, they will be required to pay only the concessional rate (AU$3.80) for further PBS prescribed items for the remainder of the calendar year. Concessional patients reaching the safety net threshold of AU$197.60 within a calendar year are provided further PBS prescribed medicines free for the remainder of the calendar year.[5]

REGULATION OF HEALTH TECHNOLOGIES IN AUSTRALIA

The complexity of the mixed responsibility for funding and delivery system for health in Australia is mirrored in the regulatory structure for health services. Both the Commonwealth and state governments have key roles. The Commonwealth directly funds non-public hospital medical and pharmaceutical services and has the responsibility for the regulation of the conditions of both supply and its reimbursement. It regulates the marketing of drugs and medical devices through the Therapeutic Goods Administration (TGA) on grounds of quality, safety and efficacy as enabled by the Therapeutic Goods Act 1989 (as amended). It regulates the conditions of subsidy for diagnostic imaging, pathology, and medical services primarily through a set of benefit tables that make up the Medicare Benefit Schedule (MBS). The Pharmaceutical Benefits Schedule (PBS) describes the conditions and level of benefit payable on TGA-approved drugs. Legislation covering the major elements of the Medicare Programme is contained in the Health Insurance Act 1973 (as amended). Current provisions governing the operations of the Pharmaceutical Benefits Scheme are embodied in Part VII of the National Health Act 1953 (as amended) together with the National Health (Pharmaceutical Benefits) Regulations 1960 made under this Act. Decisions on which drugs and technologies are used in public hospitals, however, are largely a matter for the individual hospital within the constraint of an overall budget.

CRITERIA FOR PUBLIC FUNDING OF DRUGS IN AUSTRALIA

The Pharmaceutical Benefits Scheme (PBS) subsidizes the cost of government-listed prescribed medicines dispensed by private retail pharmacies, private hospitals, and, for some specialized drugs, public hospital pharmacies. A full description of the PBS and the process of deciding whether to subsidize can be found in documents on the Department of Health and Ageing website.[6] Certain requirements must be satisfied before the Minister for Health can decide to make available a public subsidy for a pharmaceutical under the PBS. The drug must first be approved by the TGA as described above on the basis of its quality, safety, and efficacy, but not its comparative effectiveness or cost.[7] Once a drug is approved for marketing, it can be considered for public subsidy within the PBS.

The Pharmaceutical Benefits Advisory Committee (PBAC) decides whether to recommend to the Minister for Health that a benefit be provided for the drug on the PBS. Under the National Health Act, 1953, a benefit cannot be paid for a drug without such a positive recommendation. The power of an independent body to restrict national public health funding from a technology is unique to Australia. The Minister also has power to choose whether or not to accept the PBAC's recommendation.

The Pharmaceutical Benefits Advisory Committee is an independent statutory body established on 12 May 1954 under section

101 of the National Health Act 1953 to make recommendations and give advice to the Minister about which drugs and medicinal preparations should be made available as pharmaceutical benefits. The Committee currently has twelve members, all appointed by the Minister for Health. The Committee must include eight members selected from the following: (a) consumers; (b) health economists; (c) practising community pharmacists; (d) general practitioners; (e) clinical pharmacologists; (f) specialists; with at least one member selected from each of the interests or professions mentioned in (a) to (f). The remaining members of the Committee must be persons whom the Minister is satisfied have qualifications or experience: (a) in a field relevant to the functions of the Committee; and (b) that would enable them to contribute meaningfully to the deliberations of the Committee. The PBAC is currently chaired by Emeritus Professor Lloyd Sansom, the former Head of School of Pharmacy and Medical Sciences at the University of South Australia.[8]

In making its recommendations, the PBAC may take into account advice from a number of sources, including its subcommittees. The PBAC established the Economics Sub-Committee (ESC) in November 1993 under Section 101A of the National Health Act 1953 to: 1. review and interpret economic analyses of drugs submitted to the PBAC; 2. advise the PBAC on these analyses; and 3. advise the PBAC on technical aspects of requiring and using economic evaluations. In 1988, the PBAC also established a Drug Utilisation Sub-Committee (DUSC) to: 1. collect and analyse data on drug utilization in Australia for use by the PBAC; 2. make inter-country comparisons of drug utilization statistics; and 3. assist in generating information relating to rational use and prescribing of medicines.

Implementation of the PBAC's listing recommendations involves a number of steps, including negotiation between the government and the manufacturer to agree on a mutually acceptable price; clearance of chemistry and quality-control matters; preparation of the necessary legal declarations and determinations; and, in the case of the more expensive drugs, consideration by Cabinet.

The pricing of new drug products and review of prices for existing products is carried out by the Pharmaceutical Benefits Pricing Authority (PBPA). Following PBAC meetings, the Pricing Authority secretariat is provided with a summary of products that have been recommended for listing on the PBS, and advice regarding their therapeutic effectiveness and cost effectiveness relative to alternatives. Sponsors are contacted by the secretariat and asked to provide cost information and other data considered relevant by the sponsor for their new products.

Submissions to the PBAC requesting PBS listing or amendments to listings of drug products are normally made by the sponsor or manufacturer who will hold the necessary data required to substantiate listing. However submissions from medical bodies, health professionals, and private individuals and their representatives may also be considered. The PBAC has published comprehensive guidelines to guide the preparation of submissions.[9]

Since 1993, economic considerations have been part of the formal criteria that the PBAC have used to make a recommendation. The PBAC was the first national authority to include economic evaluation as a step in the process of reimbursement decisions for health technology. It remains the only national authority where it is mandatory to demonstrate that a health technology is of acceptable cost effectiveness prior to reimbursement. The criteria that the PBAC considers for recommendation of drugs for subsidy are shown in Table 2.1. The Committee is required by the National Health Act 1953 to consider the effectiveness and cost of a proposed benefit compared to alternative therapies. In making its recommendations, the Committee, on the basis of community usage, recommends maximum quantities and repeats of drugs and may also recommend restrictions as to the indications where PBS subsidy is available. In essence, the main criteria for the PBAC are comparative effectiveness, comparative safety, and comparative cost effectiveness. Other relevant factors also apply, but are not specifically identified in the legislation.

Once a medicine has been recommended by the PBAC, a number of processes need to be completed before the medicine can be listed on the PBS. These include:

• Consideration by the PBPA. The pricing of new drug products and review of prices for existing products is carried out by the Pharmaceutical Benefits Pricing Authority. Following PBAC meetings, the Pricing Authority Secretariat is provided with a summary of products that have been recommended for listing on the PBS, and advice regarding cost effectiveness and therapeutic relativity with alternatives. Sponsors are contacted by the Secretariat and asked to provide cost information and other data considered relevant by the sponsor for their new products.
• Pricing negotiations by the manufacturer and representatives of the Commonwealth government.

- Consideration by government. (If a drug is expected to cost more than AU$5 million per year, it is considered by the Commonwealth Department of Finance and Administration. If a drug is expected to cost more than AU$10 million per year, it is considered by Cabinet).
- Clearance of chemistry and quality control matters.
- Preparation of the necessary legal declarations and determinations.

Table 2.1 Factors that the Pharmaceutical Benefits Advisory Committee takes into account when considering submissions

---

When considering a submission for listing a medicine on the Pharmaceutical Benefits Scheme (PBS), the Pharmaceutical Benefits Advisory Committee (PBAC) takes into account a number of factors, including:

- The conditions for which the drug has been approved for use in Australia by the Therapeutic Goods Administration. The PBAC only recommends the listing of a medicine for use in a condition which is in accordance with the Australian Register of Therapeutic Goods.
- The conditions in which use has been demonstrated to be effective and safe compared to other therapies.
- The costs involved. The PBAC is required to ensure that the money that the community spends in subsidizing the PBS represents cost-effective expenditure of taxpayers' funds.
- A range of other factors and health benefits. These factors may include, for example, costs of hospitalization or other alternative medical treatments that may be required, as well as less tangible factors such as patients' quality of life.

Source: Department of Health and Ageing (2004), 'Outcomes of Pharmaceutical Benefits Advisory Committee Meetings'. www.health.gov.au/pbs/healthpro/outcomes_full.htm (accessed March 2004).

Currently, the usual minimum time for these processes to be completed is around five months. This means that the overall process from submission to subsidy consumes a minimum time period of about eight months. In 2004, there have been moves to extend this period to take account of the concerns of industry about the ability of the process to consider their views at various points in the process. This is discussed in more detail below when we consider the review and appeals processes.

A number of key features distinguish this process. First the emphasis on evidence-based decision-making is expressed in very detailed, comprehensive guidelines for the preparation of submissions. The guidelines, although expressly non-prescriptive, request the highest available standard of evidence on the incremental costs and benefits of the proposed subsidy on a drug. The aim of the guidelines is to ensure transparency and rigorous analysis of both clinical and economic issues. In terms of clinical effectiveness, the emphasis is on a hierarchy of evidence with head-to-head randomized controlled trials at the apex. In the case of the economic evidence, the emphasis is on using standard unit costs and reliable techniques to model costs and final health outcomes. The aim is to encourage the production of credible economic evidence that is consistent with the clinical trial evidence, but also provides information beyond its limitations.

The Department of Health and Ageing publishes and regularly updates the list of drugs for which a benefit is payable and the conditions of payment as the Schedule of Pharmaceutical Benefits.[10]

MEDICAL SERVICES

The Medical Services Advisory Committee (MSAC) was established in April 1998 to advise the Minister for Health and Ageing on the strength of evidence on new medical technologies and procedures in terms of their safety, effectiveness, and cost effectiveness, and under what circumstances public funding under the Medicare Benefits Scheme should be supported. The Committee is appointed by the Minister of Health and has 21 members. Members come from a range of medical specialities with one clinical epidemiologist, and also include two economists and a consumer.[11] The Committee has the capacity to assemble and review available evidence and, in some circumstances, support conditional funding to collect data within an agreed research framework to establish the evidence base. The MSAC receives submissions from commercial sponsors of technologies and groups of doctors. It also undertakes health technology assessment work referred by other areas of the Department of Health and Ageing as well as the Australian Health Ministers' Advisory Council (AHMAC), and reports its findings to AHMAC. It operates with a secretariat in the Department of Health and Ageing, but contracts assessment reports to a number of organizations. These reports are prepared with the assistance of an Advisory Panel for each technology which includes clinicians expert in the relevant area of speciality, other clinicians, a consumer representative, members of MSAC, and members of the secretariat. The terms of reference of the Medical Services Advisory Committee are to:

* advise the Minister for Health and Ageing on the strength of evidence pertaining to new and emerging medical technologies and procedures in relation to their safety, effectiveness, and cost effectiveness, and under what circumstances public funding should be supported;
* advise the Minister for Health and Ageing on which new medical technologies and procedures should be funded on an interim basis to allow data to be assembled to determine their safety, effectiveness, and cost effectiveness;
* advise the Minister for Health and Ageing on references related either to new and/or existing medical technologies and procedures; and
* undertake health technology assessment work referred by the AHMAC, and report its findings to AHMAC.

Table 2.2 outlines the MSAC assessment process.

The MSAC process is still relatively new. It has some similarities with the PBAC process such as an emphasis on evidence-based decision-making that includes clinical and economic considerations, but there are some significant differences. A number of authors have commented on the apparent differences between the assessment of medical technologies and pharmaceuticals.[12] The most obvious are the technical differences in the evaluation process, the legal framework underpinning the two processes, and the political influence of the actors. In the drug market there is a historical culture of evaluation (at least of safety and efficacy), including the analysis of high-quality evidence produced and presented with the financial sponsorship of private companies. The evidence provided to the PBAC in submissions and the associated commentaries on the clinical efficacy and cost effectiveness of drugs is therefore of a relatively high quality. Although there are often problems with the analyses, the depth of information and analysis provided to the PBAC is usually of a standard and an extent that exceeds that of the best academic journals.[13] Original trial data are often re-analysed, meta-analysis is conducted of trial data, and detailed computer analytic models of cost effectiveness are constructed and deconstructed as part of the evaluation process. Experience and

Table 2.2 MSAC assessment process

Stage 1 – Eligibility

The first stage of the MSAC assessment cycle involves consideration within the Department of Health and Ageing of an application's eligibility for assessment by MSAC.

Stage 2 – Assessment

If an application is considered eligible for review it moves on to the second stage-assessment. MSAC utilises independent contractors to conduct the majority of the evidence-based assessment. This involves the development of an evaluation protocol and assessing the available evidence on the safety, clinical effectiveness, and cost effectiveness of the technology or procedure.

MSAC appoints a specialist Advisory Panel, chaired by a member of MSAC, to assist in the assessment of each application. This provides expert input into the assessment process as well as ensuring that the contractor's assessment is clinically relevant.

Stage 3 – Formulation of Advice to the Minister

In formulating recommendations to the Minister, MSAC considers a range of information. This includes the assessment report and any feedback on the report received from the MSAC applicant or the Department. MSAC recommendations generally fall into one of three categories:

- the evidence is strong and supports public funding;
- the evidence does not support public funding; or
- the evidence is inconclusive but suggests that the procedure could be safer, more effective, and more cost-effective than comparable procedures that attract public funding. In these circumstances, MSAC may recommend interim funding to enable data collection and further evaluation of the procedure.

Stage 4 – Decision

The Department makes a submission to the Minister for Health and Ageing that combines MSAC's final assessment report and recommendations with policy advice from the Department. The Minister considers this information and makes a decision to endorse or reject the MSAC recommendations. To date, the Minister has endorsed all MSAC recommendations.

Stage 5 – Implementation

If the Minister endorses a recommendation for Commonwealth funding of a new medical service, the appropriate consultative committee draws on MSAC's findings to determine funding levels. The appropriate committee is determined primarily by the nature of the service. Relevant committees include the Medicare Benefits Consultative Committee, the Consultative Committee on Diagnostic Imaging, and the Pathology Services Table Committee.

Source: Department of Health and Ageing (2004), 'Medical Services Advisory Committee – Evaluation Cycle'. http://www.health.gov.au/msac/evaluation.htm (accessed 31 March 2004).

---

familiarity with this level of analysis has been largely absent in the non-drug medical services sector.

Evaluation of comparative effectiveness is often harder for non-drug medical services because the process of administration is usually more complicated and involves more potential confounding factors and variability from patient to patient. This is made worse by the fact that, in most cases, the clinical advantage of a new treatment or diagnostic test is quite small. Demonstrating an advantage or even that it is no worse than an alternative can be difficult without a large well-controlled direct comparative study. The scientific literature is often confined to case series or poorly controlled clinical studies. This makes it difficult to establish the superiority of one treatment over another.

In addition, there remains considerable resistance to use of evidence-based medicine to target resources in health if this conflicts with clinical freedom. There is even less enthusiasm for the use of cost-effectiveness considerations where it has an impact on both clinical freedom and medical income. With comparatively low regulatory requirements on medical services, a pattern of care may have become established prior to an evaluation of effectiveness and cost effectiveness. This is particularly the case in the Australian health care system where out-of-hospital medical services are largely privately provided. This can lead to a *de facto* reversal of the burden of proof in the evaluation process (compared to pharmaceuticals). In the pharmaceutical evaluation process in Australia, the sponsor needs to demonstrate evidence of comparative effectiveness and cost effectiveness. In the medical services evaluation process, particularly where a technology is currently part of clinical practice, the MSAC may need to demonstrate to the profession that the service does not have a comparative advantage in terms of clinical or cost effectiveness if it is not to recommend public funding. When combined with a profession that directly provides services and has a popular public profile (compared with large pharmaceutical companies in Australia, for example), it has been more difficult to establish and maintain an evidence-based decision-making culture in medical services compared to pharmaceuticals. Nevertheless Australia has achieved a high level of acceptance among the providers of medical care that demonstration of effectiveness and cost effectiveness should be among the determinants of public funding decisions.

ACCEPTANCE OF EVIDENCE-BASED DECISION-MAKING IN HEALTH

Not all participants have been satisfied with evidence-based reimbursement decisions. The Australian Society of Anaesthetists, for example, was very upset with the MSAC recommendation that public funding for Intraoperative Transoesophageal Echocardiography (TOE) be withdrawn, except for interim funding where used specifically to assess valve competence following valve surgery. In its annual report of October 2003, the Economics Advisory Committee of the Society complained that, in spite of 1. the protests of the Society and the Australian Medical Association (AMA) 'at every level up to and including the Minister herself', and 2. the fact that in August 2002 the Department of Health and Ageing (or the Minister) agreed to have the assessment (May 2002) re-examined by MSAC, with a seat at the table for the anaesthetists, MSAC did not alter its recommendation to the Minister. In the words of the Society: 'The whole MSAC process has been most unsatisfactory and should be a cause for concern for all sections of the profession if this Committee is to be involved in examining further areas of the MBS.'[14] It is interesting to note that the report from the Society made no mention of the clinical or economic evidence on TOE. Indeed, the final report from MSAC did not question the technical accuracy of the evidence in the original report. Rather funding was sought on the basis that TOE represented the current international consensus of the standard of care.

There have been some complaints about the length of time taken to assess the evidence, formulate advice, and implement funding from those with an interest in the therapy. However, with respect to the PBAC process, the Australian National Audit Office reported in 1997 that the total time allowed for processing major applications for PBS listing had been reduced from between 170 and 185 days prior to 1993 to between 145 and 160 working days from 1993 to 1997, concluding that the process was efficient.[15] The Department guarantees that any application for listing received by a given cut-off date will be fully assessed at the next PBAC meeting. This is a considerable commitment as it does not depend on the complexity of the submission or the quality of the information provided. The MSAC process, although it aims to have a three-month assessment period, appears to be subject to far less rigid timeframes and does not make any such commitments. For example an application for public funding for hyperbaric oxygen therapy (HBOT) was received in 1999, and the Minister accepted the report in February 2001. MSAC began to review the evidence on nuchal translucency screening in pregnancy (NTS) in February 2000. It made a recommendation on the public funding of NTS in May 2002, which was accepted by the Minister in October 2002. There are a number of sources of delay in the MSAC process. The initial screening of applications and setting up a new balanced Advisory Panel for each review has made it difficult to have rigid scheduling. The number of meetings and the terms of reference of the Advisory Panels are very flexible and can extend the assessment. There can also be political appeals outside of the process that can lead to a re-assessment of the evidence as in the example of TOE discussed above.

The MSAC Annual Report, April 1998 to June 2000, shows that by the January–March quarter 1999, MSAC had received a cumulative total of 20 applications and by the April–June quarter 2000, MSAC had finalized a cumulative total of 21.[16] Of the 35 applications received between April 1998 and June 2000, 40 per cent were from industry, 31 per cent from professional medical organizations, and 29 per cent from individuals. By 2001/2002, MSAC had received 64 applications or references for review and had completed 42 health technology assessments since its establishment in April 1998.

The MSAC completed 16 reports in 2001/2002, which the annual report says took on average 14–16 months to complete from submission of application or reference to final MSAC recommendation.[17] It may be that the MSAC process is becoming faster as the backlog of assessments is dealt with and experience leads to greater efficiency. The time taken in the evaluation process is considerably longer than the (technically no less complex) PBAC assessment process, but perhaps more in line with other countries which have a similar (more open and less adversarial) review process.

ASSESSING VALUE FOR MONEY

Both the PBAC and MSAC require high-quality explicit information on the existence and size of the incremental costs and benefits associated with the intervention. Both committees have published guidelines on what is expected in submissions to the listing process. Although the principles are similar, the expectations are higher in the case of the PBAC, not only because of the likelihood of the existence of such evidence and the culture of evaluation discussed above, but also the availability of sponsors to provide that evidence. In assessing likely value for money, each takes a similar approach. Incremental costs and benefits are assessed compared to the medical treatment most likely to be substituted (or, in the case of drugs where there may be a number of alternative drugs in that class available, the most commonly prescribed pharmacological analogue used for the same indication). A societal perspective is taken in principle, but in practice both processes take a more pragmatic approach including all health system costs and patient payments. Health outcomes are assessed both in terms of the measures reported in the most scientifically rigorous clinical studies available and often as the results of decision analytic models. The former are often surrogate outcome measures while the latter may extrapolate the clinical study measures over time, translate them into more patient-relevant outcomes, or assign a value on them based on the strength of preference for some health outcomes over others.

Figure 2.1 shows the process of listing a new drug on the PBS. In 2004, an extra step was added to allow more time for a sponsor to comment on the documents reviewing its application prepared by the Department of Health and Ageing prior to the consideration of the application by the PBAC's subcommittees. This also requires a reduction from four to three PBAC meetings per year, which extended the time for the PBAC evaluation process to 17 weeks from submission to the PBAC meeting, with written brief advice provided to the sponsor three weeks after the PBAC meeting. The time from submission to listing is now a minimum of 38 weeks.

Provided the submission is received at least 17 weeks prior to the PBAC meeting, a commentary will be prepared and it will be considered at that meeting. Many drugs are rejected on the first submission and are re-submitted (with changed indication, price, or data) one or more times before eventually being listed by PBS or withdrawn from offer by the sponsor.

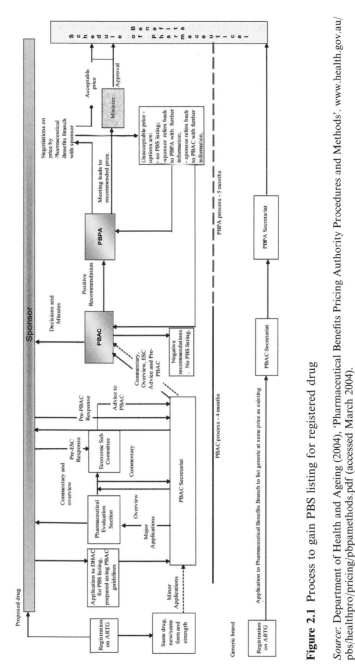

Figure 2.1 Process to gain PBS listing for registered drug

Source: Department of Health and Ageing (2004), 'Pharmaceutical Benefits Pricing Authority Procedures and Methods'. www.health.gov.au/pbs/healthpro/pricing/pbpamethods.pdf (accessed March 2004).

Cookson described six key characteristics of what he terms the Pharmaceutical Evaluation Scheme (PES) in 2000:

> The key features of the PES initiative are (1) semi-adversarial evaluation procedure, (2) high priority to industry and expert consultation, low priority to public consultation, (3) strong emphasis on rigorous evidence of comparative efficacy from head-to-head randomised trial evidence and to deal with uncertainty, but not to combine rigorous with less rigorous evidence, (5) no evaluation of cost–utility, equity, or 'leakage' due to inappropriate prescribing, and (6) sufficient funding to achieve fairly rigorous evaluations within guaranteed short time lines, but with staff capacity stretched to the limit.[18]

Some of these have been discussed, but it is worth looking at two of these and comparing them with the MSAC process. The adversarial nature of the process is in part an outcome of the fact that the PBAC decision-making process is defined by the terms of reference under National Health Act, 1953 as described above. As Cookson puts it:

> The PES can be seen as a semi-adversarial procedure, in which the sponsor's health economics department puts the case for listing, the PES secretariat puts the case against listing, the ESC sums up, and the PBAC then makes a decision. To pursue the legal analogy, the sponsor's health economics department acts as defence lawyer, the PES as prosecuting lawyer, the ESC as judge, and the PBAC as jury.[19]

There are elements of truth in this characterization. The sponsor certainly has an incentive to put the best case forward for their product within the limits of the evidence available. The onus is on the sponsor to demonstrate that public money should be spent on their product. The Secretariat subjects the evidence produced by the sponsor to demonstrate their case to a rigorous critical examination and looks for weaknesses in it. The prosecutorial analogy is not perfect since the Secretariat does not see its role as preventing the listing of all drugs. It does not try to prove that the sponsor is trying to steal public money. Rather, as a part of the Commonwealth government, it has the more balanced objective of the PBS overall, which is to improve the health of the population at a reasonable cost. The Pharmaceutical Evaluation Section may even present an implicit case in its commentary to the ESC and the PBAC that the drug should be listed as proposed or with some amendments to the sponsor's proposal, for example in terms of the drug's indication or place in therapy. We would suggest that a better analogy is one of a bargaining relationship between the sole supplier of a patented product and a large purchaser. Bargaining takes place under imperfect competition with less than full information on product quality, cost and the potential for alternative therapies. The task of the supplier is to convince the purchaser of the quality of the good for the price, while the task of the purchaser is to appraise the quality, determine if the price is acceptable, and the maximum price they are willing to pay (and the minimum acceptable to the supplier). The role of the evaluation process is to provide information on the quality (health outcomes including risk) and the total social cost of the proposed subsidy, and thereby reduce the uncertainty for the purchaser. The role of the PBAC is to make an assessment based on that evidence. The role of the PBPA is to negotiate a price no greater than the maximum suggested by that information.

The information provided by the evaluation is in principle not limited to that contained in the sets of guidelines, but in practice drug sponsors are encouraged to follow the guidelines closely. The guidelines focus on clinical effectiveness, cost and incremental cost per extra unit of health outcome gained. There are no requirements to set out equity implications in a systematic manner, or to quantify them in either the PBAC or the MSAC process. As Cookson points out,[20] there is no requirement to analyse patient characteristics such as age, social class, and lifestyle from an equity point of view. Anecdotal evidence suggests that treatments for life-threatening illnesses, especially where there are no satisfactory alternative treatments available, might be considered more favourably compared to those for less severe conditions with alternative drug or other effective treatments available. It may be that more favourable consideration is given to drugs for severe illnesses that are relatively rare, both because there are few alternative treatments and also because the budgetary implications of an expensive treatment in rare conditions are seen as of less consequence. While some have questioned the ethical basis of the so-called 'rule of rescue',[21] the PBAC has adopted a principle like this. In the example of Glivec®, the PBAC made specific reference to that concept. It may be that in the future the committee will require quantification of how rare a disease has to be, how severe, and how effective alternative treatments must be, before a submission will be treated differently. This may be difficult because neither the PBAC nor the MSAC currently have a formal cut-off value for an acceptable incremental cost-effectiveness ratio in any condition or for broad measures of incremental cost per extra life saved, incremental cost per extra life-year gained or incremental cost per extra quality-adjusted life-year gained. It seems likely that the probability of listing on the PBS or MBS is affected by the incremental cost effectiveness of the technology as assessed by the committees, but given the confounding factors in decisions, this is difficult to establish.[22]

TRANSPARENCY OF THE PROCESS

Transparency in public funding decisions is desirable, not only because of the accountability that it brings to the process, but also because transparency can improve information quality and thereby reduce analytical uncertainty. This means that disagreements can be reduced to judgements about values and less about empirical evidence. There may be a conflict between the public interest and private commercial interests if the general disclosure of information might give a commercial advantage to a rival. Submissions to both the PBAC and MSAC are treated as confidential.

A sponsor of a submission to the PBAC has rights of review during the process in that it can comment in writing on the assessment of its submission before the PBAC subcommittee meetings and again before the PBAC meeting. In the case of the MSAC, applicants have a month in which they can comment on the draft assessment prior to the MSAC meeting. Other interested parties do not have a right to comment in either process before the decision is made. In the case of the PBAC, the application is confidential. In the case of the MSAC, while there is notice that the evaluation is proceeding and interested parties could in principle make a submission to the MSAC, the parties are not routinely provided with the application from a sponsor, a reference from a government agency, the detailed considerations of the Advisory Panel, or the evaluators. To the extent that documentation would be available under the Freedom of Information Act, 1982, however, the Secretariat would be unlikely to refuse access to that documentation.

The public accountability of the process has been hindered by a strong concern by industry with commercial confidentiality. Submissions to the PBAC, commentaries on the submissions provided by the Department of Health and Ageing, advice from the ESC and DUSC, and the minutes of the PBAC are all confidential documents and not publicly available. Until very recently it was not possible for the public (or other sponsors) to know which drugs are or have been considered (except of course those that were listed on the Pharmaceutical Benefits Schedule[23]). This has led to an appeal by one drug sponsor on the grounds that they had been denied natural justice insofar as the PBAC had considered their product along with another without the opportunity for the sponsor to offer evidence on a direct comparison. Legal opinion suggested that the PBAC had indeed breached the rules of natural justice. The PBAC had not revealed the existence of the parallel submission because of the constraint of commercial confidentiality. The sponsor was allowed to resubmit an application for the PBAC to consider anew under extraordinary circumstances.

In 1999, industry agreed to allow the reasons behind a recommendation to list a drug to be published. PBAC decisions not to recommend listing along with a summary of the reasons have been published since June 2003. The discussion of imatinib (Glivec®) below includes some examples of the information that it made available following a decision whether to recommend listing.

MSAC has had less of an issue with confidentiality, largely due to the small number of commercial sponsors, but has had some inherent problems with conflict of interest. The PBAC and MSAC take advice from expert technical committees. In the case of the PBAC, the ESC is a standing committee of 12 members, made up of clinicians with expertise in evidence-based medicine, a biostatistician, economists, and a non-voting member from the industry association, Medicines Australia. While ESC members may have an interest in a clinical area, they do not take part in the discussion of any product for any company in which they have a financial interest. In the case of the MSAC, however, the Advisory Panels are made up of clinicians who earn their income from providing medical services. Some are deliberately chosen for their expertise in the area concerned, even in the use of the technology concerned. They, for example, may be a director of a hyperbaric oxygen facility. They may have a declared direct or indirect financial interest in the technology, or they may simply have strong views on the appropriate medical specialty to perform a procedure or order a test. While reports and commentaries are prepared by independent consultants, they are guided by these Advisory Panels. The final decision is made by the MSAC taking into account the evidence in the report, but there is a potential for bias in the reports associated with the makeup of the Advisory Panel. There are safeguards built into the system to minimize the potential for bias. These include the professionalism of the independent consultants, a department advisor on the panels, publication of the assessment reports, and perhaps most critically, the panels are chaired by a member of MSAC. However, given that the Advisory Panel members are likely to be the most informed about the technology, there is the possibility that the assessment reports will unduly reflect the views of the profession.

REVIEW OF DECISIONS BY THE PBAC AND MSAC

Decisions by the PBAC to reject a submission are final (until such time as a resubmission can be considered), and cannot be overruled by the Minister, while decisions to recommend PBS listing require further approval by the Minister. Recommendations by MSAC are advice to the Minister and are not binding. There is a statutory opportunity for appeal against all government decisions, which can be initiated on the grounds of procedural irregularity, for example that all the relevant information was not considered or that irrelevant information was considered. To date no judicial review of an MSAC recommendation has been initiated. Perhaps the most publicized case for the PBAC was that of sildenafil. Amongst other things, Pfizer claimed that the Committee wrongly took into account the fact that, in its view, the cost of subsidizing Viagra® under the Scheme was likely to be unacceptably high, particularly as the Committee thought that there was a risk that the usage of the drug could not effectively be limited to the people for whom it was medically indicated. Pfizer also claimed that the Committee had acted unfairly in taking into account some particular information without first disclosing that information to Pfizer and giving it a chance to respond.

The trial judge rejected all of Pfizer's arguments and dismissed the application for judicial review.[24] Pfizer then appealed to a Full Court of the Federal Court challenging most, but not all, of her conclusions. The members of the Full Court, in a joint judgement, concluded that the original judgement was correct on the main points upon which the case was decided. In particular, they considered that the trial judge was correct in rejecting Pfizer's contention that the Committee was wrong in taking into account the likely overall cost of subsidizing Viagra® under the Scheme.[25]

The Full Court considered that the requirements of procedural fairness in this context meant that the Committee was obliged both to inform Pfizer that it intended to take into account certain information that was potentially detrimental to Pfizer's interests, and to allow Pfizer an opportunity to respond to that information. In essence, that information concerned the fact that another drug for the same condition was used at a considerably higher rate than originally predicted. This information contributed to the Committee's conclusion that Viagra® would be used at a greater rate than that estimated by Pfizer and hence cost the Commonwealth more than the figures submitted by Pfizer. The Full Court concluded that the Committee's failure to inform Pfizer that it intended to rely on this information with respect to the alternative drug, and to allow Pfizer to respond to that information, deprived Pfizer of natural justice, and so the Court allowed Pfizer's appeal.

The Full Court's conclusion that the Committee failed to accord natural justice to Pfizer means that the Committee was obliged to reconsider, in a manner consistent with the law as the Court had interpreted and applied it, whether to make a recommendation to the Minister that Viagra should be declared a pharmaceutical benefit. As the Court's reasons for judgement make clear, the function of the Court in a case of procedural review is to determine whether a decision such as that made by the Committee in this case was made according to law. It is not the function of the Court to say whether or not Viagra should be listed on the Pharmaceutical Benefits Scheme.

As this case demonstrates, this judicial appeals process is lengthy, and unlikely to overturn a PBAC recommendation largely because the PBAC has such a rigorous process for gathering and analysing information. Another interesting feature of this case is the conflict between the requirements of natural justice and the rights of commercial privacy. It could be argued that for the PBAC to reveal to Pfizer the utilization projections for another drug would be to breach a commitment to maintain the commercial confidentiality of information provided as part of submissions to the PBAC. In this case, the court found that natural justice was not served by keeping information from Pfizer. The issue of commercial-in-confidence is one that has prevented full public discussion and justification of PBAC processes and decisions and has at times been a source of great frustration. As discussed above, only recently has the PBAC been able to publish any information on drugs that were rejected. Even then the amount of information published is limited to the bare bones of the reasons for positive or negative recommendations.[26] The discussion of Glivec® below gives an indication of the information available from the PBAC.

Industry has long argued that there should be a special, swifter appeals process against PBAC decisions not to list a drug. This formed part of the argument put by the US government on behalf of the industry in the recent round of talks on a free-trade agreement between Australia and the US. The argument is that this would reduce the damage and unfairness caused when the PBAC makes mistakes, and would increase the accountability of the overall procedure.

An interesting objection to an independent review mechanism is that, from a public perspective, this is a one-sided appeals mechanism that favours the sponsors. There is no possibility of appeal by other affected parties, such as the taxpayer, against decisions to recommend funding. A one-way appeals process (that is, against refusals to list but not against recommendations to list) is in principle inappropriate in the context of purchasing decisions. As Cookson observes, this is not like the criminal law where the right of appeal is conditioned by a concern to avoid punishing the innocent. In the context of a purchasing decision, we are concerned not to waste public money on cost-ineffective treatments or diagnostic tests, perhaps as much as we are concerned to fund treatments or tests that offer value for money. In a world where we are uncertain about the expected net benefits of any medical treatment, to allow a one-sided appeals system would place far greater emphasis on one type of potential error compared to the other.

Nevertheless, as part of the Australia United States Free Trade Agreement (AUSFTA), it was announced in February 2004 that Australia would establish an 'independent process' to review decisions on drugs recommended for subsidies under the scheme. At the time of writing it is unclear what the words 'independent' or 'review' represent.[27] Certainly some may hope that this independent review will be able to overturn decisions, but the intention may be only to allow independent comment back to the PBAC. If this were to lead to long delays (compare for example the National Institute for Clinical Excellence (NICE) process in the UK), then it might be an infrequently used mechanism, no more effective from the sponsor's perspective than resubmission of an application. At present, resubmissions of proposals to the PBAC to fund a drug are common (see Glivec below) and, in the case of the MSAC, reconsiderations following comments from interested parties have occurred (see hyperbaric oxygen therapy below).

CASE STUDY 1: HYPERBARIC OXYGEN THERAPY (HBOT)

The MSAC assessed the arrangements in place in 2000 for the funding of HBOT. The assessment report by the MSAC on HBOT (application 1018–1020) in November 2000 recommended that public funding should be supported for HBOT administered in either a multiplace or monoplace chamber, as appropriate, for the following indications:

- decompression illness, gas gangrene, air or gas embolism;
- diabetic wounds including diabetic gangrene and diabetic foot ulcers;
- necrotizing soft-tissue infections including necrotizing fasciitis and Fournier's gangrene;
- the prevention and treatment of osteoradionecrosis.

These are serious conditions in which HBOT provides a non-invasive treatment option which may have a beneficial effect and offer cost savings. HBOT is widely accepted as standard clinical care in the management of these life-threatening conditions for which there are limited alternative treatment options. The decision by MSAC recognized that further studies are required to provide more conclusive evidence of an effect, but that these are difficult to undertake due to the ethical and practical constraints of conducting trials in these conditions. They were convinced that there was stronger evidence that HBOT is effective in promoting wound healing, and reducing the length of hospital stays and the likelihood of major amputations in patients with diabetic wounds. There may also be cost savings associated with these treatment benefits. They supported public funding for HBOT use in these conditions until conclusive evidence becomes available that indicates it is not effective or that other treatments are preferable and more cost-effective.

The Minister for Health and Aged Care accepted this recommendation on 9 February 2001. HBOT providers were concerned that the Committee had not taken sufficient account of evidence for the effectiveness of HBOT in soft-tissue radionecrosis and non-healing wounds in non-diabetic patients. It appears that they were concerned that a reduction in the range of indications available for subsidy would affect the financial viability of HBOT. Following discussions with the HBOT providers, it was agreed to maintain interim funding for those indications pending a further MSAC review. In December 2001, a second submission was received that sought to extend the indications for which HBOT was funded. Advice was formulated at the May 2003 meeting of MSAC and has been transmitted to the Minister. The decision on HBOT demonstrates the understanding of the MSAC that public funding decisions need to be made on the best evidence available, but they remain hesitant to fund a technology where there is insufficient evidence of effectiveness. It also demonstrates that considerations of cost effectiveness, while important, are not the only criteria and in this case the fact that this may be a last-line treatment for some severe conditions may have influenced the decision.

CASE STUDY 2: POSITRON EMISSION TOMOGRAPHY (PET)

In 1990, the National Health Technology Advisory Panel (NHTAP) – the Australian Health Technology Advisory Committee's predecessor – reviewed the safety, clinical and cost effectiveness of PET as a diagnostic tool. The review concluded that there was a lack of evidence to justify the routine clinical use of PET in Australia; further evaluation of PET as a clinical tool was required; and PET should be subject to a co-ordinated evaluation of clinical and cost benefits involving the then two Australian units (at the Austin and Royal Prince Alfred (RPA) hospitals).

In response to the NHTAP review, the Commonwealth, New South Wales, and Victoria jointly funded a multi-centre evaluation project involving the PET units at the Austin and RPA. The project encountered serious difficulties in relation to establishing an appropriate protocol for a multi-centre trial, and the inability of the centres to recruit sufficient patients to participate in the trial.

The Department of Health and Aged Care (Diagnostics and Technology Branch) then conducted a review with the guidance of a Steering Committee comprising representatives of the medical profession, state and territory governments and consumers. An integral part of the review was a technical evaluation of PET, conducted by a supporting committee of the MSAC. The review involved extensive consultation with a diverse range of stakeholders. A public call for public submissions resulted in some 50 responses.

In March 2000, MSAC[28] found that PET has improved diagnostic accuracy over conventional imaging in a number of indications:

* detection of mediastinal and distant metastases not detected by conventional imaging in the staging of non-small-cell lung cancer (NSCLC);
* detection of metastatic disease in patients with potentially resectable metastatic melanoma;
* detection of local recurrence, hepatic metastases and extrahepatic metastases in patients with suspected recurrence of colorectal cancer;
* medically refractory epilepsy;
* assessment of viable myocardium that may respond to reperfusion in patients being considered for coronary revascularization.

The Steering Committee subsequently presented its own report, incorporating consideration of the broader policy issues raised by the review, to the Minister. The Minister agreed to the implementation of the review's recommendations in August 2000.[29]

The Steering Committee recommended public funding of PET services, but recommended that the high capital costs of the technology be recognized through the allocation of separate funding streams for capital and recurrent costs. The Steering Committee further recommended that PET providers' eligibility for interim funding be dependent on:

* meeting relevant accreditation standards;
* satisfying data-collection requirements specified by the Commonwealth to enable the further evaluation of PET;
* funding being restricted to seven dedicated PET facilities.

In August 2001, the MSAC published a second assessment report recommending public funding for PET[30] and commenting that there is currently insufficient evidence on the clinical and cost effectiveness of PET to warrant unrestricted funding. Despite this, the evidence suggests that PET is safe, potentially clinically effective and potentially cost-effective for the indications reviewed. As such, interim funding was recommended for:

- staging of newly diagnosed or previously untreated disease, evaluation of residual mass after treatment and restaging of suspected recurrent/residual Hodgkin's and non-Hodgkin's lymphoma;
- primary staging, suspected residual or recurrent SCC of the head and neck and evaluation of metastatic SCC involving cervical nodes from an unknown primary site; and
- guiding biopsy of suspected bone or soft-tissue sarcomas where structural imaging suggests lesion heterogeneity, staging of biopsy-proven bone or soft-tissue sarcoma being considered for resection of the primary or limited metastatic disease, evaluation of suspected residual or recurrent sarcoma on the structural imaging after definitive therapy.

PET provides an example where uncertainty in the clinical literature led to an inability to come to a firm conclusion on the cost effectiveness of the technology. Interim funding was granted in the expectation that new evidence from randomized clinical trials would provide better evidence within the next few years, but it is not clear that the trials would be able to answer the questions of the link between diagnostic accuracy and patient outcomes in the indications suggested.

CASE STUDY 3: GLIVEC®

The PBAC's considerations of applications requesting subsidy of imatinib (Glivec®) are a good illustration of how the process of submission and resubmission can be seen as a bargaining process over the appropriate place of a technology in the treatment pathway taking account of cost effectiveness.

An application was submitted to the PBAC in September 2001 requesting subsidy of imatinib when used in the treatment of patients with chronic myeloid leukaemia (CML). The PBAC recommended subsidy of imatinib when used in the treatment of adult patients in either the accelerated phase or the blast phase of CML. Listing was recommended on the basis of acceptable, but high cost-effectiveness ratios in these patient groups. According to media reports Glivec was considered by the PBAC for gastrointestinal stromal tumour and rejected for subsidy at least three times before July 2003.[31; 32] A series of published considerations by the PBAC followed in September 2002, June 2003, September 2003, and December 2003 that related to extending the CML indication, initially to second-line treatment for the chronic phase of CML (following failure of prior treatment with interferon alfa, an indication that had been granted marketing approval alongside the accelerated and blast stages), and when that was accepted, to first-line treatment. They also sought to extend the indication to the treatment of unresectable malignant gastrointestinal stromal tumour (GIST) and then to modify the restrictions on age group and the rules for continuing treatment.

In large part, these resubmissions were successful in expanding the groups and indications eligible for subsidy. The PBAC recommended subsidy for GIST on the basis of an acceptable, but high, incremental cost-effectiveness ratio. The PBAC considered that the 'rule of rescue' was applicable in this case, given that no other effective treatments exist for this condition. The introduction of a continuation rule that allows PBS-subsidized treatment with imatinib to continue only in patients who have achieved a partial response also meant that the cost-effectiveness ratio was more favourable than if this continuation rule were not implemented. Further, although the revised cost-effectiveness ratio was not quality-adjusted, the PBAC considered that patients who achieve a partial response would also achieve a benefit in quality-of-life terms during the period that the partial response is maintained.[33]

The experience of Glivec over a 12-month period illustrates the way in which the process of application and re-application for subsidy gradually expanded eligibility and the indications available on the basis of evidence and argument provided to the PBAC. The case also illustrates that the PBAC is willing to recommend the subsidy of treatments that have a comparatively high incremental cost-effectiveness ratio if there are other relevant considerations in favour of listing. In the case of GIST, the life-threatening nature of the disease combined with the lack of alternative therapies was sufficient to persuade the committee that the high incremental cost-effectiveness ratio was acceptable. The case also illustrates the concern of the committee to restrict the use of high-cost drugs to patients likely to benefit most and moreover to ensure that individual treatment is only subsidized if it continues to be effective. The use of so-called continuation rules with clear and preferably objective clinical criteria, backed up by a prior approval system, has become critical in decisions involving high-cost drugs.

CONCLUSION

The past 20 years have seen the beginnings of a revolution in the attitude to the systematic use of evidence in public decision-making on health technology in Australia. The root causes of that birth are not hard to discern, even if the conditions for its implementation are more complex. They lie in the concerns over the marked rise in expenditure on health in general in the 1980s and more particularly with new health technologies, especially pharmaceuticals. It was particularly of concern in the Australian context where both drugs and medical services have long been subject to an open-ended subsidy with few means of capping expenditure outside of co-payments. This provided the political backing within the health portfolio to include economic considerations to be taken into account when making decisions on whether to fund drugs and at what price.[34] The 1987 amendment to the National Health Act, 1953, that required the PBAC (and by implication the government) to 'take account of comparative effectiveness and cost in recommending drugs as pharmaceutical benefits' was therefore a landmark event. For the first time anywhere, economic criteria became a mandatory part of the decision to provide public funding for medical care. The overall success of the formal pharmaceutical evaluation scheme is not easy to assess.[35; 36; 37; 38] It has survived for more than ten years, in spite of one short period of disharmony[39; 40] and occasional sniping from some parts of industry. Indeed, the formality of the system has the support of industry insofar as the system is widely regarded as procedurally fair. There are still some in the health sector who regard the listing criteria as opaque, and some who regard the evidentiary standards as overly stringent. Attitudes have shifted over time, however, as the experience and skills of participants have increased. There does seem to be recognition of an imperative to assess the value for money of medical technologies that often only offer minimal therapeutic benefit but at a high cost. The fact remains that even after more than ten years of evaluation in Australia, expenditure growth on medical services and pharmaceuticals has remained high and has followed similar trends in other countries. Figure 2.2 shows that both government expenditure and the volume of health service use accelerated in the late 1990s, particularly in the area of pharmaceuticals. This was a world-wide phenomenon associated with a number of new high-cost, high-volume drugs such as cholesterol-lowering and anti-inflammatory agents. If the original rationale for the introduction of a more rigorous evaluation system was to cap expenditure, then this has not been a success. Even if one of the original key aims was to restrain expenditure, the way in which the evaluation system has evolved with cost effectiveness as a key objective, has meant that new treatments that offer health gains, even at a high cost, have been accepted for public subsidy. The evaluation system may have prevented the subsidy of some medicines as not being acceptably cost-effective and may have delayed some expenditure while evidence was collected, analysed and assessed. It may have restricted

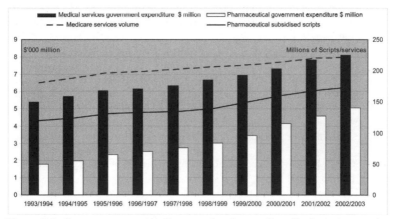

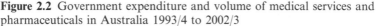

Figure 2.2 Government expenditure and volume of medical services and pharmaceuticals in Australia 1993/4 to 2002/3

Source: Constructed from Australian Government Health Insurance Commission utilization data on Medicare and pharmaceutical benefits.

subsidy of some medicines to indications where treatment is more effective and may have maintained lower prices for some drugs in Australia, but it has not restrained the community's increasing willingness to pay for new treatments that have some apparent health gain.

The health technology evaluation process in Australia has become extremely rigorous, with standards of analysis at least equal to the best peer-review medical journals, with information requirements that often exceed many of those journals. The emphasis on evidence-based decision-making, including economic considerations, has spread internationally, and within Australia now includes all medical services provided under the Medicare Programme.[41] In the early 1990s, the conditions were ripe for the introduction of a rigorous evaluation process prior to subsidy of drugs in Australia, and its rapid success influenced the decision to extend the process to include medical services with the creation of MSAC. The challenge now is to maintain and extend that experience of evidence-based policy making across all health services that receive a public subsidy.

References

1 The chapter has benefited from comments by Andrew Mitchell on an earlier draft. The authors take responsibility for all views expressed here.
2 S. Duckett (2000), *The Australian Health Care System*. Melbourne: Oxford University Press.
3 < www.health.gov.au/pubs/mbs/mbsnov2003_DHTML/MBS_Book_ 1_November_2003_22.htm?contents + 6 > (accessed 25 Mar. 2004).
4 < www.health.gov.au/mediarel/yr2004/ta/abb010.htm > (accessed 25 Mar. 2004).
5 < www.health.gov.au/pbs/general/index.html > (accessed 12 Mar. 2004).
6 < www.health.gov.au/pbs/pharm/listing.htm # necessary > (accessed 10 Mar. 2004).
7 Therapeutic goods are regulated through a variety of legislative instruments. Details are provided at < www.health.gov.au/tga/docs/ html/legis.htm > (accessed 10 Mar. 2004). Membership and procedures of the Australian Drug Evaluation Committee are set out in the Therapeutic Goods Regulations 1990 – REG 36. Details of the regulatory process for drugs and other therapeutic goods are given at: < www.health.gov.au/tga/docs/html/tga/tgaginfo.htm > (accessed 10 Mar. 2004).
8 < www.health.gov.au/pbs/general/listing/pbacmembership.htm > (accessed 1 Apr. 2004).
9 Department of Health and Ageing (2002), *2002 Guidelines for the Pharmaceutical Industry on Preparation of Submissions to the Pharmaceutical Benefits Advisory Committee Including Major Submission Involving Economic Analysis.* < www.health.gov.au/pbs/pharm/pubs/ guidelines/index.htm > (accessed 24 Feb. 2004).
10 < www.health.gov.au/pbs/general/schedule.htm > (accessed 10 Mar. 2004).

11 < www.health.gov.au/msac/membership.htm > (accessed 10 Mar. 2004).
12 D. Henry and S. Hill (1999), 'Assessing New Health Technologies: Lessons to be Learned from Drugs', *Medical Journal of Australia*, 171: 554–6.
13 S.R. Hill, A.S. Mitchell, and D.A. Henry (2000), 'Problems with the Interpretation of Pharmacoeconomic Analyses: A Review of Submissions to the Australian Pharmaceutical Benefits Scheme', *Journal of the American Medical Association*, 283: 2116–21.
14 Australian Society of Anaesthetists (2003), *Economics Advisory Committee Annual Report*. < www.asa.org.au/uploadedfiles/eac%20report%20agm%208%20oct%2003.pdf > (accessed 1 Apr. 2004).
15 Australian National Audit Office (1997), *Pharmaceutical Benefits Scheme*. Canberra: National Audit Office.
16 Commonwealth Department of Health and Ageing (2000), *Medical Services Advisory Committee Annual Report 1998–2000*. < www.health.gov.au/msac/pdfs/msac_report.pdf > (accessed 1 Apr. 2004).
17 Commonwealth Department of Health and Ageing (2002), *Medical Services Advisory Committee Annual Report 2001–02*. < www.health. gov.au/msac/pdfs/msacrep0102.pdf > (accessed 1 Apr. 2004).
18 R. Cookson (2000), *ASTEC Non-EU Case Study in Australia*. < www.lse.ac.uk/collections/LSEHealthAndSocialCare/pdf/astec/oz. pdf > (accessed 10 Mar. 2004).
19 Cookson (2000), p. 13.
20 Cookson (2000), p. 13.
21 J. McKie and J. Richardson (2003), 'The Rule of Rescue', *Social Science & Medicine*, 56: 2407–29.
22 B. George, A.H. Harris, and A. Mitchell (2001), 'Cost-Effectiveness Analysis and the Consistency of Decision Making: Evidence from Pharmaceutical Reimbursement in Australia', *Pharmacoeconomics*, 19(1): 1–8.
23 *Schedule of Pharmaceutical Benefits*. < www1.health.gov.au/pbs/index. htm > (accessed 24 Feb. 2004).
24 *Pfizer Pty Ltd* v. *Birkett* [2000] FCA 303 (20 Mar. 2000).
25 *Pfizer Pty Ltd* v. *Birkett* [2001] Federal Court of Australia 828 (2 Jul. 2001).
26 < www.health.gov.au/pbs/general/outcomes_full.htm # recent > (accessed 10 Mar. 2004).
27 M. Metherell (2004), 'Backdown on Drug-Subsidy Scheme Sickens Experts', *Sydney Morning Herald*, 10 Feb.
28 MSAC Reference 2. *Assessment Report ISSN 1443–7120*.
29 < www.health.gov.au/haf/pet/petrec.htm > (accessed 20 Mar. 2004).
30 MSAC Reference 10 part 2(ii). *Assessment Report ISSN 1443–7120*.
31 ABC Radio (2003), *Health Report*, 21 Jul. < www.abc.net.au/rn/talks/ 8.30/helthrpt/stories/s905390.htm > (accessed 30 Mar. 2004).

32 (2003) *Sydney Morning Herald*, 21 June. < www.smh.com.au/articles/
    2003/06/20/1055828490824.html > (accessed 30 Mar. 2004).
33 < www.health.gov.au/pbs/general/listing/pbacrec/sep03/positive.
    htm > (accessed 25 Feb. 2004).
34 G. Salkeld, A. Mitchell, and S. Hill (1998), 'Pharmaceuticals', in G.
    Mooney and R. Scotton (eds.), *Economics and Australian Health
    Policy*, p. 123. Sydney: Allen and Unwin.
35 Australian National Audit Office (1997).
36 Industry Commission (1996), *The Pharmaceutical Industry*. Canberra:
    AGPS.
37 George, et al. (2001).
38 D. Birkett, A. Mitchell, and P. McManus (2001), 'A Cost-Effective-
    ness Approach to Drug Subsidy and Pricing in Australia', *Health
    Affairs*, 20(3): 104–14.
39 B. Loff and S. Cordner (2001), 'Australian Government Loosens its
    Grip on the Pharmaceutical Industry', *Lancet*, 357(9254): 452.
40 Four Corners ABC TV (2001) *Paying the Price*, 19 Feb., transcript at:
    < www.abc.net.au/4corners/archives/2001a_Monday19February2001.
    htm > (accessed 23 Mar. 2004).
41 A.H. Harris, M. Buxton, B. O'Brien, F. Rutten, and M. Drummond
    (2001), 'Using Economic Evidence in Reimbursement Decisions for
    Health Technologies: Experience of 4 countries', *Rev. Pharmacoeco-
    nomics Outcomes Res*, 1(1): 7–12.

3

A COMPLEX TAXONOMY: TECHNOLOGY ASSESSMENT IN CANADIAN MEDICARE

Eric Nauenberg, Colleen Flood and Peter Coyte[1]

INTRODUCTION

As new health care technologies and procedures evolve, both public and private insurers must decide whether or not to insure them. Part of the goal of health technology assessment (HTA) and in particular economic analysis is to maximize the benefit stream given limited health care resources. Simply put, money spent on one service cannot be spent on another and trade-offs have to be made between services and treatments. New technologies often require significant up-front investment and ongoing operational outlays, but down-stream savings resulting from technical efficiencies, fewer adverse events, and quicker recovery times may offset these additional expenditures. But the results of HTA, based on an economic analysis alone, will rarely be sufficient to inform policy. Publicly funded health care systems, like Canada's, must wrestle with the public's simultaneous desire for the best health care system possible and the lowest tax rates possible. From the perspective of Canadian public insurers, then, it is important to analyse not only the *relative* cost and benefits of treatments and services but also their impact on the government's budget (as opposed to total public and private spending). Because of the extremely political nature of Medicare, governments will also be sensitive to the political implications of decisions to fund or not fund new technologies and treatments. In addition, and underscoring the political consequences of decision-making vis-à-vis new technologies, legal considerations, such as the prospect of judicial review of decisions not to fund new treatments, will also affect decision-making.

Over the past ten years, Canada's institutional capacity to conduct HTA has significantly strengthened[2, 3] but there is significant variability in both the parameters that are considered in HTA assessment and the uptake of those assessments. A particular HTA may encompass only a few or all aspects of a use for a technology: intrinsic safety and technical performance; nature and probability of health benefits and risks; efficacy, effectiveness, and safety of the innovation; cost-effectiveness, cost–utility, and cost–benefit analysis;[4] impact on the health care system at public health, organizational, social, and economic levels; social and cultural dimensions, including ethical, legal, and social issues; anticipated effects of adoption of the technology on the behaviours, attitudes, institutions, and values of health care professionals, client groups, and the public; and acceptability of these changes, i.e. whether they dovetail with the values and ideals of the community or society as a whole.[5] The variety of possible approaches to HTA is amply demonstrated in the Canadian system by the cornucopia of approaches taken by different decision-makers at multiple levels. The benefit of this variety is the possibility of learning from experimentation. As Martin and Singer note, however, the problem is that there is no co-ordinated way to compare the merits or disadvantages of different approaches or to consider at what point and by whom these decisions are best made.[6]

One of the most noticeable features of HTA in Canada is that quite different approaches are taken to HTA within different *sectors* of the health care system. For example, economic evaluation has become of greater importance in the approval of new drugs for listing on the public formularies in provinces across Canada but plays a much less significant role in the listing of new physician services. Possible explanations for the sectoral approach include the silence of the governing framework for publicly insured physician and hospital services (the Canada Health Act) on the importance of economic analysis in those sectors. Decision-makers may also be sceptical about the values underpinning economic modelling and, in particular, they may be sceptical of HTA assessments, based on economic efficiency modelling, which fail to address the impact on the government's budget should a particular technology be adopted. In other words, adoption of a new technology may be efficient (looking at public and private costs and benefits) but it may not necessarily be feasible given limited public resources. Given this, Lehoux and others have argued that HTA must expand beyond economic modelling and embrace the socio-political dimensions of health care technologies.[7]

This paper provides a taxonomy of health care decision-making vis-à-vis the adoption of new health technologies across Canada and explores some of the issues raised in this introduction. We organize our discussion by level of decision-making from top (federal level) to bottom (hospitals and physicians) in order to examine the cascade or compounding of constraints imposed by one level on those underneath. While this hierarchy of decision-making often holds true, it is also important to recognize that at times decisions are shared across two or more levels of government and some decisions are initiated from below rather than from above. To help illustrate these processes, vignettes within each level will be provided to help illustrate points made and to delineate various processes for making decisions.

THE LEVELS AND PROCESSES OF DECISION-MAKING

The following are the six levels of decision-making analysed in this report, descending from the highest to the lowest order of government and from the largest to the smallest form of provider:

1. federal
2. joint federal–provincial initiatives
3. provincial
4. regional (regional health authorities)
5. hospitals
6. physicians

We hypothesize that there are three broad sets of processes for decision-making about new technologies across Canada: 'closed-door/top-down', 'bilateral', and 'hands-off/bottom-up'. 'Closed-door/top-down' decision-making is defined as decision-making done by the governing body with control – constitutionally ordained or otherwise – over a particular decision without publicly transparent consultation with stakeholders. 'Bilateral' decision-making includes the governing body *and* stakeholders or other levels of government in some type of publicly visible process for arriving at an agreement. This process can either be combative or amenable through consensus-building negotiations. 'Hands-off/bottom-up' decision-making involves the governing body over a particular decision deferring to stakeholders to make the decision by which it agrees to abide.

THE FEDERAL ROLE

The Canadian way of drawing boundaries between the private and public financing of health care is unique among advanced industrial nations. The Canadian model creates three realms of finance that can be best illustrated by three concentric circles.[8] The first ring, or the 'core', contains fully publicly funded hospital and physician services; the second ring is a mix of public and private funding covering services such as home care, long-term care and pharmaceuticals; and the third ring contains all other services provided through private funding (for example, physician services like cosmetic surgery that a province has deemed as not medically necessary and thus wholly outside the purview of the Canada Health Act).[9] A single-payer, sectoral model of health care does have some problems. For example, the public funder can be slow to respond to technological changes while the private sector adopts new technologies more readily, leading to what some call 'passive privatization', a process we more fully describe below.

This sectoral model has evolved in part in response to the courts' interpretation of the Constitution and the efforts of the federal government to create national standards in health care in the absence of constitutional authority to impose these standards directly. Although the federal government does not have constitutional responsibility for the insurance and delivery of health care, through the use of its taxing and spending powers, it is able to impact provincial health policy.[10] The primary mechanism for this is the Canada Health Act (CHA), which provides for the transfer of federal funds to the ten provinces and three territories if they comply with the general criteria set out in the CHA in the administration of their respective health insurance plans (portability, universality, accessibility, public administration, and comprehensiveness). However, by far the most important provisions of the

CHA are those that effectively prohibit any form of private financing for 'medically necessary' hospital services and 'medically required' physician services.[11] 'Medically necessary' and 'medically required' are not defined in the CHA and it is left largely to provincial discretion to determine whether a physician or hospital service is a service that is 'medically necessary' and thus required to be fully publicly funded. The net result is that Canada effectively prohibits a parallel private sector for medically necessary hospital and physician services; indeed, it is illegal in a number of provinces to sell private insurance covering medically necessary physician and hospital services.[12]

As a consequence of the CHA, the Canadian health care system is one characterized by a sectoral approach to the funding of health care, i.e. public funding is concentrated in the hospital and physician sectors and there is a mix of private and public funding in other sectors.[13] Prescription drugs required outside of hospitals, home care, genetic testing, and other newer areas of health care are not protected by the CHA and as a consequence provincial governments do not necessarily provide full public insurance coverage for these services. Provinces *may* provide, for example, prescription drug coverage to the elderly and to the poor (and most provinces do) but there are no national standards with regard to the level of co-payments allowed, the range of drugs covered, and so on. The consequence is that a much greater proportion of funding for services such as prescription drugs, home care, genetic tests is sourced in the private sector (for example, 60 per cent of total spending on prescription drugs comes from the private sector). Reflecting the sectoral approach to funding, there is, as we will discuss further below, a sectoral approach to HTA, with significantly different approaches being taken, for example, to the assessment of new physician services as opposed to new prescription drugs. Most of the focus on HTA has been concentrated in the increasingly important 'newer' sectors of the system, like prescription drugs, diagnostic equipment, and genetic therapies. Given the heightened scrutiny of newer technologies compared to scrutiny of services and treatments already publicly funded, it is perhaps not surprising to find that Canada ranks in the bottom one-third of OECD countries vis-à-vis the availability of sophisticated technology like MRI scanners.[14]

More directly, the federal government affects the uptake of new technologies through its role of protecting and promoting health and safety standards and overseeing a number of very specialized aspects of health care. For example, Health Canada assesses new medicines to ensure that they conform to the quality and safety standards of the Food and Drug Act and accompanying regulations. To be approved a drug must be both safe and effective, and the drug's benefits must be shown to outweigh potential risks.[15] A drug, however, does not have to be a 'breakthrough' to be approved.[16]

The federal government does not take cost effectiveness into account in listing a new drug for general distribution in Canada. The decision to approve for general distribution, however, has cascading consequences throughout the system as it puts pressure on both provincial insurance plans and private insurers to list the new drug. The federal government, through its procedures, declares a drug to be safe and of benefit. A provincial government may then have the Herculean task of persuading their respective populations that although a drug is of some benefit it is not sufficiently beneficial to warrant public funding.

The federal government also has some impact over the diffusion of new prescription drugs through the Patented Medicine Prices Review Board (PMPRB), an entity charged with regulating the maximum manufacturer's prices for patent drugs in the Canadian market.[17] Considerations of effectiveness influences the maximum price allowed by the PMPRB in two ways. First, if a drug shows greatly increased efficacy over previous treatments it is declared a 'breakthrough' drug or a drug that offers 'substantial improvement'. Breakthrough medicines are subject to less stringent price control than other medicines. The maximum allowable price for a 'breakthrough' drug is normally set by reference to the median of the prices the drug is sold at in the seven countries listed in the *Regulations* (International Price Comparison Test).[18; 19] Second, medicines deemed to provide 'little or no therapeutic advantage' cannot have a price that exceeds the prices of comparator medicines. Efficacy may be taken into account when deciding which medicines currently on the market can serve as comparators.

It is important to note that the PMPRB does not control the prices of non-patented medicines. It also has no role in making recommendations as to the effectiveness of the drug, when the drug should be utilized, or if a third-party should cover the drug under an insurance scheme. Furthermore, unlike the United Kingdom's Prescription Price Regulation Scheme, the PMPRB is not directly concerned with limiting pharmaceutical company profits or scrutinizing expenditures.[20] The PMPRB merely approves the maximum price at which a patent drug can be sold by the manufacturer; each province uses their own market power to negotiate the price they will pay distributors to include a drug in the list of drugs they fund. Finally, it must be recognized that the PMPRB has no control over the volume of new drugs sold. As the PMPRB has noted, while patented drug prices increased by 0.2 per cent in 1999, the quantities sold increased by 21.2 per cent from 1998.[21; 22] Thus, even though prices have been held in check, total expenditures on drugs are increasing because of a rise in consumption.

The federal government also has a role through its criminal law power in regulating the diffusion of health technologies by way of regulating health and safety. For example, under the Assisted Human Reproduction Act, the federal government regulates and extremely restricts stem-cell research through criminal sanctions on the manufacture of human clones, including embryos.[23]

JOINT FEDERAL–PROVINCIAL AND PAN-CANADIAN INITIATIVES

There are an increasing number of joint bodies, representing both provincial and federal governments, which have a role in HTA. This is likely because of a desire to reap the benefits of economies of scale that come from information-sharing across provinces; the desire to present a more consistent approach to the issues of what is in and out of publicly funded Medicare; and to present a united front to help resist pressures from special interests, like pharmaceutical companies and others, who pressure provinces to publicly fund newer treatments.

The federal, provincial, and territorial Ministers of Health established the Canadian Coordinating Office for Health Technology Assessment (CCOHTA) in 1989. This is governed by a Board of Directors that includes a director appointed by each Deputy Minister of Health.[24] CCOHTA is intended to be a forum for national information exchange, resource pooling, and co-ordination of the assessment of health care technologies to ensure their appropriate use.[25] As will be discussed further below, CCOHTA's mandate has recently been extended to include responsibility for managing a common drug review process and making funding recommendations for new drugs submitted to participating federal, provincial and territorial drug benefit programmes. The CCOHTA is funded by contributions from both the provincial and federal governments.

Concern has grown about inconsistencies in drug formularies across the different provinces. As part of their action plan for health system renewal in September 2000, the first ministers (being the Prime Minister of Canada and all the provincial and territorial premiers) agreed to create an intergovernmental process to assess drugs for potential inclusion in publicly funded provincial plans. The Common Drug Review (CDR) is comprised of two parts, the first being a critical assessment of the best available clinical and pharmaco-economic evidence and the second being listing recommendations made by the new Canadian Expert Drug Advisory Committee (CEDAC).[26] Beginning in 2003, the CCOHTA will be responsible for reviewing new drugs either in-house or externally by contractors. In addition to conducting reviews, CCOHTA will provide support for the CEDAC, which will make listing recommendations to participating provincial, territorial and federal[27] drug plans. Under this scheme, provincial advisory committees may be relegated to the role of advising the provinces and territories as to 'how to list' (for example, general use, limited use) rather than 'what to list'. However, the final decision regarding a positive recommendation will still rest with the provinces, taking into account factors relevant to their jurisdiction such as population needs, other drugs on their formulary, and budgetary, political, or legal considerations.

To clarify, the federal government, although a funder and facilitator of the CDR, does not have any power in law to impose the CDR on the provinces – this process is very much in the spirit of a voluntary intergovernmental arrangement. It is also important to reiterate that CCOHTA, although a national organization, has no national authority. Its reports are resources that decision-makers at all levels of the health care system *may* choose to rely on but are not required to follow. Moreover, CCOHTA does not have formal oversight of the various HTA bodies that exist in the different provinces. (A list of formal HTA authorities, operating at provincial, regional and local levels across Canada, is included in Appendix 3.1.) In the absence of some level of formal oversight of co-ordination, HTA authorities are free to determine their own priorities for assessment, determine their own parameters for assessment, and engage in their own type of dissemination tactics. The process of decision-making is illustrated in Figure 3.1. It is also important to note that a national body like CCOHTA often finds it

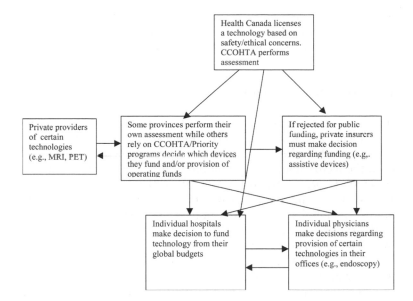

Figure 3.1 Cascading levels of decision-making in HTA

difficult to accommodate the specific culture of decision-making in each province, which may individually require slightly different types of analyses (for example, a quicker turn-around time than CCOHTA's average of 18 months per HTA); as a result, some provinces, such as Quebec and Ontario, have pushed ahead with their own HTA bodies to assist in decision-making.

The work of CCOHTA and other HTA agencies is carefully scrutinized by affected stakeholders. For example, CCOHTA decided to review a statin drug called Pravastatin, manufactured by Bristol-Myers Squibb (BMS). BMS was unhappy with the review, questioning whether CCOHTA had legal authority to advise that all statins can be expected to reduce coronary events or to have a class effect on coronary events. From the perspective of BMS, unfounded assertions of equivalent clinical benefit can lead to substantial loss of market share, revenue, and profit. Thus, BMS tried to obtain an interim injunction to prevent CCOHTA from publishing its report, arguing negligent misstatement. They were unsuccessful.[28] Despite BMS's lack of success in this instance, significant questions are raised about the chilling effect this kind of activity has on the willingness of HTA agencies to render negative reviews and, in particular, the willingness of academics and other researchers to contribute, often on an unpaid basis, to this review process given potential threats of litigation.

THE PROVINCIAL ROLE

The courts have interpreted the Constitution such that provincial governments have constitutional responsibility for both health insurance and health delivery within their respective provinces.[29] Given the increasing pressures on the health care system, including demographic pressures, cost escalation in the pharmaceutical sector, and new technologies, provincial governments are concerned about sustainability, particularly in light of other pressing needs for social services and education and a strong desire to maintain, if not lower, existing taxation levels.

Provincial health care is publicly administered by provincial ministries of health (although in all provinces except for Ontario some of these administrative responsibilities have been devolved to regional health authorities, as discussed further below). Provinces effectively define what services will be publicly funded (and thus described as 'medically necessary'), set fee schedules for payment to physicians, and set global budgets for hospitals.

Adoption of HTA at the provincial level is affected by certain constraints. The first is that of limited public dollars. Consequently, provincial governments are concerned not just with economic evidence about the effectiveness of efficiency of a new technology but the total impact on public spending. The second set of constraints is the political difficulties that provincial governments face in delisting (removing certain health services and treatments from the schedule of insured benefits). In order to be able to fund newer technologies and treatments, accepting there is a limited number of public dollars, it is essential that older, *relatively* less cost-effective treatments be delisted. But there is presently little or no capacity for delisting in provinces across the country, particularly with regard to physician and hospital services protected by the CHA.

Decisions over provider services and hospital funding

Decisions regarding provider remuneration and what services to cover are largely made in a bilateral process that involves intense negotiations between organizations representing provider interests and provincial governments. For example, every three or four years, the Ontario Medical Association (OMA) conducts these negotiations on behalf of Ontario physicians. Other provider groups, including those representing nurses, hold similar negotiating sessions across the country. Member hospitals of the Ontario Hospital Association now submit utilization data every four years to the Ontario Ministry of Health and Long-Term Care (MOHLTC) in order to assist the latter in determining global budgets over multiple years.

In 1991, the OMA was designated the exclusive bargaining agent for the medical profession in Ontario[30; 31; 32] and MOHLTC has historically consulted and negotiated with the OMA regarding the 'tariffs' or fees to be paid to physicians for the provision of publicly funded services. This process indirectly determines what physician services are 'medically necessary' and thus publicly funded.[33] A recent review of these process concluded that HTA seems to be playing a greater role in determining both fee increases and changes to the Schedule of Benefits; however, the process still remains quite private, shielded from public input and scrutiny, and one in which, for better or worse, the medical profession continues to exert significant control over the policy agenda and outcomes.[34] In contrast, hospitals, whose global budgets are profoundly affected by decisions reached about what physician services are or are not publicly funded, are not privy to these negotiations.

Decisions about what services should be included in the list of publicly insured services and decisions about what services to delist have their genesis in the OMA itself. Therefore, the OMA is effectively (amongst its other functions) an HTA agency, although usually not formally recognized as such. The OMA has a wealth of economists and other researchers who gather evidence from other jurisdictions, clinical trials, and other sources, and the OMA produces annual reports recommending changes to the Schedule of Benefits. The committee within the OMA that does this is called the Central Tariff Committee (CTC); a ten-person committee, all of whom are physicians or physician economists. Reports of the CTC are in turn reviewed by the Physician Services Committee (PSC). The PSC is intended to allow a 'broad and structured process for regular liaison and communication between the Ministry and the Medical Profession'.[35] The PSC consists of five members appointed by the OMA and five members appointed by the MOHLTC, and it performs a range of functions. Most importantly for the purposes of this paper, the PSC reviews the utilization of services and ultimately makes recommendations regarding changes to the Schedule of Benefits. The Schedule of Benefits of Physician Services (SOB-PS) is a list of medical services for which eligible Ontario residents will be publicly insured. The SOB-PS lists approximately 4800 insured physician services and contains a description of the service, a billing code, the amount payable, and any applicable conditions or restrictions.[36; 37]

The capacity for adoption of new health technologies into any provincial health insurance plan is restricted by the limited public dollars available for spending on medical services. Thus, in order for relatively more cost-effective technologies to be publicly funded it is important that older and less effective technologies and treatments be delisted. However, political, legal, and cultural institutions make it more difficult to delist than to list, leading to stickiness in the system whereby older, less effective treatments continue to be funded at the expense of potentially more effective and newer technologies.[38] For example, the CTC has become more 'gun-shy' in recent years in recommending delisting, mostly as a result of litigation brought by Ontario audiologists and other groups to contest the delistings (it should be noted that this is said to be the case even though the litigation was unsuccessful).[39] Reportedly, the CTC has not forwarded a report to the MOHLTC recommending any delistings since 1998.

Governments can be forced to fund new technologies if claimants are successful in appealing the negative decision of a provincial ministry. In Ontario, if the MOHLTC turns down a claim, a disappointed patient who wishes to obtain care that is not presently available in Ontario, or for which there are long waiting times, can appeal to the Health Services Appeal and Review Board. The relevant section of the Heath Insurance Act[40] states:

(i) Pre-Approved Treatment
     (2) Services that are part of a treatment and that are rendered outside Canada at a hospital or health facility are prescribed as insured services if,
     (a) the treatment is generally accepted in Ontario as appropriate for a person in the same medical circumstances as the insured person; and
     (b) either,
         i. that kind of treatment is not performed in Ontario by an identical or equivalent procedure; or

ii. that kind of treatment is performed in Ontario but it is necessary that the insured person travel out of Canada to avoid a delay that would result in death or medically irreversible tissue damage.

Thus, for a claimant to succeed in an appeal with respect to section 28.4, the Board must answer two seemingly similar questions, the first in the positive and the second in the negative. The Board must first determine that the treatment is generally accepted in Ontario as appropriate for a patient in the same medical circumstances, and second, it must then determine that the treatment is not performed in Ontario, either as an objective or practical matter. This presents a Catch-22 for most patients, as the Board seems to use evidence that a particular treatment is *not* performed in Ontario to indicate that treatment is thus not generally accepted in Ontario. When the treatment in question is new it is, of course, not surprising that it is difficult to surmount the first part of the test.[41] This provision underscores the difficulties faced by those seeking funding for new technologies and treatments and the systemic bias in the political and legal structures against funding newer treatments as opposed to older, established services.

Decisions vis-à-vis prescription drugs

The federal government has responsibility for approval of new drugs as safe; however, the provincial governments have the ultimate responsibility for deciding what approved drugs to place on their own publicly funded formularies. Provinces have advisory committees which individually assess whether or not to include new drugs within the public formulary. In Ontario, the Drug Quality and Therapeutics Committee (DQTC) advises the MOHLTC on which products to include in Ontario's formulary. As the Canada Health Act does not cover prescription drugs needed outside of hospital walls, the Ontario plan does not cover all residents. Ontario's formulary is a listing of products that are covered by the provincial government for residents over 65, for those on welfare, and for those for whom drug costs represent a certain percentage of their income.

Beta interferon is an example of a drug for which coverage varies across the country due to each provincial drug programme making widely varying decisions regarding coverage. This drug is a part of the treatment regimen for individuals with multiple sclerosis that helps prevent the risk of acute attacks. The federal Health Protection Branch approved this drug in 1995 and public provision is available in Ontario under the Section 8 process, which is designed to allow 'individual clinical review' by members of the DQTC on a case-by-case basis.[42] Quebec is the only province that fully funds beta interferon for those patients whose physicians prescribe it for them.[43]

With the advent of a common drug review at a national level, DQTC and the other provincial advisory committees may increasingly be relegated to the role of advising the provinces and territories as to 'how to list' (for example, for general or limited use) rather than 'what to list'.[44; 45] However, a final decision on whether to list a prescription drug with a positive recommendation from CEDAC ultimately rests with each province, while a negative recommendation is considered tacitly binding on all of the provinces. Generally, decisions regarding drug coverage are 'closed-door/top-down' in nature even though input from stakeholders is taken into consideration (see Figure 3.2).

In contradistinction to the approach taken to physician services, more attention is paid to HTA in determining whether to list or delist prescription drugs. In 1996, Ontario's provincial government required pharmaceutical manufacturers seeking to list their products to provide a formal economic analysis documenting the product's cost effectiveness. However, even though economic evidence is viewed as an extremely important consideration, there are limitations on the extent to which it is relied upon.[46] As PaussJensen, Singer, and Detsky note in their review of decision-making by the DQTC, although economic evidence is always considered, evidence of clinical efficacy is in fact what most often drives decision-making.[47] Reasons economic evidence does not drive decision-making to a greater degree, according to PaussJensen, Singer, and Detsky, include methodological problems with the use of economic analysis, particularly in studies generated by the manufacturers of the drugs. Related to this problem is the limited ability of DQTC members to critique economic reports because of a lack of formal training (in response to this problem, the MOHLTC has now increased the number of members with training in health economics). Other reasons include concerns about the values (utilitarian, population-based) that underpin an economic analysis and the reality that considerations of equity, access, politics, and law must also be taken into account in the final determination of what drugs to list in the public formulary.

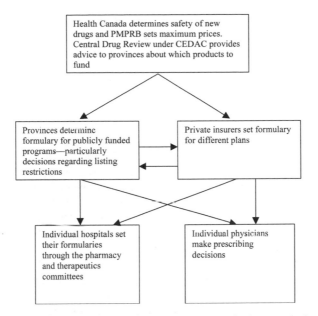

Figure 3.2 Cascading levels of decision-making vis-à-vis prescription drugs

Just as CCOHTA has faced challenges by stakeholders upset at its recommendations at the national level, so too have HTA authorities been challenged at a provincial level. For example, pharmaceutical companies have used the threat of litigation to fight back against unfavourable reviews by the DQTC and other HTA experts consulted by the Ontario government. One researcher who advised the Ontario government that a relatively expensive ulcer drug, Losec, was essentially equivalent to two cheaper medications was threatened with legal action by Losec's manufacturer, AstraZeneca.[48]

Provincial decisions vis-à-vis specific health care technologies

In the following section we focus on specific case studies of health technology adoption at the provincial level: cochlear implants, MRI scanners, PET scanners, and genetic testing. Through vignettes, largely based in Ontario, we will illustrate the tensions involved in HTA given the structure and dynamics of the larger Canadian system, and in particular the pressures that are bought to bear on the public system once a technology is available in the private sector. We will then proceed to examine more specifically health technology adoption on the part of regional health authorities, within hospitals and other transfer agencies, and on the part of physicians.

Cochlear implants and MRI services

Public hospitals in Canada are, in general, private for-profit corporations, but they receive nearly all their operating funds from provincial governments through global budgets. There are some important exceptions to this general rule, however, and provincial ministries *directly* fund some hospital-based health care services, known in Ontario as 'Priority Programmes' that are typically associated with high cost and high growth. Ontario currently manages 15 Priority Programmes, including acquired brain injury, bone marrow transplantation, cardiovascular services, cleft lip & palate and craniofacial dental, cochlear implants, end stage renal disease, haemophilia ambulatory clinics, hip & oncology, the provincial regional genetics programme, regional geriatric programmes, sexual assault treatment centres, and trauma.[49] Thus, whilst normally difficult choices of which new technologies or treatments to fund are left to hospitals within the confines of a global budget, through the Priority Programmes initiative certain technologies and treatments are elevated above this rationing process and qualify for direct provincial funding. Two services of interest are cochlear implants and magnetic resonance imaging (MRI) services, both of which combine direct Ministry funding with hospital funding.

Cochlear implants are used to provide hearing assistance to individuals with profound bilateral sensorineural hearing loss. These expensive implants constitute only a small part of the care required for these patients; therapy and rehabilitation are integral to a successful surgical outcome. The MOHLTC will fund the device portion of the surgery while the services that go along with the surgery are funded through the hospital's global budget.[50] The Priority Programmes Unit provides designated hospitals with the operating funds to deliver MRI insured services. In return, hospitals are expected to comply with a number of conditions, including service level requirements. Hospitals typically purchase MRI machines through their own fundraising efforts. The decision to fund cochlear implants and MRI services is thus a combination/bilateral funding decision by the provincial government and the hospital. With cochlear implants, the government will pay for the implant device while the hospital must fund the remaining services associated with the surgery through their global budget. Conversely, the provincial government will fund MRI operational services while it is the responsibility of hospitals to find funding, either within their global budgets or through fundraising initiatives, to buy and maintain the MRI machines.

Genetic testing

Genetic testing services provide another example of where provision of services in the private sector puts pressure on the public sector. Provincial governments have yet to establish clear principles to guide decisions about which genetic services to fund.

In 1999, one woman successfully appealed the Ontario provincial government's refusal to fund BRCA1 and BRCA2 tests (genetic markers for breast cancer) at the Health Services Appeal and Review Board (the administrative tribunal that hears such claims in Ontario).[51] The consequences flowing from this decision have been significant. Quite quickly the Ontario government moved to establish a domestic supply of genetic tests rather than purchase the tests from the US. The Ontario government now faces litigation by Myriad Genetics Ltd, which claims that the government is breaching Myriad's patent rights by allowing testing in Ontario laboratories without licensing the test from Myriad. Myriad's procedures cost CA$3850 per test whereas Ontario's procedures cost CA$1100 per test; the consequences for the provincial health budget are clearly much more significant if the province has to pay the former rather than the latter price for all women who qualify for testing. The provincial government in British Columbia, facing similar legal threats on the part of Myriad, backed down from its plans to offer testing in British Columbia without a license. Instead it now sends its patients to Ontario for the test! This vignette illustrates how HTA within a health care system is a function of the structure of that system, including its legal system, and is also a product of the political and other values held in the system. To put it more crudely, quite different conclusions about the relative cost effectiveness of the genetic tests will be reached depending on whether or not a public insurer is compelled to pay the patent-holder's monopoly price for the test in question.

With the evolution of private markets for genetic testing services, it is also important to evaluate the impact of allowing a two-tiered system for genetic testing (in other words where people can use private insurance or private resources to purchase additional or more timely treatment).[52] After an individual receives a test result in the private sector, he or she might proceed to the public sector for advice and treatment, or make lifestyle choices that in the long run might impose further costs on the public system.[53] The decision to publicly insure genetic testing could thus help limit downstream costs that impact the public sector over the longer run. Within the evolving private-sector markets for genetic testing, there is no control of the diffusion of testing. This too puts pressure on the government to control the growth of genetic tests by publicly insuring these services for fear that once 'the genie is let out of the bottle' in terms of diffusion and utilization in the private sector, the long-run costs to the public sector will be even higher.

CASE STUDY: PET SCANNERS

There is heated debate about the merits of public funding for Positron Emission Tomography (PET) scanners, a highly innovative technology used to test for cancer, heart disease, and Alzheimer's disease. As of 15 July 2001, the CCOHTA reported that there were nine PET machines operating in Canada, but only two being used for non-research purposes. The Quebec government fully funded the first machine in Sherbrooke, while use of the second machine, in Vancouver, requires patients pay CA$2500 a test. Nobody as of yet can receive PET in Ontario as a publicly insured service outside of participation in a research project or on compassionate grounds. One private company, CareImaging, is in the process of applying to Health Canada for approval of clinical trials for FDG (the drug used in PET scanning). Upon approval, the company plans to open a private PET centre in Ontario, charging CA$2500 per test. The emergence of these private facilities supplying new technologies is creating a precedent under which some provinces will allow private clinics to charge their patients while other provinces will not (in other words, some provinces are treating PET scans are 'medically necessary' and are publicly funding them in full whereas others are not).[54] Thus while provinces are probably viewing the same evidence of cost effectiveness they are reaching different conclusions about whether to publicly fund PET scans. It is also clear that the availability of PET scans in the private sector puts pressure on provincial governments to publicly fund the scans, at least for some indications.

In recent months, Ontario has adopted a strong stance of evidence-based decision-making regarding PET scanning and has announced that PET scanners may be introduced to the province on a limited basis, but only as a part of this evaluative process. At a conference in June 2003, the CEO of the Institute for Clinical Evaluative Sciences (ICES) (see Appendix 3.1) discussed planned clinical studies of PET scanning to be conducted in Ontario. ICES is an independent non-profit corporation based in Toronto that provides HTA services. A PET Steering Committee, commissioned by the Ontario MOHLTC and ICES, is supervising a process that continuously provides updates of the published literature involving PET, determines whether the literature is convincing enough to allow PET scanning to specific individuals as an insured service, and funds PET studies.[55] As a result, four protocols are being finalized for situations where PET has been deemed integral to answering clinical questions. This hands-off decision-making strategy is in response to, on the one hand, the public pressure to pay for PET scans in Canada given their adoption in other jurisdictions, and, on the other hand, dissatisfaction with the existing published and unpublished HTAs of PET scans.

THE REGIONAL ROLE

In the 1990s, most provinces and territories in Canada decentralized some health decision-making through regionalization and creation of regional health authorities (RHA).[56] RHAs were initiated as a means for provinces to contain costs and improve service integration.[57] RHAs receive funding from the provincial governments through annual budgets that are based on the historical spending levels of the population served. RHAs do not have any role in raising revenue, other than private fundraising for internal use, but all are responsible for local planning, priority setting, fund allocation, service management, and delivery for the defined range of services.[58]

A review of evidence in the primary and secondary literature indicates that devolution across Canada resulted in a mixture of successes and failures. As Flood, Sinclair, and Erdman note, the failures can be attributed to two primary reasons.[59] First, rhetorical rather than substantive devolution of powers has often occurred. Second, no Canadian RHA receives funding for key elements of the health care system (such as physician or pharmaceutical services); RHAs thus lack the levers essential to effective management of their responsibilities.

Nonetheless, all the RHAs do have significant control over hospitals within their regions and thus over HTA decision-making within hospitals. For example, at the Winnipeg RHA, there is a single drug formulary and single pharmacy and therapeutics review process for all hospitals. This closed-door/top-down decision-making method has been highly effective at establishing consistency, although it is not a popular process: many believe that institutional differences are not given due consideration.

Although Ontario has not, unlike the other nine provinces in Canada, embraced regionalization, there is decentralization of responsibility for disease management. Cancer Care Ontario (CCO) and the Cardiac Care Network (CCN) are provincial institutions that manage the delivery of care for patients with those diseases across Ontario. The CCN was founded in 1990 as an advisory body to the Ontario MOHLTC and it co-ordinates the provision of advanced cardiac services to patients across Ontario with the aid of a computerized patient registry. A co-ordinator at each cardiac centre uses this database to triage and monitor access to services by patients. The CCN also advises the Ontario MOHLTC on the planning and delivery of care and provides advice about what new services and treatments to fund for cardiac patients. Similarly, CCO, a provincial statutory corporation created in 1997, has as its mandate the co-ordination of cancer services in Ontario, including surveillance programmes, screening procedures, systematic chemotherapy, and new and expensive pharmaceutical treatments. Through its mandate, and with a budget approximating 23 per cent of traceable costs in the province's cancer system, the CCO's practices and policies have a significant impact on the management and co-ordination of Ontario's cancer control strategy and management.[60] CCO also plays a role in advising the Ontario government on what new cancer services and treatments to fund. In this regard, Martin and Singer report in their analysis of the Cancer Care Ontario Policy Advisory Committee that cost-effectiveness analysis was rarely used formally, but the concept was used informally and combined with other considerations. In particular, the capacity of the Committee to request and obtain budget increases from the government profoundly affected the range of considerations to which the Committee gave weight.[61] Martin and Singer noted that just as rationales changed when the size of the budget increased, so did they change as costs increased:

> the committee decided to fund an expensive drug for myeloma patients but not for patients with breast cancer. The evidence of benefit of the drug in the two diseases was very similar; the primary difference was the increased total cost related to the large number of breast cancer patients.[62]

HOSPITALS

Though the majority of health care delivery typically falls within provincial and territorial jurisdiction, governments devolve certain authority to transfer agencies such as hospitals, home care agencies, and long-term care institutions. Here we will focus on hospitals only. In most provinces, hospital funding is based primarily on a principle of global (or base) funding budget provided to each hospital annually. These budget allotments are based primarily on past allocations and annual adjustments to reflect changes in costs. For the most part, physicians are not paid by the hospital's global budget but through fee schedules negotiated between provincial governments and physician groups.

Through their global budgets, along with additional funding through fundraising or charitable contributions, hospitals must decide on the adoption of new technologies through their respective pharmacy and therapeutics committees. With the exception of those few managed by a regional health authority (for example, Winnipeg), hospitals have the power to establish an internal formulary for drugs with advice from their individual pharmacy and therapeutics committees. The hospital drug benefit list is intended to expand on the provincial formulary as required to meet the special requirements of hospitals. This list is monitored and maintained by a specific advisory committee comprised of the Canadian Society of Hospital Pharmacists, the drug quality assessment committee of the particular province, and representatives of the Ministries of Health. In general, however, technology adoption by hospitals is an example of closed-door/top-down decision-making.

PHYSICIANS

In the Canadian health care system, as in many other pre-
dominantly publicly funded systems, the physician acts as gate-
keeper to the rest of the system by writing prescriptions, making
referrals, admitting patients to hospitals, and sending patients for
diagnostic tests and x-rays.

As has been discussed throughout this paper, there are significant
impediments to delisting of services. This in turn has an effect on
the capacity and willingness of public insurers to fund newer
technologies and treatments. Soderlund notes that the debate about
rationing publicly funded health care often vacillates between
macro-rationing (black and white decisions about what is in and
out of the publicly funded basket) and micro-rationing, under
which 'guidelines, protocols and prior authorization by third party
payers determine which individuals have access to which services in
which disease context, usually on a case by case basis'.[63] In the
Canadian context, given the significant difficulties associated with
macro-rationing, HTA seems to be increasingly orienting itself
towards micro-rationing. This is demonstrated in the several cases
discussed in this paper where the diffusion of new technologies (e.g.
PET scanners, beta-interferon, MRIs, etc.) is allowed on a very
limited basis and micro-managed centrally. This is to be compared
to simply allowing the incorporation of new technologies or treatments within the list of publicly insured services and leaving it to the
discretion of individual physicians to prescribe or recommend the
treatment.

Why central management rather than physician guidelines?
Physician guidelines would allow greater flexibility, reduce administration costs, and speed up the process of decision-making.
However, in the absence of reform of the financial incentives physicians face in the Canadian system (fee-for-service) it seem likely
that the promulgation of guidelines will have little impact in the
utilization of newer treatments and technologies. Physicians may
take cognizance of guidelines regarding medical efficacy (and this
duty is reinforced by professional ethical codes and the law) but
why, without incentive, would they change established patterns of
practice to follow guidelines that speak to cost effectiveness?

CONCLUSION

The Canadian system of HTA must be considered in the light of the structure and dynamics of the system within which it is enmeshed. As Battista and colleagues point out, 'technology management within a health care system is a function of the structure of that system and its surrounding cultural milieu'.[64] In the Canadian system, there is a strong sectoral division in the funding of health care, with 'medically necessary' hospital and physician services being almost fully publicly funded, and other services and technologies, such as prescription drugs, genetic therapies, and devices, falling into a mixed private and public system. This sectoral approach to funding is also reflected in the variety of approaches taken to HTA. Most HTA efforts have been directed towards therapeutic technologies (primarily drugs) and diagnostics (including genetic tests[65]). HTA efforts with regard to physician services are relatively new and are focused only on assessment of new procedures; there is little or no momentum for considering the relative cost effectiveness of physician services that are presently funded. This leads to stagnation in a publicly funded health care system, as new technologies and treatments are viewed with a more demanding eye than would be the case if it were possible to delist *relatively* less cost-effective procedures that are already publicly funded. This stagnation is perpetuated by the political and legal systems. It is politically extremely difficult to take away established entitlements and much easier to ration prior to the entitlement become vested. Similarly, the fear of legal challenges (even if not successful) underscores this political reluctance.

HTA within the Canadian system is very complex, reflecting the different approaches taken to the insurance and delivery of health care across the ten provinces and three territories and reflecting the multiple levels of decision-making regarding HTA that occur throughout the system. Decisions about the diffusion of technologies and HTA are shaped through a cascade of decision-making and pressure from higher government levels limits decision-making by the government below. Decision-making with regard to health technology occurs at three levels: the federal level with regard to safety and assessments; the provincial level with regard to the decision of whether to publicly fund new technologies (and how to regulate the diffusion thereof if left to the private sector); and at the hospital/physician level with regard to use or adoption of particular technologies. Each level constrains the level below in terms of the range of choices.

There are also some lateral pressures between the public and private sectors (for example, a province may face pressure to publicly fund a technology once it is available in the private sector). If a province or territory does not act prior to private providers moving in, it may lose control over diffusion of the technology and face pressure to publicly fund it; moreover, existing providers are usually grandfathered into the public insurance scheme. Examples of such lateral pressure include the cases of genetic services, diagnostic imaging, and PET scanning.

Throughout the layers of decision-making that draw on HTA, economic analysis is viewed as a valuable tool for programme evaluation and decision-making. But ultimate decisions are rarely made on the basis of an economic analysis alone. This is partly due to methodological problems: data are often insufficient and techniques are prone to debate, such that there is a lack of confidence that results are valid for the decision at hand. This technical difficulty is compounded by a general perception that health care is of priceless value and that by applying an economic evaluation you draw a line as to which lives are more valuable. Therefore, the impact of economic evaluations are often more subtle, having more of an impact on decision-making trends rather than on particular decisions. If the CHA were amended to include a 'medically necessary and reasonable' provision, instead of the current 'medically necessary' provision, it is possible that this would provide a top-down impetus and endorsement for the greater use of economic modeling.

For HTA to have a greater impact in decision-making, there arguably needs to be greater integration of social, political, legal, and ethical dimensions of health technologies into the process of technology assessment.[66; 67] But this raises the question of whether this is a good use of resources and whether those who work in HTA could adequately anticipate the variety of considerations that policy-makers and decision-makers may wish to take into account. At the moment, the concern is that decision-makers respond on an *ad hoc* basis: they make decisions (albeit after having received an HTA report) and then justify them subsequently. A better and more robust solution would be to develop a principled framework that would assist decision-makers (as opposed to those who generate HTA) to balance economic evidence and political, economic, ethical, legal, and distributive considerations in a transparent and rigorous way.

APPENDIX 3.1: SOME OF THE ORGANIZATIONS THAT CONDUCT FORMAL HTA IN CANADA

- Canadian Coordinating Office for Health Technology Assessment (CCOHTA – National) http://www.ccohta.ca/ (funded by federal and provincial governments)
- Agence D'Évaluation des Technologies et des Modes D'intervention en Santé (AETMIS – Quebec) http://www.aetmis.-gouv.qc.ca/en/index.php (government-funded)
- Institute for Clinical Evaluative Sciences (ICES – Ontario) http://www.ices.on.ca (funded by government through an annual grant (on a five-year renewable term that expires at the end of 2005), through competitively-derived grants and awards, and from contributions (mostly in kind) of a number of hospitals and universities)
- Manitoba Centre for Health Policy and Evaluation (MCHPE – Manitoba) http://www.umanitoba.ca/centres/mchp/ (university-based; competitively-derived grants and awards; two thirds funded by government contract)
- Health Services Utilization and Research Commission (HSURC – Saskatchewan) http://www.hsurc.sk.ca/ (government-funded)
- Alberta Heritage Foundation for Medical Research (AHFMR – Alberta) http://www.ahfmr.ab.ca/ (government-funded)
- The Institute of Health Economics (IHE – Alberta) http://www.ihe.ca/ (some government funding and funding from large pharmaceutical companies)
- Calgary Health Region Health Technology Implementation Unit (CHRHTI – Alberta) http://www.crha-health.ab.ca/htiu/program.html (funded by the Calgary Regional Authority, University of Calgary, and government)
- Centre for Health Evaluation and Outcome Sciences (CHEOS – St Paul's Hospital, British Columbia) http://www.cheos.ubc.ca/main.html (no information on funding)
- British Columbia Office of Health Technology Assessment, Centre for Health Services and Policy Research (CHSPR – University of British Columbia) http://www.chspr.ubc.ca (university-based; competitively derived grants and awards and government funding)

- Hospital Report Research Collaborative (University of Toronto – Ontario) http://www.hospitalreport.ca/index.html (government funding and funding from the Ontario Hospitals Association)

References

1   This report was funded by the Canadian Health Services Research Foundation under grant no. RC2–0861–06 for the project entitled: Defining the Medicare 'Basket'. This paper reflects the views of the authors and does not necessarily reflect the opinions of the Canadian Health Services Research Foundation nor the Ontario Ministry of Health and Long Term Care. We would like to thank our research associates, Dara Zarnett, Andrée Mitchell, and Simon R. Rabinovitch.

2   D. Menon (2000), 'An Assessment of Health Technology Assessment in Canada', *Canadian Journal of Public Health*, 91(2): 120.

3   D. Menon and L. Topfer (2000), 'Health Technology Assessment in Canada', *International Journal of Technology Assessment in Health Care*, 16(3): 896–902.

4   Cost-effectiveness, cost–utility, and cost–benefit analysis are three types of economic evaluation differing primarily in the methods used to measure the benefits or consequences of alternative choices. Cost-effectiveness analysis involves calculating the direct cost of direct intervention per unit of effectiveness, for example, cost per life years saved, cases successfully treated, or cases averted. Because only one effect can be related to the cost of intervention and the effect must be identical for each appraised choice, cost effectiveness is more useful for comparing between interventions for a single condition than for comparing the relative value of a given intervention for different conditions. Cost–utility analysis combines morbidity and mortality (illness and death) data into a single outcome measure (for example, quality adjusted life year, QALY), allowing comparison of the relative efficiency of an intervention for different conditions. Cost–benefit analysis is theoretically the gold standard of economic evaluation, allowing determination of the absolute benefit of a choice by calculating all direct, indirect, and intangible costs and benefits; problematically, however, this requires the monetary valuation of intangibles, such as alleviation of pain, and the outcome measure, such as lives saved. D. Coyle and L. Davies (1993), 'How to Assess Cost-Effectiveness: Elements of a Sound Economic Evaluation', in M.F. Drummond and A. Maynard (eds.), *Purchasing and Providing Cost-Effective Health Care*. Edinburgh: Churchill Livingstone.

5   R. Battista, V. Déry, R. Jacob et al. (2003), *Health Technology Assessment in University Teaching Hospitals* (*Translated from L'éva-*

luation des technologies et des modes d'intervention en santé dans les hôpitaux universitaires). Montréal: AETMIS.

6 See D. Martin and P. Singer (2003), 'Canada', in C. Ham and G. Robert (eds.), *Reasonable Rationing: International Experience of Priority Setting in Health Care*. Maidenhead: Open University Press, 42–63.

7 P. Lehoux and S. Blume (2000), 'Technology Assessment and the Sociopolitics of Health Technologies', *Journal of Health Politics, Policy and Law*, 25(6): 1083–120.

8 The metaphor of 'concentric circles' for describing the Canadian health care system was first advanced by Carolyn Tuohy.

9 C.M. Flood, M. Stabile, and C. Tuohy (2004), 'What Is In and Out of Medicare? Who Decides?' Working paper No. 5 – Defining the Medicare Basket. < www.law.utoronto.ca/healthlaw/basket/docs/working5_inandout.pdf > (accessed 5 Apr. 2004).

10 A. Maioni (2002), 'Roles and Responsibilities in Health Care Policy', Discussion Paper no. 34, Commission on the Future of Health Care in Canada. < www.hc-sc.gc.ca/english/pdf/romanow/pdfs/34_Maioni_E.pdf > (accessed 5 Apr. 2004).

11 For a discussion, see C.M. Flood (2002), 'The Anatomy of Medicare', in J. Downie, T. Caulfield, and C.M. Flood (eds.), *Canadian Health Law & Policy*. Toronto: Butterworths.

12 C.M. Flood and T. Archibald (2001), 'The Illegality of Private Health Care in Canada', *Canadian Medical Association Journal*, 164(6): 825–30.

13 C. Tuohy, C.M. Flood, and M. Stabile (2004), 'Marshalling the Evidence', *Journal of Health Politics, Policy and Law*, 29(3) (forthcoming).

14 D. Harriman, W. McArthur, and M. Zelder (1999), 'The Availability of Medical Technology in Canada: an International Comparative Study', Public Policy Source Paper No. 28. Vancouver: Fraser Institute.

15 Health Canada (2001), 'Tough Tests for Drugs', *Health Canada Magazine*, March. < www.hc-sc.gc.ca/english/feature/magazine/2001_03/2001_03_hc.pdf > (accessed 5 Apr. 2004).

16 See, for example, the Patented Medicine Prices Review Board (2003), *Compendium of Guidelines Policies and Procedures*. Ottawa: Patented Medicine Prices Review Board. < www.pmprb-cepmb.gc.ca/CMFiles/2004compendium-e21LTW–152004–1350.pdf > (accessed 5 Apr. 2004).

17 This memorandum is specific to pharmaceuticals for human use and does not explore the PMPRB's role in the control over pharmaceuticals used in animals.

18 See, for example, Patented Medicine Prices Review Board, 'Report on New Patented Drugs – Gleevec', < www.pmprb-cepmb.gc.ca/

CMFiles/gleevec-e21IPD–632003–2630.pdf> (last accessed 5 Aug. 2004).

19 For details, see Patented Medicine Prices Review Board (2003), pp. 35–6, Schedule 3 – International Price Comparison.

20 For example, the PPRS looks at the volume of drugs sold as well as the price of drugs. The United Kingdom also restricts the amount of money that companies can spend on promotion.

21 Patented Medicines Price Review Board (2000), *Annual Report*. Ottawa: Patented Medicine Prices Review Board. <www.pmprb-cepmb.gc.ca/CMFiles/ar00e612NOJ–482003–1747.pdf> (accessed 5 Apr. 2004).

22 IMS Health Canada reports that there were 270 million prescriptions filled in Canada in 1999. IMS Health Canada (2000) Annual report on diagnoses, treatments, and the pharmaceutical industry. <www.imshealthcanada.com/htmen/pdf/4_2_1_18.pdf> (accessed 5 Apr. 2004).

23 The act became law on 29 March 2004 but will be phased into effect over 2004–5. Reproductive treatments underway at the time the act became law are 'grandfathered'. See <www.hc-sc.gc.ca/english/protection/reproduction> (accessed 5 Apr. 2004).

24 J.M. Sanders (2002), 'Challenges, Choices, and Canada', *International Journal of Technology Assessment in Health Care*, 18(2): 199–202.

25 D. McDaid (2003), 'Co-ordinating Health Technology Assessment in Canada: A European Perspective', *Health Policy*, 63: 205–15.

26 The CDR process is described at <www.ccohta.ca/CDR/cdr_intro_e.ASP> (accessed 5 Apr. 2004).

27 The federal government provides drug insurance coverage for some Aboriginal peoples and the military.

28 Bristol-Myers Squibb Canada Inc. v. Canadian Coordinating Office for Health Technology Assessment [1998] O.J. No. 1404.

29 Flood (2002).

30 Health Care Accessibility Act, R.S.O. 1990, c. H.3, ss. 3(1) and 3(2).

31 Health Insurance Act, R.S.O. 1990, c. 1, Sched. H, ss. 19 and 27.

32 Physicians Services Delivery Management Act, S.O. 1996, c. 1.

33 Pursuant to s. 3.1 of the Health Care Accessibility Act, R.S.O. 1990, c. H.3, the Minister may enter into agreements with the OMA 'to provide for methods of negotiating and determining the amounts payable under the [Ontario Health Insurance] Plan in respect of the rendering of insured services to insured persons'.

34 See T. Archibald and C.M. Flood (2004), 'The Physician Services Committee – the Relationship Between the OMA and the Ontario Ministry of Health and Long-Term Care', Working Paper No. 2, Defining the Medicare Basket. <www.law.utoronto.ca/healthlaw/basket/docs/working2_oma.pdf> (accessed 5 Apr. 2004).

35 OMA-MOHLTC 2000–2004 Agreement at s. 2.01. <www.srpc.ca/librarydocs/omaagrmt.htm> (accessed 5 Apr. 2004).

36 When the Health Insurance Act was adopted in 1972, there was no SOB-PS. Rather, the government paid physicians a discounted fee based on the OMA schedule of fees. The Ministry published the SOB-PS in 1978 and has subsequently modified it over the years.

37 Archibald and Flood (2004).

38 Flood, Stabile, and Tuohy (2004).

39 Shulman v. College of Audiologists and Speech Language Pathologists of Ontario, [2001] O.J. No. 5057. Among other grounds, the applicant sought a declaration that the decision of the Ontario government to stop insuring costs of hearing-aid evaluations and re-evaluations and to attach conditions to terms of payment to physicians for diagnostic hearing tests violated equality rights of persons with a hearing disability as guaranteed by s. 15(1) of the Charter of Rights and Freedoms. The Court deferred to the government on policy-making grounds, concluding (at paragraph 43) that the 'healthcare system is vast and complex. A court should be cautious about characterizing structural changes to OHIP which do not shut out vulnerable persons as discriminatory, given the institutional impediments to design of a healthcare system by the judiciary.' In this case, the changes to the Schedule of Benefits were found not to discriminate within the meaning of s. 15(1) of the Charter and the application was dismissed on that ground.

40 R.S.O. 1990, c. H.6, s. 28.4.

41 Flood, Stabile, and Tuohy (2004).

42 B. Otten (1996), 'Technology Overview: Pharmaceuticals – Interferon Beta 1-B and Multiple Sclerosis. Ottawa: CCOHTA. < www.phru. medicine.dal.ca/briefs/beta1b.pdf > (accessed 5 Apr. 2004).

43 In Britain, the government's advisory body has found that Beta Interferon treatment is not cost-effective, and has recommended that it should not be made available unless there is new money allotted to fund this drug therapy. The National Health Service (NHS) has subsequently decided to fund this drug, but has made special arrangements with the pharmaceutical companies that manufacture the drug to share financial risk. Should Beta Interferon prove to be ineffective, the NHS can reclaim profits for the drug from the pharmaceutical companies.

44 L. Dunn and N. Pilla (1998), 'Understanding the Classes–Focus on Cholesterol Lowering Agents', *Provincial Reimbursement Advisor*, November.

45 < www.ccohta.ca/CDR/cdr_intro_e.ASP > (accessed 5 Apr. 2004).

46 There is, however, some evidence that even in the arena of drug assessment, cost-effectiveness analysis is not consistently used. Rather, evidence of clinical efficacy is what primarily drives decision-making. See A. M. PaussJensen, P. A. Singer, and A. S. Detsky (2003), 'How Ontario's Formulary Committee Makes Recommendations', *Pharmacoeconomics*, 21(4): 285–94.

47 As an example of this, in 1999 the DQTC completed a review of all antibiotics listed in the Ontario Drug Benefit Formulary/Comparative Drug Index to ensure that all antibiotics listed in the formulary were being used in agreement with current clinical evidence. Ontario Ministry of Health and Long Term Care (2002), *DQTC Bulletin: Antibiotic Review and ODB Formulary Listing Changes*, November. As a result, several changes have been made to antibiotic listing in the ODB formulary. The most significant listing change affects the flouroquinolone antibiotics, some of which were formerly listed as general benefit products. The committee was particularly concerned about the increasing rates of resistance to this class of antibiotics and the spread of cross-resistance from older to newer flouroquinolones. Other provinces, including Saskatchewan, Manitoba, Nova Scotia and Prince Edwards Island, have also restricted the use of flouroquinolone antibiotics for similar reasons as those given by Ontario.

48 See M. Shuchman (1999), 'Drug Firm Threatens Suit over MD's Product Review', *The Globe and Mail*, 17 November, p. A5.

49 Provincial submission to the Canada Health Act Annual Report 2001–2. < www.hc-sc.gc.ca/medicare/ont-n-all.htm > (accessed 5 Apr. 2004).

50 Provincial submission (2001–2).

51 C. Abraham (1997), 'Tenacious Woman Scores Medical Victory: Fiona Webster's Fight Opens Access to Genetic Breast-Cancer Test', *The Globe and Mail*, 27 August, p. A1.

52 T. Caulfield, M. Burgess, B. Williams-Jones, et al. (2001), 'Providing Genetic Testing through Private Sector – a view from Canada', *ISUMA–Canadian Journal of Policy Research*, 2(3): 72–82.

53 Caulfield, et al. (2001).

54 B. Laghi (2002), 'The Patchwork of Care in Canada', *The Globe and Mail*, 4 December, p. A4. < www.globeandmail.com/servlet/Article News/spec3/RTGAM/20021204/wconsistent/SpecialEvents3/roma now BN/breakingnews > (accessed 5 Apr. 2004).

55 A. Laupacis, W. Evans, L. Levin, et al. for the PET Evaluation Steering Committee of Ontario (2003), 'A Strategy to Evaluate the Diagnostic Role of Positron Emission Scanning in Canada'. Paper presented at the International Society of Technology Assessment in Health Care Conference, Alberta, June 2003.

56 C. Frankish, B. Kwan, P. Ratner, et al. (2002), 'Social and Political Factors Influencing the Functioning of Regional Health Boards in British Columbia', *Health Policy*, 61(2): 125–51.

57 J. Lomas, J. Woods, and G. Veenstra (1997), 'Devolving Authority for Health Care in Canada's Provinces: An Introduction to the Issues', *Canadian Medical Association Journal*, 156(3): 371–7.

58 This is to be compared to the advisory role of the District Health Councils in Ontario, the only province not to embrace regionalization.

59 C.M. Flood, D. Sinclair, and J. Erdman (2004), 'Steering and Rowing in Health Care: The Devolution Option?' Working Paper. Original paper prepared for the Role of Government Panel, Ontario, 2003.
60 T. Sullivan, E. Holowaty, and W. MacKillip (2004), *Cancer Care in Ontario*. Toronto: Canadian Healthcare Association Press.
61 Martin and Singer (2003), p. 54.
62 Martin and Singer (2003), p. 54.
63 N. Soderlund (1998), 'Possible Objectives and Resulting Entitlements of Essential Health Care Packages', *Health Policy*, 45: 196.
64 R. N. Battista, H. D. Banta, E. Jonnson, et al. (1994), 'Lessons from the Eight Countries', *Health Policy*, 30: 401.
65 M. Giacomini, F. Miller, and G. Browman (2003), 'Confronting the "Gray Zones" of Technology Assessment: Evaluating Genetic Testing Services for Public Insurance Coverage in Canada', *International Journal of Technology Assessment in Health Care*, 19(2): 301–16.
66 M. Johri and P. Lehoux (2003), 'The Great Escape? Prospects for Regulating Access to Technology through Health Technology Assessment', *International Journal of Technology Assessment in Health Care*, 19(1): 179–93.
67 Lehoux and Bloom (2000).

4

EVALUATING NEW HEALTH TECHNOLOGY IN THE ENGLISH NATIONAL HEALTH SERVICE

Christopher Newdick

INTRODUCTION

Until the creation of the National Institute for Clinical Excellence (NICE) in 1999, the National Health Service (NHS) had no systematic mechanism by which to appraise new health technology. As a result, responsibility for evaluating and introducing new technology was devolved to a large number of local commissioners, clinicians, and hospital managers. Unsurprisingly, this led to variations in uptake throughout the service. NICE was created in order to create greater national harmony in the use of health technology in the NHS. Its capacity, however, is limited. There will always be a large number of technologies NICE is not able to review. Evaluations of these technologies remains subject to *local* discretion. Bearing in mind that health technology appraisal in the NHS is not simply a national responsibility, we discuss: 1. health care coverage in the UK and the statutory duty to promote 'a comprehensive health service'; 2. NICE and national health technology appraisal; 3. local health technology appraisal in respect of the many technologies which are not subject to NICE guidance.

NHS HEALTH CARE COVERAGE: A 'COMPREHENSIVE HEALTH SERVICE'

Under the National Health Service Act 1977, the Secretary of State is under a duty 'to continue the promotion in England and Wales of a national health service'[1] and to provide certain other services 'to such extent as he considers necessary to meet all reasonable requirements'.[2] These services shall be free of charge, unless Parliament provides otherwise.[3] Since the 1950s, for example, there has been a flat co-payment for prescriptions drugs (currently around £6).[4] In *R v. N and E Devon HA, ex p Coughlan*[5] the Court of Appeal noted that the duty is to 'promote' (but not to 'provide') a comprehensive health service and that the obligation is to provide the specified services to the extent that the Secretary considers *necessary* to meet *all reasonable requirements*. Therefore:

> [T]here is scope for the Secretary of State to exercise a degree of judgment as to the circumstances in which he will provide the services. ... [T]he fact that the service will not be comprehensive does not mean that he is necessarily contravening [the 1977 Act]' ... [A] comprehensive health service may never, for human, financial and other resource reasons, be achievable...

Thus, the Act does not impose an absolute duty to provide the specified services. 'The Secretary of State is entitled to have regard to the resources made available to him under current government economic policy.' Clearly, this provides the Secretary of State with much discretion in selecting the quality and quantity of services to be provided within the NHS.

Crucially, however, the actual business of NHS priority setting is not performed by the Secretary of State, but by local health authority decision-makers. This is because the National Health Service Act delegates the Secretary of State's duties to health authorities (currently called primary care trusts (PCTs)).[6] In addition, health authorities are subject to an additional duty not to exceed their annual financial allocations.[7] The combination of delegated authority and financial restraint means that many difficult and unenviable choices have to be made between deserving patients at local level. This delegated system of health care management has the advantage of enabling local decision-makers to respond to the needs of local communities. But it also creates differentials within the NHS and the risk of what is called 'post-code rationing'. There are currently some 300 PCTs, all of which possess the power to allocate resources in their own discretion. PCTs may react to identical clinical evidence in differing ways. Some may be persuaded by evidence about which others remain equivocal.[8] Even if they agree about the veracity of the clinical evidence, PCTs may disagree as to the place particular treatments commands in the resource-allocation process.

In a national health service, is it not reasonable to have national expectations as to the treatment that will be available within the NHS? Government is blamed when patients' rights of access to care depend on their health authority and, perhaps, on which side of the road they live. NICE was created to ease this concern by advising PCTs throughout the NHS whether or not to fund a particular technology, having regard to 'the promotion of clinical excellence and of the effective use of available resources in the health service'.[9] We now turn to the nature and meaning of this duty by considering the impact of NICE on health technology assessment at national level.

NICE AND HEALTH TECHNOLOGY ASSESSMENT AT THE NATIONAL LEVEL

The following section considers: (a) selection procedures for appraisal by NICE, (b) substantive decision-making by NICE, (c) the legal status of NICE guidance, and (d) the impact of NICE on NHS disinvestment.

Selection and appraisal procedures

Given the significance of NICE approval, independence and transparency are essential to its status and authority. How are topics chosen, against what criteria are they assessed, and by whom? Is the agenda driven by government, the pharmaceutical industry, health authorities, patients, or other pressure groups?

Bear in mind that the pharmaceutical industry makes a significant contribution to UK gross domestic product. Concern that the selection process could be distorted by 'political' considerations was expressed in 1999. In a 'rapid appraisal', NICE recommended that zanamivir (a treatment for influenza) should not be used in the NHS. The refusal caused the pharmaceutical manufacturer (GlaxoSmithKline Ltd) to express misgivings about the viability of maintaining its base in the UK. A year later NICE issued new guidance reversing its previous decision and recommending the treatment as suitable for some patients. Many suspected that NICE had been subjected to pressure from government.[10] In 2002, the chairman of NICE, Professor Sir Michael Rawlins conceded that 'the process is still somewhat opaque and obscure'[11] and the House of Commons Health Committee recommended procedures be made more open and robust.

Accordingly, as of 2004, NICE has introduced new systems for selecting and appraising technologies that are clearer both as to procedures and substantive decision-making.[12] Topics put forward for selection may originate from three sources: 1. 'specialty mapping' by the National Coordinating Centre for Health Technology Assessment (NCCHTA), which responds to the need for guidance in the main clinical areas; 2. 'horizon scanning' by the National Horizon Scanning Centre, which reacts to new clinical innovations likely to have a significant impact on patient care and the NHS; 3. proposals from individuals, patient groups, professional groups, the NHS and industry.[13] The final decision as to which matters to refer to NICE is taken by ministers guided by the Advisory Committee on Topic Selection (ACTS). ACTS is composed of around 30 members with a broad composition representing the Department of Health, NHS bodies, patient groups, and the pharmaceutical industry.[14]

The Department of Health and Welsh Assembly have identified criteria to guide ACTS in recommending which technologies to refer to NICE. First, is the technology likely to result in significant health benefit taken across the NHS as a whole? For example, would it address a condition that is associated with significant disability, morbidity, or mortality; would it tend to improve existing clinical practice or improve the efficiency with which health resources were used? Second, is the technology likely to result in a significant impact on other health-related Government policies such as the reduction of health inequalities? Third, is the technology likely to have a significant impact on NHS resources (financial or other) if given to those for whom it is indicated? Fourth, is NICE likely to be able to add value by issuing national guidance (for example, is there sufficient clinical evidence on which to develop robust guidance, or such divergent practice amongst clinicians as to make further guidance desirable)? ACTS may also advise whether NICE should issue a firm and mandatory technology appraisal guidance or rather a broader discretionary guideline; the time at which an appraisal should be undertaken; and, if clinical evidence is still developing, whether the balance of advantage favours delaying an appraisal until further data become available.[15; 16] Once specific technologies have been selected by the Secretary of State, NICE envisages three stages of 'appraisal'. The first is the 'scoping process' in which NICE sets the parameters of its appraisal. It defines, for example, the clinical problem; it identifies whether the technology is used in hospital or the community and relevant comparator technologies; it describes principle outcome measures and the means for determining effectiveness. It identifies a range of 'consultees', for example, the manufacturer (or sponsors) of the technology in question, national professional organizations and national patient organizations to whom it may turn for guidance.[17] Each consultee may submit a dossier of evidence to NICE. Sponsors are required to declare that no pertinent information has been withheld and patient and carer consultees are offered financial support in preparing submissions. In addition, 'commentators', such as manufacturers of comparator technologies, related research groups and relevant NHS bodies, may be invited to join the appraisal process without submitting a dossier of evidence. NICE will not accept evidence from 'non-consultees' (that is those from whom it has not requested evidence).[18] Once the scope of the appraisal is defined, the process moves to the second stage in which NICE commissions a 'technical assessment' of the evidence of clinical and cost effectiveness from independent centres with acknowledged expertise.[19] During this stage, consultees and commentators nominate experts to make submissions to the assessors and may comment on the final report to NICE. The purpose of the assessment and the responses is to assist NICE's Appraisal Committees evaluate the technology, but not to advise it as to its conclusions.[20]

The third stage is the 'appraisal' proper, led by Appraisal Committees with a range of expertise. The appraisal committees are 'standing' committees appointed for three years and composed of experts from the health professions, patient-focused organizations, health economists, NHS managers and the pharmaceutical industry. Members with conflicts of interests are excluded from a particular process. The Appraisal Committees produce an Appraisal Consultation Document (ACD) which contains an initial evaluation of the technology. Consultees and commentators may submit further observations during a four-week consultation period. In particular, consultees and commentators may comment on whether the ACD has properly considered the evidence submitted to it, whether the summaries of clinical and cost effectiveness are reasonable, whether the ACD provides a sound basis for the preparation of NICE guidance, and whether the assessment of impact on NHS resources is reasonable.[21] Commercially sensitive and other confidential information may be considered by NICE as part of the appraisal process. Clearly, this has the advantage of providing additional information, but it may also obscure the transparency of the decision-making process.[22] In the light of this consultation, the Appraisal Committee produces a further Final Appraisal Determination (FAD) for submission to NICE. Again the FAD is distributed to consultees and commentators for comment. If NICE accepts the FAD, it will form the basis of its guidance to the NHS.

Substantive criteria

One of the most challenging aspects of health technology appraisal is to identify the substantive criteria by which assessments should be made; particularly when a decision to recommend one technology may have significant impact (or opportunity costs) elsewhere in the NHS. For example, a medicine may be clinically effective, but only for a small proportion of relevant patients, and only in varying degrees of efficacy. Current therapies can often slow, but not reverse, the progress of disease, and the proportion of patients for whom they are effective may be small. Thus, many patients may need to be treated in order to secure improvements in the health of relatively few. Under a cost per quality adjusted life year (QALY) analysis, the overall cost of achieving improvements in the quality of life of individual patients is high. How should the value to an individual be weighed against its opportunity costs?

Recall that NICE advises on the basis of two criteria: '[1.] the promotion of clinical excellence and [2.] of the effective use of available resources in the health service.'[23] NICE will consider the full hierarchy of clinical evidence from authoritative, large-scale, randomized trials, to the anecdotal experience of carers, but greater weight is given to evidence from high-quality studies with methodology designed to minimize bias.[24] With respect to NICE's duty to promote 'cost effectiveness', NICE takes account of:

The overall resources available to the NHS when determining cost effectiveness. Therefore, decisions on the cost effectiveness of a new technology must include judgments on the implications for healthcare programmes for other patient groups that may be displaced by the adoption of the new technology. [It] does not consider the affordability of the new technology but does take account of how its advice may enable the more efficient use of healthcare resources.[25]

It is not clear entirely how this principle enables NICE to consider the impact of its decisions on the resources available to health authorities. Estimates of cost effectiveness are often imprecise. NICE will consider the plausibility of the economic models presented to it, its own preferred approach and any critique of the manufacturer's analysis. It has been suggested that NICE has adopted a QALY threshold of around £30,000 per patient as a guide to the limit at which approval will usually be given.[26; 27] The World Health Organisation's (WHO) review of NICE, however, considered the cost-thresholds used by NICE to be unclear. It recommended 'NICE must resolve the confusion related to the use of a value-for-money threshold. If a threshold is to be used as the basis for recommendations, it needs to be specified and justified for reasons of transparency.'[28] However, NICE explains that it does not use a fixed incremental cost-effectiveness threshold, above which a technology would automatically be rejected. Instead, it takes a more flexible approach, so that:

> [B]elow a most plausible ICER [incremental cost-effectiveness ratio] of £20,000/QALY, judgments about the acceptability of a technology as an effective use of NHS resources are based primarily on the cost-effectiveness estimate. Above [that figure] judgments ... are more likely to make more explicit reference to factors including the degree of uncertainty surrounding the calculation of ICERs, the innovative use of the technology, the particular features of the condition and population receiving the intervention [and] ... appropriate wider societal costs and benefits. Above an ICER of £30,000/QALY, the case for supporting the technology on these factors has to be increasingly strong.[29]

As we see in the appendix in connection with *imatinib* for chronic myeloid leukaemia, costs considerably in excess of these figures may still be considered acceptable. Having considered the evidence, NICE guidance may take a number of different forms. It may recommend the use of the technology for all patients for whom it is intended, recommend its use for a limited category of patients only, indicate that further clinical trials should be undertaken, or where evidence of clinical and cost effectiveness is not persuasive, recommend the technology not be adopted in the NHS.[30] The latter option presents the greatest challenge. Hard-pressed PCTs will soon request NICE to appraise technologies with a view to their being *de-commissioned* from the NHS. Clearly, guidance which supports the *withdrawal* of treatment from the NHS is likely to present more controversy than that which mandates that new technologies be adopted.

In an area so dominated by incomplete or uncertain clinical and economic evidence, strong differences of opinion between differing stake-holders are inevitable. NICE accepts the need to include patient experience in its appraisal system and has established a 'Citizens Council' composed of 30 members of the public who are broadly representative of the population of England and Wales.[31] The Council meets to consider matters of general interest to NICE and advises on the basis of evidence supplied by experts in the field. Short of saying, however, that individual patients should have anything they want (which would destroy the whole *raison d'être* of NICE) what features of the patient should be taken into account in determining patient need?[32] The Council identified the following (in no particular order):

> What values does the patient have? What is the patient's informed decision? What is the age of the patient? How fit is the patient to undergo treatment? What are the patient's other conditions? How able is the patient to self-manage their condition? What is the family history and are there any genetic or hereditary issues for the patient? Has a holistic approach for the patient been considered?[33]

This seems unlikely to provide significant help. WHO has suggested two means of improving the clarity of factors relevant to substantive basis of decision-making. First:

> The principle of transparency requires that NICE codifies and justifies the specific criteria used in decision-making. Difficult but important elements of this task are the articulation of the ethical and social value judgements, and definition of the interaction of these judgements with the appraisal of the scientific evidence used by the Appraisal Committee in reaching its decision.[34]

In truth, this is a very difficult task and so replete with political and social ingredients that it may better be suited to government, rather than an unelected body composed mainly of scientists. Nevertheless, as long as government refuses to muddy its hands in these controversies, it seems inevitable that others will have to do so on their behalf.

Second, WHO noted that 'it is important to develop methods for budget modeling that would enable NICE to provide more detailed information on the implementation costs to the local [health] authorities.'[35] As we shall see in our discussion of the impact of NICE on NHS *disinvestment*, it would be beneficial for the NHS to be more sensitive to the cost-pressures imposed by NICE on PCT's fixed financial allocations. Perhaps in this way the Service could develop a more comprehensive system for identifying and implementing health priorities.

Rights of appeal to the NICE Appeal Panel are available for any of the consultees (but not others) who have a complaint concerning the FAD, or the way in which the appraisal was conducted.[36] The Appeal Panel comprises five members drawn from the NICE's Appeals Committee who have had nothing to do with the appraisal in question and will adopt an 'inquisitorial' style of hearing. The right should be exercised within 15 working days from the day the guidance is received by consultees. The grounds of appeal are: (a) NICE has failed to act fairly and in accordance with its own procedures, (b) the FAD or guidance is perverse in light of the evidence submitted, or (c) NICE has exceeded its powers. Appeal is not available simply to have the matter re-heard by a differently constituted board and is not an opportunity to re-open the substantive arguments in the case. The right to appeal may be refused if the chairman of the board of NICE is not satisfied of these matters. Appeals should normally be heard within 28 days of the appeal being lodged and a decision will normally be determined within 21 days of the hearing. Publication of NICE's guidance may be postponed pending the outcome of the appeal. If an appeal is successful, the matter may be resolved by an adjustment to specific wording in the guidance; alternatively, the entire appraisal may be referred back to the Appraisal Committee for a further FAD. We consider a specific appeal engaging these procedures in the appendix at the end of this chapter. Those dissatisfied with the results of these procedures may bring proceedings for judicial review.

The legal status of NICE guidance

In 2002, NICE technology appraisal guidance was given the status of 'directions'. Secretary of State's directions have mandatory force so that those to whom the directives are issued are bound to comply with them.[37] Directions enable the centre to retain control which would otherwise be delegated to PCTs. The NICE directions read as follows:

> [A] Primary Care Trust shall, unless directed otherwise by the Secretary of State ... apply such amounts of the sums paid to it ... as may be required to ensure that a health intervention that is recommended by [NICE] in a Technology Appraisal Guidance is, from a date not later than three months from the date of the Technology Appraisal Guidance, normally available (a) to be prescribed for a patient on a prescription form for the purposes of his NHS treatment, or (b) to be prescribed or administered to any patient for the purposes of his NHS treatment.[38]

First, note that NICE guidance is not binding on individual clinicians, each of whom must assess whether it is appropriate for the needs of individual patients. However, if the clinician decides to use it, then the guidance is binding to the extent that PCTs must make funds available to support it. Thus, it is no longer open to PCTs to choose not to implement NICE guidance. As the directions make clear, within three months PCTs 'shall' make the relevant funds available to enable the treatment to be given to patients in primary and secondary care ... 'normally'. Clearly, the three month time limit requires PCTs to have contingency funds available to enable them to absorb the additional costs imposed by NICE.[39] In practice, however, financial constraint means that there are many approved technologies in many PCTs that are not automatically available to patients.[40] It is only a matter of time before litigation will require a PCT to adhere to the directions.

NICE may also publish more generic guidelines (as opposed to 'technology appraisal guidance'). NICE guidelines do not have mandatory force and compliance with them remains at the local discretion of PCTs. Do not, however, underestimate the political encouragement from the centre to implement these guidelines. Recent guidelines concern the provision of in vitro fertilization (IVF).[41] The pressure imposed by the Secretary of State on PCTs to implement this 'voluntary' guideline is quite obvious in his statement:

> Our immediate priority must be to ensure a national level of provision of IVF is available wherever people live. As a first step, by April next year I want all PCTs, including those who at present provide no IVF treatment, to offer at least one full cycle of treatment to all those eligible. In the longer term I would expect the NHS to make progress towards full implementation of the NICE guidance.[42]

In reality, PCTs may be constrained to adopt it, notwithstanding its discretionary status. Many PCTs will sympathize with couples who need IVF but, given the financial pressures upon them, set aside little resource to provide IVF treatment. NICE guidelines on the subject will now exert considerable pressure on PCTs to change that approach and to divert resources from other areas of care which they consider to deserve greater support.

Clearly, NICE can impose very different financial stresses and strains in different parts of the country depending on local patterns of morbidity and mortality and some patients may claim to have been adversely affected by its guidance. At present, no legal challenge in judicial review has been brought to clarify any aspect of its powers. This brings us to the sensitive question of the extent to which NICE merely redivides the slices of the NHS cake by giving to some and taking from others. In so doing, it may impose upon local PCTs duties of disinvestment.

Impact of NICE on health care disinvestment

Obviously, the duty to fund the costs of NICE guidance imposes its own cost-pressures on PCTs. It does not perceive itself as being a rationing body and, for this reason, has approved the majority of procedures which have been brought before it. In 2002, NICE estimated that its recommendations had cost the NHS around £570 million since it had commenced work three years earlier.[43] This is a significant proportion of the £7.8 billion spent on pharmaceuticals in the NHS in 2001 (which accounts for 12.3 per cent of total NHS spending).[44] These figures indicate the impact of NICE on finite PCT budgets. When PCTs have a duty to so many in respect of such expensive products, NICE has the potential to destabilize a local health economy. And looking to the future, what will be the cumulative cost of NICE guidance in five, or ten years? Clearly, along with other central government initiatives, it will consume ever-increasing proportions of PCT budgets. Treatments that win NICE approval clearly enjoy a significant advantage and 'shall' (normally) be made available within three months. Yet the fact that something works does not necessarily mean that it should take automatic priority over competing treatments that have yet to be brought before NICE. NICE focuses on the efficacy of individual treatments, not on the needs of the NHS as a whole. What about the many other treatments which have not obtained NICE approval? Some may be of great and undoubted value. By definition, however, they must take second place to the treatments with NICE approval, no matter what their priority. This confuses efficacy with priority. For example, NICE has approved treatment for influenza which reduces the symptoms of the illness by about one day.[45] If the treatment is recommended by doctors, it must be funded by the responsible PCT. Should such a treatment take automatic priority over a effective treatment for cancer that has yet to come before NICE? The logic of conferring 'blanket' priority on certain treatments regardless of the merits of others is clearly driven by the concern for post-code rationing discussed above. It does not, however, necessarily lead to the sensible development of health care priorities.

The implication of 'blanket' priority is that a treatment which does not have the support of NICE is subject to greater resource-pressure and increased risk of post-code disparity between PCTs – precisely the reverse of what was intended by the creation of NICE. On what basis should NICE and the PCTs undertake this process of disinvestment? If NICE has power to divert substantial sums of NHS resources, it is essential that NICE has a clear set of principles and objectives around which it should operate and be measured. The author put this point to the House of Commons Health Committee who responded as follows:

> NICE raises difficult issues by introducing a systematic process for prioritisation in one area without extending the principles and expertise ... more widely. Mr Newdick suggested that primary care trusts need to be given a framework within which to consider new drugs and treatments which are not subject to NICE guidance. ... Our inquiry has persuaded us that that, with so many competing interests vying for attention and funding in an area where resources are finite, it is not sufficient to have implicit healthcare prioritization. ... The Government

must work to achieve a comprehensive framework for health-care prioritisation underpinned by an explicit set of ethical and rational values to allow relative costs and benefits of different areas of NHS spending to be comparatively assessed in a informed way.[46]

Consistent with its Conservative predecessors, however, the Labour government declined the invitation to introduce a priorities framework for the benefit of PCTs.[47] The government responded simply that '[t]he NHS does have sufficient funding to meet the cost of NICE recommendations'.[48] In these circumstances in which 'rationing' tends to be someone else's fault, it will always be difficult to address the problems of health care resource allocation. In consequence, post-code differentials for non-NICE treatment are likely to become more extreme as PCTs struggle to manage the resources that remain within their discretion.

Note, however, that such decisions are being made every day in over 300 PCTs without any framework of guidance from government. Clearly, it is pointless for PCTs to have to perform this rationing function in isolation from one another, in effect, to reinvent the same wheel over 300 times. If the government is unable to assist PCTs, they are capable of assisting themselves by combining together in consortia which adopt open and accountable systems describing how the resource allocation process should take place. The voluntary ethical framework offers a significant contribution to quality in the resource allocation process, and it is to that process that we turn next.

HEALTH TECHNOLOGY ASSESSMENT AT THE LOCAL LEVEL

NICE has issued guidance on about 50 technologies per year. Although this capacity may expand, this leaves many more technologies for which it is unable to give an appraisal and around which local discretion remains intact. What mechanism exists for appraising the many health technologies that are not reviewed by NICE? Pharmaceutical manufacturers will seek to influence PCT purchasers with evidence of the benefits of products that have not been assessed, as will clinicians, patients, MPs, and pressure groups. We noted the concern with 'post-code rationing' in the NHS and that PCTs are capable of developing different responses to the pressures of resource allocation. How should such local discretion be managed? Cases have begun to create a legal framework around PCT resource-allocation and to develop broad principles within PCTs should operate.

First, they inform PCTs as to the proper response to non-binding NHS 'circulars'. From time to time, the Department of Health may advise (but not mandate) that certain treatments should be provided within the NHS. What is the status of such advice? The question arose in *R v. N. Derbyshire HA, ex p Fisher*,[49] in which the Secretary of State for Health issued a health service circular recommending the drug beta interferon for the treatment of multiple sclerosis (MS).[50; 51] However, given the drug's profile of clinical benefits and financial costs, the health authority, exercising the discretion it believed was available to it, resolved not to fund the drug for local people in the NHS. The applicant suffered from MS. His responsible doctor had recommended that he be prescribed beta interferon. By means of judicial review, the applicant challenged the refusal to fund the drug. The court confirmed that the advice imposed no obligation upon the health authority to fund the drug and that the matter remained within its own reasonable discretion. Nevertheless, the case succeeded on another ground. The health authority had failed to bear in mind a material consideration in coming to its decision, namely NHS policy set out in the circular. It had effectively shut its eyes to the policy and thereby come to an irrational decision. When the matter was referred back to the authority, it reversed its original decision and provided funding for the drug (though whether its reasons for doing so were more political than clinical is not known). This stresses the importance of taking governmental circulars properly into account when assessing new technology.

Second, hard decisions between competing demands are unavoidable. Giving a particular condition or treatment low priority or indeed, denying it treatment altogether, is not irrational, provided that the process recognizes the possibility of patients with exceptional clinical need. In *R v. NW Lancashire HA, ex p A, D and G*[52] the applicants suffered from 'gender identity dysphoria'. The Authority accepted that the condition was an illness, but it adopted a policy that allocated low priority to procedures it considered to be clinically ineffective. The applicants sought judicial review of the refusal of the health authority to pay for sex reassignment surgery. The policy was explained on the perfectly reasonable basis that the authority had limited financial resources and could not afford to fund all services of proven clinical effectiveness. The Court of Appeal confirmed the general principle that hard choices have to be made between deserving cases.[53] Nevertheless, the Court overturned the decision and referred it back to the health authority to be reconsidered in the light of its judgement. The court observed that the authority had failed to consider the merits of the applicants' circumstances and, in doing so, had ignored a relevant consideration. Thus:

> [T]he more important the interests of the citizen that the decision effects, the greater will be the degree of consideration that is required of the decision-maker. A decision that, as is the evidence in this case, seriously affects the citizen's health will require substantial consideration, and be subject to careful scrutiny by the court as to its rationality. That will particularly be the case in respect of decisions ... which involve the refusing of any, or any significant, treatment. ...[54]

The coverage process should consider, for example, the nature and seriousness of each type of illness, the relative effectiveness of various forms of treatment for it, and the costs of the treatment.[55] In particular, however, it should consider the individual patient and be sufficiently flexible to accommodate those with exceptional needs. In the circumstances of this case, the applicants had effectively been subject to a blanket ban on the procedure, which had led the health authority to ignore the possibility that the applicants might have presented exceptional circumstances which merited an exceptional response.

Third, the procedures involved in 'exceptional cases' were considered in *R (on the application of F) v. Oxfordshire Mental Healthcare NHS Trust.*[56] The court emphasized the need for balance between the need for fairness and openness as to the reasons for the decision, but stressed the danger of turning the process into a trial. It said:

> Fairness requires that the claimant should have the opportunity to tell the Forum in writing why it was contended that resources should be allocated to her. ... A meeting of the forum is essentially a discussion between medical experts. It is not to be equated with a contested hearing, and rules of disclosure which might be appropriate for such a hearing should not be imposed upon the Forum's deliberations. ... Decisions on funding affect lives, not just liberty. That is not a good

reason to judicialise them. They are agonisingly difficult decisions, and they will not be made any easier or better if they are encumbered with legalistic procedures.[57]

Thus, the matter should receive fair and impartial consideration by a properly constituted committee sensitive to the requirements of natural justice, but it does not require the formality of a judicial hearing. Fourth, the transsexuals' case dealt with technologies about which there is no systematic and reliable clinical data. The authority had refused the patients access to surgery. One of its reasons for doing so was that there was insufficient clinical evidence of clinical efficacy to support the procedure. In common with many treatments, exhaustive randomized trials were not available because none had been conducted. Yet a body of doctors regularly performed such surgery and supported making it available to suitable patients. How should health authorities assess a new technology in the absence of authoritative clinical trials, or guidance from NICE? The court reasoned that it was not sufficient to exclude every such treatment from consideration. After all, time may not have permitted proper advances in medical opinion to have been endorsed by large-scale randomized controlled trials. The court held that where a body of opinion supported the use of a technology, 'it is . . . not open to a rational health authority simply to determine that the procedure has no proven clinical benefit while giving no indication of why it considers that is so'.[58] Thus, even in the absence of reliable clinical evidence and not withstanding the differences of view that existed, the authority was duty-bound to subject the proposed treatment to proper consideration and to assess it according to the fair and consistent values discussed above.

These processes of clinical appraisal and assessment, and the need to review exceptional cases, are time-consuming, expensive and depend on considerable specialist input. PCTs serve relatively small populations of people (around 100,000) and may not have the time and expertise to accommodate a comprehensive response of this nature. In the absence of central guidance, PCTs should collaborate in matters of health technology appraisal. In the county of Berkshire, for example, a 'Priorities Committee' acting within the guidance of an 'Ethical Framework', acts as a non-statutory source of guidance to the six PCTs in the county. Membership of the committee is comprised of senior representatives of the county's six PCTs, with financial, clinical, and managerial expertise, as well as lay representatives of patients and the public. In this way, the cost and expertise required by such an advisory committee can be accommodated. The advantage of the process is that PCTs can more easily learn from one another and quickly know if their own policies are inconsistent with those of their neighbours. In such a case, they can review the reasons and justification for their different response, improve the quality of their decision-making and develop procedures sufficiently robust to withstand judicial scrutiny.

CONCLUSION

NICE guidance may require PCTs to disinvest from established areas of care. The previous Secretary of State acknowledged the political implications of its decisions but has indicated that NICE should not engage itself with matters of affordability. He has said with respect to NICE:

> There are two quite separate distinctions ... [one] which is about assessing clinical and cost effectiveness and a quite separate set of decisions which are around affordability issues. In the end you would want ... affordability decisions to be located with an accountable politician who has to answer to the House of Commons and to Parliament. It just so happens that accountable politician is me.[59]

Laudably, this recognizes the sensitivity of health care priority setting and suggests that 'hard' *rationing* decisions are for the Secretary of State alone. In reality, however, Secretaries of State almost never engage themselves in the rationing debate, preferring to delegate the matter to local health authorities.[60] Ideally, government should be more transparent in the priority setting process and offer both NICE and PCTs a substantive framework within which to make decisions. In truth, however, given the uncertainties surrounding the weighing of clinical and economic evidence in these cases, and the competing demands of patients, it will always be difficult to make entirely transparent the bases on which decisions have been made. Nevertheless, the creation of NICE makes transparent the processes at work in decision-making and this is a valuable step in understanding who makes decisions and how. The next is to develop a regulatory structure which accommodates the financial implications of its guidance within finite PCT budgets.

CASE STUDY 1: NICE APPEAL PANEL ON ZANAMIVIR, OSELTAMIVIR, AND AMANTADINE

Recall that NICE was criticized in 2000 for its guidance on zanamivir. NICE undertook to review its guidance and did so in September 2002. It expressly compared the clinical and cost effectiveness of zanamivir with the other anti-viral drugs, oseltamivir and amantadine. NICE's Appraisal Consultation Document (ACD) and the Final Appraisal Document (FAD) closely match one another. They conclude that zanamivir and (more restrictively) oseltamivir should be used during influenza epidemics for at-risk patients but that amantadine should not be used.[61] The appeal against the appraisal was brought by the manufacturers of amantadine and oseltamivir (Alliance Pharmaceutical Ltd and Roche Products Ltd). The matter was heard in December 2003. The NICE Appeal Panel consisted of the chairman of NICE, two non-executive directors of NICE's board, a patient representative and an industry representative. Both of the appellants were represented.

The decision is detailed, carefully reasoned, and runs to 13 single-spaced pages.[62] This brief analysis demonstrates the nature of the Appeal Panel and its willingness to refer matters back to NICE for reconsideration. Appeal was made under the three grounds available to appellants under the appeal procedure, namely that NICE (1) failed to act fairly and in accordance with its procedures, (2) came to conclusions which were perverse in the light of the evidence submitted, and (3) exceeded its powers.

NICE failed to act fairly and in accordance with its procedures

In its FAD, NICE recommend that anti-viral drugs should not be used prophylactically in healthy adults because of the resource implications of doing so and the additional work it would impose on GPs. The appeal alleged that NICE had failed to explain how that conclusion had been reached and how NICE had considered 'the effective use of available resources' in the Health Service, as required by the NICE

Directions. NICE responded in two ways. First, it said that any estimation of a likely increase in public demand was bound to be speculative. The Appeal Panel agreed with this and held that such a judgement was not improper.[63] Second, NICE said that in no appraisal had it ever received guidance from the Secretary of State on available resources. It argued that, in reality, the complaint sought to require NICE to consider the issue of 'affordability', which, it argued, it was not able to do. Agreeing with NICE, the Appeal Panel rejected the complaint and ruled that

> [T]here was an important distinction between 'the effective use of available resources' and 'affordability'. The former encompassed considerations of the opportunity costs of adopting a particular technology both in monetary and other (e.g. manpower) respects, within whatever overall resources were available. The latter related to whether, or not, the NHS had sufficient *additional* financial resources available to meet the additional costs that would be incurred by adopting a particular technology. The Panel considered that the Appraisal Committee, in drawing its conclusions, had recognised this distinction and acted in accordance with the Institute's Directions from the Secretary of State.[64]

We noted the imprecise nature of this distinction above. It empowers NICE to produce guidance without knowing whether additional resources will be made available to the NHS; but this is inevitable – as a general rule, no such additional resources will ever be made available ear-marked for NICE guidance. Thus, appraisals will often be based on incomplete information, guess-work, and instinct, and appeals for failing to consider the resource implications of a decision will always be difficult to sustain.

NICE's guidance was perverse in the light of the evidence submitted

The NICE FAD stated that: 'No evidence was found to show that treatment of influenza A with amantadine reduces the frequency of complications or hospitalisation secondary to influenza.'[65] Complaint was made that this was factually incorrect because evidence of efficacy supported the use of high doses of amantadine (200 mg). NICE's response was that its guidance referred only to the dose of amantadine licensed for use in the UK (that is 100 mg). The Panel decided that NICE had not acted 'perversely', but that it should clarify its guidance by stating that it concerned 100 mg doses only.[66] The appellants also argued that the FAD ought to have included guidance on the efficacy of higher doses of amantadine. However, the panel considered that it would be inappropriate to make recommendations on doses higher than those licensed in the UK and dismissed this aspect of the appeal.[67]

A successful complaint was made that NICE gave disproportionate emphasis to the risks of side-effects presented by amantadine. The FAD said: 'the potential for adverse effects of amantadine in the at-risk population would ... outweigh the clinical benefits.'[68] Yet, this view was expressed in the absence of any clear evidence as to efficacy. The Appeal Panel endorsed NICE's view of the incidence of side-effects, but said that the observations as to risk-benefit were perverse: 'In the absence of any significant quantitative or qualitative evidence for the efficacy or effectiveness of amantadine at a dose of 100 mg daily (or less), it was inappropriate to postulate an adverse (or indeed any) risk-to-benefit ratio.'[69] The Panel recommended, therefore, that this part of the FAD should be removed.

With respect to oseltamivir, the complaint of perversity concerned the limitations on its proper use. NICE recommended that the drug should not be used prophylactically, but failed to distinguish between routine 'seasonal' and specific 'post-exposure' prophylaxis. The appeal succeeded. The Appeal Panel said that the Appraisal Committee had been perverse both 'in formulating its guidance on the prophylactic use of oseltamivir'[70] and in its assessment of the cost effectiveness of the drug.[71] Similarly, the appeal was upheld as to the recommendation that oseltamivir should be limited to those 'who are not effectively protected by vaccination'.[72] The Appeal Panel considered that NICE 'had failed to appreciate that the efficacy of influenza immunisation may be reduced in the frail elderly population'.[73] In respect of these successful complaints, therefore, the Appeal Panel recommended that they be referred back to the Appraisal Committee for reconsideration so that further guidance could be issued.

NICE exceeded its powers

A general complaint was made that NICE had exceed its powers because its guidance amounted to a general ban on amantadine and a selective ban on oseltamivir. This ground of appeal was rejected. The Appeal Panel endorsed NICE's view that its guidance to clinicians has persuasive weight only and that doctors are not obliged to adhere to it. Further, each set of NICE guidance had (and still has) attached to it a reminder to clinicians expressly reminding them of the need to exercise clinical judgement and not to regard appraisals as overriding clinical discretion. The Appeal Panel did not consider that NICE guidance could be considered to be a *de facto* ban on some treatments.

In the case of amantadine, it was argued that the drug possessed a product license from the Department of Health as being safe and efficacious for patients and that accordingly, NICE ought not reach negative conclusions concerning its use. The Appeal Panel said however that NICE performed a different role than that of the medicines licensing authority and that each considered a different set of factors. In particular, under its Directions, NICE 'must include a consideration of the broad balance of benefits and costs to society',[74] but these are matters outside the statutory jurisdiction of the medicines licensing authority.[75] Clearly, NICE is capable of having a significant impact on the nature and extent to which clinicians prescribe particular medicines, but could never forbid them from doing so. This ground of complaint was, therefore, rejected.

CASE STUDY 2: APPRAISAL OF IMATINIB (GLIVEC®) FOR CHRONIC MYELOID LEUKAEMIA (CML)

The study of Glivec presented NICE with the challenge of providing guidance on a drug intended to treat a potentially fatal disease when the clinical evidence surrounding the product was incomplete. CML is one of the most common forms of luekaemia in England and Wales. There are around 2600 cases, or 1 in 100,000 patients. But the relative rarity of the disease presents the difficulty of organizing reliable controlled trials to test the efficacy of medicines. Interferon-alpha is an alternative treatment for CML; however, in some patients it is ineffective and others it provokes adverse side-effects. Thus, the European Medical Evaluation Agency (EMEA) granted a product license to Glivec in the exceptional circumstances that it would be unreasonable to require persuasive clinical evidence from the manufacturer (Novartis Ltd). Accordingly, it agreed to conduct a specific programme of studies on its efficacy.

NICE considered that the QALY costs of imatinib were as follows:

- between £36,000 and £38,000 for the chronic phase,
- between £21,000 and £56,000 for the accelerated phase, and
- between £33,275 and £64,750 for the blast phase.

Clearly, costs of this magnitude suggest that NICE should require good evidence of effectiveness in order to avoid the possibility of large sums of money being spent on ineffective medicine. At the ACD stage of appraisal, therefore, NICE was minded to recommend Glivec for the treatment of patients with accelerated phase CML, but found that there was 'insufficient evidence on which to recommend the routine treatment of patients in the chronic or blast-crisis phase of CML. Until adequate clinical and cost effectiveness data become available ... the use of imatinib for these indications should be restricted to ongoing or new clinical trials. ...'[76] On this basis it considered that the cost to the NHS of its recommendation would be (at its upper limit) approximately £6.8 million per year, based on an average dose of 600 mg per day.[77]

In preparing the FAD, NICE reconsidered data of clinical and cost effectiveness, evidence from people with CML and those representing them, evidence of clinical experts, the nature of the condition, and patients' perceptions of the value and effects of Glivec. Doing so, it was mindful of the need to consider the efficient use of available resources.[78] It was conscious too of the 'lack of alternative treatments ... and the potential value of imatinib therapy in the context of delivering useful disease palliation with minimal side-effects. ...'[79] This inclined NICE to take a more a more sympathetic view of the limited evidence available to it. Given the absence of clear evidence of survival, NICE used cytogenic response (CR) and haematological response (HR) as alternative measures for efficacy:

> The extent to which CR (particularly) and HR as intermediate outcomes, predict survival is central to the judgment about the clinical and cost-effectiveness of imatinib ... [and concluded] that the relationship between CR and HR and survival is sufficiently strong to support the use of CR and HR as surrogate measures of efficacy.[80]

On this basis, for patients intolerant or resistant to interferon-alpha, the FAD endorsed imatinib for use with patients with chronic phase and blast phase CML. These revised recommendation were estimated to carry costs of £11.8 million for the first year, rising to £15.8 million (at its upper limit).[81]

A lawyer can make no sensible observation as to the substance in clinical logic for NICE's change of view between the imatinib ACD and the FAD. However, the appraisal suggests that NICE is not immune to consideration of other qualitative or intuitive, factors. In this very difficult case, NICE was required to strike a balance between the cost of the product, the incomplete clinical data and the fact that, for many patients, imatinib may offer the last hope of treatment for an otherwise fatal condition. Perhaps the last of these considerations weighed heavily in its mind. Nevertheless, a decision to invest finite resources in treatment of uncertain value will inevitably have an impact on the care available to patients elsewhere in the NHS. This profound ethical problem challenges PCTs decision-makers as well as NICE.

References

1 National Health Service Act (1977) section 1. Scotland is governed by comparable provisions in the National Health Service (Scotland) Act (1978).
2 1977 Act, Section 3.
3 1977 Act, Section 1(2).
4 However, a wide range of people are exempted from the charge and 80 per cent of prescriptions are provided without requiring the co-payment. (1993) *Priority Setting in the NHS: The NHS Drug Budget* (HC 80-vii, Session 1993–94), para. 878. London: HMSO.

5 *R v. N and E Devon HA, ex p Coughlan* [1999] Lloyd's Rep Med 306: 314.

6 See National Health Service Act (1977) as amended, section 17.

7 See NHS Act (1977), section 97C.

8 See e.g., T. Kaptchuk (2003), 'Effect of Interpretative Bias on Research Evidence', *British Medical Journal*, 326: 1453–5.

9 National Institute for Clinical Excellence (Establishment and Constitution) Order 1999, SI 1999, No 220, and No 2219.

10 See ch. 1 in (2002) *National Institute for Clinical Excellence*, vol. 1, second Report of Session 2001–02, vol I, House of Commons Health Committee, HC 515-I. London: HMSO.

11 See (2002) NICE, para. 117.

12 See NICE (2002a), *National Arrangements for Clinical Excellence Arrangements for Topic Selection – Overview of the New System*. London. NICE. < www.doh.gov.uk/nice/consultation2002 > (accessed 1 Mar. 2004).

13 See para. 23, in NICE (2002b), *Topic Selection and Timing of Guidance on New Technology*. London, NICE, para 23. Horizon scanning is conducted in the University of Birmingham.

14 See NICE (2002b), Annex B.

15 See NICE (2002a), Annex B.

16 See NICE (2004a), *Guide to the Technology Appraisal Process*. London: NICE, para. 2.2.

17 See NICE (2004a), para. 3.2.1.

18 See NICE (2004a), para. 4.4.2.1.

19 The groups are the West Midlands HTA collaboration; the NHS Centre for Reviews and Dissemination; School of Health Related Research, University of Sheffield; Southampton University HTA Centre; Health Economics Research Unit, University of Aberdeen; and the Department of Pharmacology and Therapeutics, University of Liverpool. The process is co-ordinated by NCCHTA.

20 WHO recommends that NICE introduce standard methods of assessment by all technology assessment centres. See World Health Organisation (2003), *Technology Appraisal Programme of the National Institute for Clinical Excellence*, p. 8. Copenhagen: World Health Organisation.

21 See NICE (2004a), para. 4.5.2.7.

22 WHO recommends confidential information should not be included in the process. It would also prefer members of the pharmaceutical industry not to be members of the Appraisal Committee and instead, be confined to the stakeholder's submission process. See pp. 18 and 28 respectively, (2003), *Technology Appraisal Programme of the National Institute for Clinical Excellence*. Copenhagen: World Health Organisation.

23 National Institute for Clinical Excellence (Establishment and Constitution) Order 1999, SI 1999, No 220, amended by SI 1999, No 2219.

24 See NICE (2004a), para. 6.2.5.
25 See NICE (2004a), para. 6.2.6.1 and 2.
26 See J. Raftery (2001), 'NICE: Faster Access to Modern Treatments? Analysis of Guidance on Health Technologies', *British Medical Journal*, 323: 1300–03.
27 NICE (2002c), *Guidance on the Use of Riluzole (Rilutek) for the Treatment of Motor Neurone Disease*. London: NICE.
28 World Health Organisation (2003), p. 32.
29 See NICE (2004a) para. 6.2.6.10–11.
30 See C. Ham and G. Robert (2003), *Reasonable Rationing: International Experience of Priority Setting in Health Care*. Buckingham: Open University Press, p. 73.
31 Previously speaking of the drug beta interferon, the Multiple Sclerosis Society said NICE was 'consistently unwilling to engage with people who are expert in MS by virtue of having it . . . [NICE] has taken a very hard line on the acceptability of evidence derived from studies which do not meet the rigid gold-standard of RCTs [randomized controlled trials].' See Ev. 44, paras. 4.6–4.7, *National Institute for Clinical Excellence*, Second Report of Session 2001–02, vol II, House of Commons Health Ctte, HC 515-II. London: HMSO. Subsequently, as we saw above, ACTS was created with greater patient representation.
32 See also M. Kelson (2002), 'The National Guidelines and Audit Patient Involvement Unit', *Journal of Clinical Excellence*, 4: 194.
33 See NICE (2002d), *Report of the First Meeting of the NICE Citizens Council*, London: NICE, p. 7.
34 See World Health Orgnisation (2003), p. 19.
35 See World Health Organization (2003), p 6. See also p. 33.
36 See generally NICE (2001), *Guidance for Appellants*. London: NICE.
37 See NHS Act, section 17 (as amended).
38 Secretary of State, *Directions* (undated) of 2003. London, Department of Health. These guidelines are confined to England. NICE guidance remains *discretionary* in Wales.
39 The significance of the word 'normally' is open to doubt. See (2002), *Government's Response to the Health Committee's Second Report of Session 2002–02 on the National Institute for Clinical Excellence*, p. 8. Cm 5611. London: HMSO.
40 See e.g. (2004), *Tackling Cancer in England – Saving More Lives*, National Audit Office, HC 364, Session 2003–04. London: The Stationary Office.
41 NICE (2004b), *Fertility: Assessment and Treatment for People with Fertility Problems*, Clinical Guideline 11. London: NICE.
42 Department of Health (2004) *Press Release*, 25 February, <www.doh.gov.uk> (accessed 1 Mar. 2004).
43 S. Mayor (2002), 'NICE Estimates that its Recommendations Have Cost the NHS £575m', *British Medical Journal*, 325: 924a.

44 See P. Yuen (2002), *Compendium of Health Statistics*. London: Office of Health Economics, ch.4.1.
45 NICE (1999), *Guidance on Zanamivir (Relenza)*. London: NICE.
46 See paras 133–5, in *National Institute for Clinical Excellence*, HC 515-I, Session 2002–02. London: HMSO.
47 (2002), *Government's Response to the Health Committee's Second Report of Session 2002–02 on the National Institute for Clinical Excellence*, Cm 5611. London: HMSO, p. 16.
48 (2002), p. 10.
49 (1997) 8 Lloyd's Rep Med, 327.
50 See generally, C. Ham and S. McIver (2000), *Contested Decision: Priority Setting in the NHS*. London: King's Fund.
51 See (1995), *New Drugs for Multiple Sclerosis* EL (95)97. Leeds: National Health Service Executive.
52 (1999) Lloyd's Rep Med 399.
53 (1999) Lloyd's Rep Med 399: 408.
54 (1999) Lloyd's Rep Med 399: 412.
55 *R v NW Lancashire HA v A, D & G* (1999) Lloyd's Rep Med, 399: 408.
56 (2001) EWHC Admin. 535.
57 (2001) EWHC Admin. 535 paras 77 and 80.
58 (1999) Lloyd's Rep Med 399: 412.
59 A. Milburn (2000), Evidence to House of Commons Health Ctte, 8 November 2000, para. 336. NICE makes the same distinction: 'The Board draws a distinction ... between advising on cost effectiveness within the resources available for health care, and affordability. The latter is properly the responsibility of government and to scrutiny by Parliament.' See (2001), *Response to the Bristol Royal Infirmary Inquiry*. London: NICE, p. 3.
60 For a single example of such a decision, overturned on judicial review for contradicting statutory requirements, see *R v Secretary of State, ex p Pfizer* [1999] Lloyd's Rep Med, 289.
61 See NICE (2002e), *Appraisal Consultation Document: The Clinical and Cost Effectiveness of Zanamivir, Oseltamivir and Amantadine for the Treatment and Prophylaxis of Influenza*; and NICE (2002), *Final Appraisal Document: Zanamivir, Oseltamivir and Amantadine for the Treatment and Prophylaxis of Influenza*. London: NICE.
62 NICE (2003), *Appraisal Document: Zanamivir, Oseltamivir and Amantadine for the Treatment and Prophylaxis of Influenza; Decision of the Appeal Panel*. London: NICE, < www.nice.org.uk/pdf/Flu drugs_apeal_decision-January2003.pdf > (accessed 1 Mar. 2004).
63 See NICE (2003), para 3.8.
64 See NICE (2003), para 2.6.
65 See (2002e) *Final Appraisal Document: Zanamivir*, para. 4.1.1.3.
66 See NICE (2003), para. 3.2.
67 See NICE (2003), para. 3.4.
68 See NICE (2002e), *Final Appraisal Document: Zanamivir*, para. 4.5.4.

69 See NICE (2003), para. 3.3.
70 See NICE (2003), para. 3.9.
71 See NICE (2002e), *Final Appraisal Document: Zanamivir*, para. 3.13.
72 See NICE (2002e), *Final Appraisal Document: Zanamivir*, para. 1.6.
73 See NICE (2002e), *Final Appraisal Document: Zanamivir*, para. 3.10.
74 See NICE (2002), *Final Appraisal Document: Zanamivir*, para. 4.2.
75 Medicines Act 1968, section 20(2).
76 See paras. 1.1 and 1.2 in, NICE (2002f) *Appraisal Consultation Document: Imatinib for chronic myeloid leukaemia*. London: NICE.
77 See NICE (2002f), para. 6.2.
78 See para. 4.3.1, in NICE (2002g) *Final Appraisal Determination: Imatinib*. London: NICE.
79 See NICE (2002g), para. 4.3.10.
80 See NICE (2002g), para. 4.3.5.
81 See NICE (2002g), para. 6.3.

5

BENEFIT DECISIONS IN GERMAN SOCIAL HEALTH INSURANCE

Stefan Greß, Dea Niebuhr, Heinz Rothgang, Jürgen Wasem[1]

INTRODUCTION

The content of the benefits package in German social health insurance is determined through a two-step process. In a first step, the overall content of the package is described in very general terms in the social security code (macro-level). The Social Code on Health Insurance (Social Code Book V) requires sickness funds to cover, among other services, ambulatory medical care provided by family doctors and specialists, hospital care, drugs, medical devices, dental care, and sick pay. With minor exceptions, the contents of the benefits package at the macro-level have remained mostly unchanged for the last three decades, although there continues to be a heated discussion about reducing the scope of services (for example, excluding dental services or sick pay) due to financial constraints.[2]

Within this given framework, however, the Social Code does not determine exactly what kind of services have to be provided for the insured on the micro-level. It does, however, establish procedures and criteria for the second step of the determination of the contents of the benefits package on the micro-level. According to the Social Code, services and technologies must be 'medically necessary, effective and cost-effective'. In this paper, we focus on the application of these procedures and criteria in determining the benefits package of social health insurance.

In the first section we give a brief overview of health care financing in Germany. The second section describes the institutional characteristics that are relevant for benefit decisions. In the third section we focus on analyzing the decision-making process itself. The fourth section illustrates the decision-making process by analyzing two case studies. Finally, the fifth section describes briefly legislative changes that impact on benefit decision-procedures found in the 2003 Health Reform Act.

HEALTH CARE FINANCING IN GERMANY

Almost 90 per cent of the German population is covered by social health insurance; the rest is covered by voluntary private health insurance and special programmes – such as one that covers the armed forces – leaving only 0.2 per cent of the population without coverage.[3] All employees beneath the income ceiling (€3850 per month in 2003) are obliged to take up social health insurance, while employees above the income ceiling are allowed to opt out of social health insurance and to take up private health insurance. About two thirds of those insureds who can opt out stay in social health insurance – mostly because of its provision of family coverage. Spouses of social insurance enrolees, who are themselves without gainful employment, and children up to a certain age limit are insured for free. Social health insurance is almost exclusively financed by income-related contributions on a pay-as-you-go basis, while private health insurance premiums are risk-related and capital-funded. The burden of contributions to social insurance is equally shared between employers and employees. Pensioners pay half of the contribution, the other half is financed from pension funds; while contributions for the unemployed are completely financed by unemployment insurance. Contribution rates are calculated as a fixed per centage of gross earnings up to an income ceiling of €3375 per month (2003 figure). Contribution rates differ among sickness funds, but are the same for each member of a fund.

The benefits package of private health insurance is determined by individual health insurance contracts and is not uniform. By contrast, all sickness funds – the risk bearing entities in social health insurance in Germany – are legally obliged to offer a standardized benefits package to their insured. Except for some minor benefits – the most important of which is spa treatment – sickness funds are not allowed to include or exclude services at their discretion. Neither are they allowed to offer supplementary insurance to their members; this is the privilege of commercial private health insurers.[4] Sickness funds compete for the insured primarily by means of distinct contribution rates. Differences in the risk structure of sickness funds are adjusted by a risk adjustment mechanism mainly based on age, sex, contributory income, and number of (contribution free) family members.[5]

INSTITUTIONAL ARRANGEMENTS FOR BENEFIT DECISIONS

The institutions responsible for coverage decisions are expressions of the corporatist institutional structure in the governance of the German health care system. Government – that is, the Ministry of Health – and parliament usually limit legislation in this area to general guidelines. Details need to be filled in collectively by representatives of providers and sickness funds. Government only intervenes if both groups are unable to reach an agreement or in case of major procedural errors.[6]

There is no single entity for deciding coverage policy in Germany. Responsibilities are divided along the line of health care sectors. Ambulatory care coverage decisions are made by the Federal Committee of Physicians and Sickness Funds (*Bundesausschuss Ärzte und Krankenkassen*), one of Germany's self-governing bodies. Its directives (*Richtlinien*) are legally binding and must be followed by physicians who provide ambulatory medical care, as well as by sickness funds. This Committee is also responsible for the coverage of pharmaceuticals. However, since there is no explicit provision in the Social Code allowing the Committee to exclude coverage for drugs,[7] the Federal Social Court has overruled the Committee's decision to exclude specific drugs completely from the benefits package. Instead, the Committee is only able to specify the circumstances when pharmaceuticals may be prescribed. For example, it can limit the prescription of pharmaceuticals to specified indications and/or patient subgroups.

The Hospital Committee (*Ausschuss Krankenhaus*) is responsible for making coverage decisions for hospital care.[8] There is one very important difference between ambulatory care on the one hand and hospital care on the other: in hospital care, all services are covered unless the Hospital Committee excludes the service. In ambulatory care, no service is covered unless the Federal Committee of Physicians and Sickness Funds includes the service.

The Federal Committee of Physicians and Sickness Funds has been active with regard to defining the benefits package since the early 1990s.[9] The Hospital Committee was only founded in 2001. Accordingly, our analysis of the decision-making process (see the next section) is restricted to the former Committee and its coverage decisions for ambulatory care.

The Federal Committee of Physicians and Sickness Funds consist of 21 members. Nine members are nominated by the federal organizations of sickness funds, another nine members are nominated by the Federal Association of Panel Doctors (*Kassenärztliche Bundesvereinigung*), which is an organization comprised of regional panel doctors' associations, to which all doctors in ambulatory care must belong if they want to be reimbursed for treating members of social health insurance. Three independent members are to be nominated jointly by physicians and sickness funds. One of the independent members is also the chairman of the Committee.

The Hospital Committee is constituted in a similar way.[10] Again, nine members are nominated by the federal organizations of sickness funds. The providers are represented by members nominated by the federal organization of hospitals (*Deutsche Krankenhausgesellschaft*) and by the German medical association (*Bundesärztekammer*). Again, these groups jointly choose three independent members including the chairman. Accordingly, only providers of (ambulatory and hospital) care and insurers (sickness funds) have voting power. Insureds (usually through their unions) and the employers are indirectly represented on these committees, since these groups are represented on the self-governing boards of individual sickness funds and their federal organizations. There is no direct representation of manufacturers, patients, or government.

PROCEDURES AND CRITERIA FOR BENEFIT DECISIONS

This section is split into four subsections. The first subsection examines the prioritization of health care services that are to be assessed. The second subsection analyses the procedures of the assessment process itself, while the third subsection explores the criteria for decision-making. The final subsection looks into the appeal process that is available for patients.

Prioritization of health care services

Formally, only federal organizations of sickness funds or providers are allowed to initiate a proceeding to decide whether a service will be covered or not. Neither patient groups, unions, employees, industry, nor government are authorized to start a proceeding. There are no formal criteria for prioritization of evaluation of technologies. Even after initiating a procedure, the committees of providers and sickness funds are still able to prioritize which technologies to decide on first.[11] Basically, the committees are free to decide which prioritization criteria to apply. According to the by-laws of the Federal Committee of Physicians and Sickness Funds, technologies are prioritized with respect to 'relevance for diagnostic or therapeutic services, urgency for ambulatory primary and specialist medical care, and potential economic effects.'[12; 13]

In fact, most proceedings of the Federal Committee of Physicians and Sickness Funds are initiated by the federal organizations of sickness funds. One reason for that is quite straightforward. As there is a fixed global budget for ambulatory care (which is distributed to individual physicians by their regional panel physicians' organization) sickness funds are very much interested in adding services to the benefit package of ambulatory care without enlarging the global budget accordingly. In contrast to sickness funds, providers of ambulatory care would prefer to provide extra-budgetary services which have to be paid for out-of-pocket by patients. Thus, the inclusion of any new services will diminish their opportunities to make money from extra-budgetary services without automatically increasing the budget they receive from sickness funds.

According to members of the Federal Committee of Physicians and Sickness Funds, another factor driving the initiation of proceedings is social court judgements. The increasing number of social court judgements, therefore, is an explanation for the committee's initiation of proceedings for review of various services (see below). Additionally, individual patients as well as patient groups have tried to apply pressure to providers and sickness funds to initiate proceedings. The same is true for industry – and sometimes even government. However, none of them is formally allowed to start proceedings – they must always find a 'sponsor' supporting their request formally.

Assessment of health care services

Coverage decisions are based on the result of the assessment process. While the assessment process is managed by a subcommittee of the Federal Committee of Physicians and Sickness Funds, the actual decision is made by the Federal Committee itself.

The Federal Committee of Physicians and Sickness Funds has established a standardized procedure to assess services in ambulatory medical care.[14] This procedure has also been adopted by the Hospital Committee. The starting point of this procedure is the Committee's decision to assess a new or established service (with only one exception, all assessment procedures have been concerned with new services). This decision to assess services is published. At the same time, external experts are invited to provide written statements based on scientific evidence in order to prove that the assessed service is medically necessary, effective, and cost-effective. Manufacturers are not allowed to join the hearings, nor are they asked to provide statements.

Although the subcommittee responsible for the assessment procedure itself does not consist of the same persons as the Federal Committee, it still includes representatives of panel physicians' associations and sickness funds only. A representative from the Ministry of Health is also sometimes present in committee meetings – without being a formal member. After receiving the statements of professional organizations and of independent experts, the subcommittee performs a systematic review of all available evidence which is summarized in a formal Health Technology Assessment report.

The available evidence is grouped by evidence levels according to the principles of evidence-based medicine. Randomized controlled trials (RCTs) are the gold standard for reaching a recommendation about a service under review. However, in the absence of RCTs, studies with a lower evidence level may be sufficient for the subcommittee to supply a recommendation. The subcommittee consists of highly motivated experts and bases its recommendations almost exclusively on the available evidence. This is not always true for the Federal Committee itself, which consists of high-level representatives of the federal organizations of providers and sickness funds, and consequently has in mind the interests of the stakeholders to a greater degree (see discussion of the acupuncture decision below). The decision-making process itself is highly opaque. Although the final decision and the HTA report on which the decision is based are published at the end of the process,[15] no information about the decision-making process itself is available. Meetings of the Federal Committee and its subcommittees are not open to the public, and the minutes of these meetings are held secret. Voting behaviour of individual members is secret as well, as are voting results.

The decisions and the content of the HTA report are not published in a form that is easily understandable for all groups affected by the decision – especially patients. On the other hand, sickness funds and ambulatory primary and specialist care providers are well informed about the decision, since services that are approved become part of the fee schedule while excluded services do not become part of the fee schedule.[16]

Both the Federal Committee of Physicians and Sickness Funds and the Hospital Committee have only a very small number of permanent staff to co-ordinate the assessment process. Most of the actual work collating the HTA reports is done by members of the subcommittees, who work primarily for provider organizations and sickness funds. Especially in the case of very expensive services, the committees commission HTA reports from universities or other research centres. However, compared to other countries, notably the UK, the HTA infrastructure in Germany is still rather underdeveloped. Accordingly, the time frame for the whole review and decision-making process is rather long. Usually, it takes at least 18 months from starting a review on a service until a decision is reached on that service, and sometimes much longer. In the case of PET-scanning, it took the Federal Committee 32 months to reach a decision.[17] Sickness funds are not allowed to cover services while those services are under review. Accordingly, it can take a long time for the insured to get access to new services. Alternatively, patients can pay out-of-pocket or try to convince their sickness fund to cover the service anyway. Sickness funds may pay directly in order to attract or retain attractive risks, while physicians are eager to sell services to patients directly.

Criteria for decision-making

The Federal Committee is not free to determine the criteria for its decision-making. According to the Social Code, all services covered by compulsory social health insurance have to be medically necessary, effective, and cost effective. This must be true not only for assessed services when compared to doing nothing, but also for the assessed services when compared to existing services.

Our analysis of the decision-making process – as documented in the HTA reports of the subcommittee – has shown that Committee decisions are based almost exclusively on the effectiveness of new services. Effective services are covered; services that are not effective are excluded from coverage. Cost effectiveness does not influence the decision-making of the Federal Committee. This is illustrated first by the fact that services that are slightly more effective than existing services, but that have a much higher cost, are covered, although their cost-effectiveness ratio is much worse than that of existing services. Members of the Federal Committee state that they do not dare to propose explicit rationing by excluding services with some benefit – even if the additional benefit of a particular service is very low and the additional costs are very high. Second, the Federal Committee does not add new services to the benefit package that are slightly less effective than existing services, even when those services have much lower costs so that their cost-effectiveness ratio is rather favourable in comparison with existing services.[18]

Since the Federal Committee is reluctant to exclude coverage for new services with additional benefits – even those with high additional costs – coverage decisions do not induce rationing. Rationing would occur if patients were denied access to even slightly more effective services because those services were excluded from collective financing. On the other hand, coverage decisions at this point are not able to increase the cost effectiveness of the whole benefits package.

Although the Social Code requires the Federal Committees to assess *all* services – new services and existing services – our analysis of coverage decisions rendered between 1990 and 2003 shows that 49 of the coverage decisions concerned new services, while the Federal Committee reached only one decision regarding an existing service.[19] If the coverage decision is positive, these services are added without eliminating less cost-effective services from the benefits package (although the approval of new services is usually restricted to certain indications). Approval of a new service with a low cost-effectiveness ratio may even decrease the cost effectiveness of all services. The Federal Committees consist almost entirely of stakeholders in the system. The sickness funds as well as physicians or hospitals have private interests even though they are supposed to be fulfilling public tasks. Although the Social Code provides some general guidelines as to criteria that are applicable for coverage decisions, the committees still have a lot of leeway. The subcommittee of the Federal Committee of Physicians and Sickness Funds which is responsible for the review of services in ambulatory care has, however, standardized the assessment process. Mostly, decision-makers in the Federal Committee follow the recommendation of the subcommittee, which is based on the available evidence regarding services under review. According to members of the Federal Committee, interests of the stakeholders are neutralized because they base their decisions exclusively on the available evidence.

However, if interests of the stakeholders strongly diverge from the evidence available, decisions of the Federal Committee may not be consistent with the evidence. This is illustrated by the lengthy decision-making process on the coverage of acupuncture. The subcommittee responsible for reviewing acupuncture came to the conclusion that there was no evidence to support the effectiveness of acupuncture. However, the Federal Committee decided that the sickness funds are allowed to cover acupuncture – not as a regular service but based on 'model projects' that have to be evaluated after some time.[20]

In contrast to services that are part of the standardized benefits package, payment for acupuncture is not part of the budget for ambulatory primary and specialist medical care. This is the reason why physicians opposed inclusion of acupuncture into the benefits package. They stood to lose some €300 million of extra-budgetary funding.[21] The final compromise was in the interest of both physicians and sickness funds. The former were able to secure extra-budgetary funding for acupuncture – at least temporarily; the latter are confident that they will be able to gather additional evidence for the inclusion of acupuncture after evaluation of the model projects.

Although the Ministry of Health mostly refrains from influencing the decision-making process directly, there is one notable exception. The Ministry of Health strongly supported the treatment of all drug addicts with methadone in order to decrease the need for the purchase of illegal drugs and to increase the probability of rehabilitating drug addicts. Up to this point, treatment with methadone was only covered for drug addicts with co-morbidity. The sickness funds in the Federal Committee strongly opposed the coverage of all drug addicts, since they did not want to pay for services which in their opinion should have been covered by government. On the other hand, the physician members of the committee supported the extension of coverage. The Federal Committee could not reach a decision and the Ministry of Health issued an ordinance extending coverage to all drug addicts. The committee first appealed this ordinance to the social affairs court. However, in order to avoid a lengthy appeal process, the Federal Committee finally gave in and accepted the demands of the Ministry of Health.

Appeal process

According to a judgement of the Federal Social Affairs Court (*Bundessozialgericht, BSG*), sickness funds are prohibited from reimbursing services in ambulatory care when coverage either has been rejected or has not been approved by the Federal Committee. According to the BSG, after the approval by the Federal Committee, sickness funds are automatically obligated to reimburse the service (*Verbot mit Erlaubnisvorbehalt*). The rejection of services is legally binding for sickness funds as well as for providers of ambulatory care.[22] The lower social courts, however, did not follow the ruling of the BSG immediately. Frequently they valued expert opinions more highly than decisions by the Federal Committee. Moreover, they repeatedly obligated sickness funds to reimburse therapies that had not been decided on by the Federal Committee. These decisions were also based on expert opinions by individual physicians.

Since the Federal Committee started to publish HTA reports in 2000, however, social affairs courts have mostly confirmed the decisions of the Federal Committee of Physicians and Sickness Funds on coverage or non-coverage of services in *ambulatory care*. Currently social affairs courts suspend their decisions until they are able to base their verdicts on the assessment reports of the committees, which were the result of a standardized process.

When the prescription of pharmaceuticals is excluded or restricted, either manufacturers or patients can file lawsuits against the directive of the Federal Committee. In 1998, the Federal Committee decided on a directive for the treatment of erectile dysfunction and drugs to improve sexual potency such as Viagra®. The committee argued that the treatment of erectile dysfunction fell into the domain of personal lifestyle and excluded Viagra completely. Social affairs courts, however, grant individual requests for Viagra if erectile dysfunction is caused by co-morbidity.

CASE STUDY 1: PET SCANNING

The Federal Committee of Physicians and Sickness Funds started proceedings on the review of PET scanning in May 1998. One of the peak organizations of sickness funds had applied for the review of PET scanning due to an increasing number of individual requests for coverage of PET scanning in ambulatory specialist medical care. The decision to review PET scanning was caused by the high costs – capital cost as well as running costs[23] – of PET scanners and by the high degree of diffusion of this technology. In 1985, there were only three PET installations in Germany. By 2002, this number has increased to more than 90 PET installations.[24] A considerable part of this increase has been due to a growing number of installations in the offices of ambulatory specialists after the Federal Committee started proceedings on PET scanners. Physicians and manufacturers expected the inclusion of PET scanning into the standardized benefits package and invested considerably in new installations even before the final decision of the Federal Committee came through.

The Federal Committee took 32 months to review the evidence and to reach a decision about the coverage of PET scanning. The Federal Committee found PET scanning to be no more effective than existing technologies already covered by compulsory social health insurance.[25] This decision was based on findings for five indications – three of them diagnosing specific types of cancer, one for the diagnosis of epilepsy, and one for the diagnosis of heart tissue.[26] The decision did not meet the expectations of physicians, manufacturers, and patient groups. All expert statements (from professional organizations of oncology, cardiology, neurology, nuclear medicine and radiology) favoured the coverage of PET scanning. After conducting an extensive review of the available evidence, the Federal Committee considered these statements to be biased. According to the conclusions of the HTA report, existing technologies are as effective as PET. Accordingly, the coverage of PET scanning in ambulatory specialist medical care had to be denied.

PET scanning is still covered by compulsory social health insurance if it is provided in inpatient care in hospitals. The Hospital Committee has started proceedings on PET scanning in hospitals. However, until and unless the Hospital Committee excludes PET scanning from coverage, it continues to be covered by the sickness funds. Since it may take a long time for the Hospital Committee to reach a decision on PET scanning, for the time being patients demanding PET scanning simply have to convince their physician to refer them to a hospital. Moreover, it is far from clear that the current hospital subcommittee of the Joint Federal Committee will reach the same decision as the former Federal Committee. The division of responsibilities and the divergence in procedures for coverage decisions undermines the ability to control the diffusion of progress in medical technology, and thus the ability to control costs.

CASE STUDY 2: HYPERBARIC OXYGEN THERAPY (HBOT)

The Federal Committee has excluded hyperbaric oxygen therapy (HBOT) from ambulatory medical care since 1994. It concluded at that time that there is no evidence of the effectiveness of this service. The Federal Association of Panel Doctors again applied for inclusion of HBOT in 1998, stating that sickness funds frequently pay for this service in ambulatory care, contrary to the decision of the Federal Committee. Moreover, according to the Federal Association of Panel Doctors, new data were available in order to review the decision of 1994.[27]

The subcommittee responsible for the review process reviewed HBOT for 36 individual indications and concluded that there is no evidence of medical necessity, effectiveness and cost effectiveness for any of these indications (in a review process that lasted 24 months). Several RCTs either did not confirm the effectiveness of HBOT (for example HBOT for multiple sclerosis) or recommended the need for further studies. Accordingly, the Federal Committee confirmed its decision of 1994.

By contrast, the Hospital Committee decided to maintain the inclusion of HBOT for three indications in hospital care.[28]

The Hospital Committee stated that for two of these indications (arterial gas embolism, decompression illness) there were no alternatives to HBOT. Moreover, after reviewing the available evidence, the Hospital Committee concluded that HBOT is effective for treating carbon monoxide poisoning. However, the Federal Committee concluded the evidence for the effectiveness of HBOT is rather inconclusive (carbon monoxide poisoning) or non-existent (arterial gas embolism, decompression illness) – at least for the use in ambulatory care. According to the Hospital Committee, the decision to include HBOT does not contradict the decision of the Federal Committee to exclude HBOT, since it takes into account different levels of care (for example, the lack of intensive care in ambulatory health care).

REFORM OF PROCEDURES FOR BENEFIT DECISIONS

As a consequence of legislative changes in the 2003 Health Reform Act, the institutional setting for benefit decisions has been changed. Since 2004, a single institution, the new Joint Federal Committee (*Gemeinsamer Bundesausschuss*), is responsible for benefit decisions in all health care sectors: ambulatory care, hospital care, and dental care. In principle, the new Joint Federal Committee is constituted in a similar way as the former Federal Committee and the Hospital Committee. The composition of the Joint Federal Committee depends on the sector of care that is affected. If ambulatory care is affected, representatives of sickness funds and panel physicians decide; if hospital care is affected, representatives of sickness funds and hospitals decide. There are even separate chairpersons. The Joint Federal Committee differs from its predecessors in that it also includes patient representatives. Yet patient representatives are only entitled to give their comments, and do not have votes.

Another important legislative change concerns the right of the Joint Federal Committee to exclude pharmaceuticals completely from the benefits package. Since 2004, the new Joint Federal Committee is allowed to exclude new pharmaceuticals if they are proven to be less effective than existing drugs.

Consequently, recent legislation has somewhat changed the nature of the decision-making process. However, we believe that the new joint commission is likely to function in a very similar way as the old separate commissions.

CONCLUSION

In Germany, the state has delegated the responsibility for making detailed benefit decisions to intermediate bodies. As members of these intermediate bodies, sickness funds and providers decide on the inclusion and exclusion of services. Only since the beginning of 2004 are patients represented on the Committee, too. However, they have no authority to vote on benefit decisions and can only offer comments. So far, the whole process of decision-making has been highly intransparent. This is true for the prioritization of assessments, for the decision-making process itself, and for the publication of results. Although the assessment process is standardized, the outcome of the assessment is influenced by the interests of sickness funds and health care providers. As a consequence, decisions are not entirely consistent. Until the end of 2003, separate committees were responsible for benefit decisions. This deficit has been remedied by the 2003 Health Care Reform Act and the introduction of a Joint Federal Committee. However, there are still separate procedures for including or excluding services in ambulatory and hospital care, and participating organizations differ, which inhibits the development of integrated care arrangements.

The overall efficiency of health care systems can be improved by the consistent application of *cost effectiveness* as a decision criterion for benefit decisions. If decision-making bodies want to be able to realize these potential efficiency gains, however, they have to be able to assess the incremental costs of new services as well as the incremental effectiveness. So far, German decision-making bodies focus only on effectiveness and neglect costs. They probably are aware of the trade-off between efficiency gains and rationing when more effective services have to be excluded due to an unfavourable ratio of costs and benefits. Therefore, our analysis confirms that 'the inherently political nature of priority-setting in health care precludes any easy technocratic solution'.[29]

Effects on cost-control will be rather small as long as decision-making bodies do not apply cost effectiveness more frequently. This is particularly true in Germany since benefits decisions are mostly limited to new services while existing services with low cost effectiveness remain part of the benefits package.

References

1 This article is based on the results of a research project that was financed by the *Hans-Böckler-Stiftung*, the research foundation of the German trade unions.

2 However, as a result of the 2003 Health Care Reform Act, eyeglasses and most non-prescription pharmaceuticals have been excluded from the benefits package. Sick pay and dentures are still part of the package but have to be financed solely by the insured starting in 2005 (dentures) and 2006 (sick pay).

3 Bundesministerium für Gesundheit (2002), *Statistisches Handbuch Gesundheit 2002*. Bonn: Bundesministerium für Gesundheit, Table 9.1.

4 However, since 2004 sickness funds are allowed to co-operate with private health insurers in order to offer supplementary insurance to their insureds.

5 Additionally, the claims for sick pay, and the number of pensioners receiving pensions due to disability are controlled. For details see F. Buchner and J. Wasem (2003), 'Needs for Further Improvement: Risk Adjustment in the German Health Insurance System', *Health Policy*, 65(1): 21–35.

6 K. Jung (1999), 'Bundesausschuss der Ärzte und Krankenkassen – Aufgaben, Zusammensetzung, Verfahren', in F.E. Schnapp (ed.), *Probleme der Rechtsquellen im Sozialversicherungsrecht – Tagungsband zum 7. Fachkolloquium des Instituts für Sozialrecht der Universität Bochum*. Bochum: Institut für Sozialrecht der Universität Bochum.

7 D. Hart (2001), 'Health Technology Assessment (HTA) und Gesundheitsrechtliche Regulierung', *Medizinrecht*, (1): 1–8.

8 Another separate committee is responsible for dental care (Bundesausschuss Zahnärzte und Krankenkassen). This committee is not analyzed in this paper.

9 The committee was refounded in 1956. It must be regarded, however, as the successor of the Reichsausschuss Ärzte und Krankenkassen', founded in 1923, which succeeded the 'Zentralausschuss', founded in 1913 (for details: M. Döhler/P. Manow-Borgwardt (1992), 'Korporatisierung als gesundheitspolitische Strategie', *Staatswissenschaften und Staatspraxis* 3: 64–106). Since 1989 the committee is responsible for assessing new technologies, since 1997 its assessment also should cover those technologies that are already in use.

10 M. Arnold and R. Strehl (2001), 'Wie kommen Innovationen ins DRG-System? (die Steuerungsfunktion der Bundesausschüsse), in M. Arnold, M. Litsch, H. Schellenschmidt (eds.), *Krankenhaus-Report 2000*. Stuttgart: Schattauer.

11 K. Jung, C. Gawlik, B. Gibis, et al. (2000), 'Bundesausschuss der

Ärzte und Krankenkassen – Ansprüche der Versicherten präzisieren',
Deutsches Ärzteblatt, 97(7): A365–A370.

12 See Richtlinien über die Bewertung ärztlicher Untersuchungs- und
Behandlungsmethoden (Verfahrensrichtlinien), Nr. 4.1.

13 D. Niebuhr, H. Rothgang, J. Wasem, and S. Greß (2004), *Die Bes-
timmung des Leistungskataloges in der gesetzlichen Krankenversicherung* (Band 2). Düsseldorf: edition der Hans-Böckler-Stiftung Band
108.

14 K. Jung, et. al. (2000).

15 Publication of the HTA reports on the Internet started only in the
year in 2000. See <www.arge-koa.de>

16 The basic structure of the fee schedule is agreed upon in another
corporate body (Bewertungsausschuss), which can only become active
after the Committee has approved the new service.

17 S. Greß, D. Niebuhr, H. Rothgang, and J. Wasem (2004), 'Verfahren
und Kriterien zur Konkretisierung des Leistungskatalogs in der
Gesetzlichen Krankenversicherung', *Journal of Public Health*, 12(1):
32–42.

18 Niebuhr, Rothgang, Wasem and Greß (2004).

19 Greß, Niebuhr, Rothgang and Wasem (2004).

20 In order to justify this decision, the evidence was judged as being not
completely conclusive.

21 H. Korzilius (2000), 'Bundesausschuss: Streit um Akupunktur',
Deutsches Ärzteblatt, 97(30): A-2013.

22 BSG, urteil vom 16 September 1997, Aktenzeichen 1 RK 28/95,
BSGE 81, 54–73.

23 Capital costs of a small PET installation are estimated at 1 to 3
million euros. Running costs are about €500,000 per year.

24 P. Rheinberger (2002), *Diffusion of Innovations: Positron-Emission-
Tomography (PET). Results from the Review of the Federal Standing
Committee of Physicians and the Sickness Funds*. Potsdam: Four
Country Conference 2002 (Diffusion of medical technologies: Inno-
vation and policy response).

25 Arbeitsausschuss Ärztliche Behandlung (2002), *Positronen-Emissions-
tomographie (PET): Zusammenfassender Bericht des Arbeit-
sausschusses Ärztliche Behandlung des Bundesausschusses der Ärzte
und Krankenkassen über die Beratungen gemäß §135 Abs.1 SGB V*.
Köln: Bundesausschuss der Ärzte und Krankenkassen.

26 PET scanning works with radioactive tracer drugs, which have to be
licensed by the national drug licensing authority. These tracer drugs
have only been licensed for the five indications mentioned.

27 Arbeitsausschuss Ärztliche Behandlung (2000), *Hyperbare Sauerstofftherapie (HBO): Zusammenfassender Bericht des Arbeit-
sausschusses Ärztliche Behandlung des Bundesausschusses der Ärzte
und Krankenkassen über die Beratungen der Jahre 1999 und 2000 zur*

Bewertung der Hyperbaren Sauerstofftherapie gemäß §135 Abs.1 SGB V. Köln: Bundesausschuss der Ärzte und Krankenkassen.

28 See press releases (Jan. and Feb. 2003): < www.arge-koa.de >
29 K. Syrett (2003), 'A Technocratic Fix to the "Legitimacy Problem"? The Blair Government and Health Care Rationing in the United Kingdom', *Journal of Health Politics, Policy and Law*, 28(4): 715–46.

6

HEALTH CARE COVERAGE IN THE NETHERLANDS; THE DUTCH DRUG REIMBURSEMENT SCHEME (GVS)

Tanisha Carino and Frans Rutten

INTRODUCTION

The Dutch have a long history in health technology assessment and have developed one of the most rigid and evidence-based systems in the world for making reimbursement decisions for pharmaceuticals. This chapter begins with a brief background of the Dutch health care system, its history in technology assessment, and the development of their Drug Reimbursement Scheme (*Geneesmiddelen Vergoedingen Systeem* (GVS)). This is followed by an in-depth description of the GVS system including: 1. the process for inclusion; 2. composition of decision-makers; and 3. participation of stakeholders in the process. Case studies of the drugs Glivec® (imatinib mesilate) and Relenza® (zanamivir) provide examples of this process. The chapter concludes with a discussion of the challenges faced by this coverage process and its relevancy to other technologies.

General background of the Dutch health care system

The Dutch government has long prided itself on its ability to assure the provision of equitable, accessible, and high-quality health care.[1] A high percentage (63 per cent) of Dutch health expenditures are paid for through public funds.[2] Consequently, a majority of health policy decisions are discussed at the level of the central government, particularly in the Ministry of Health, Welfare, and Sports (MinVWS).

Within the Dutch health care system, there is a strict separation between health care financing and delivery. Financing is done primarily through a mix of public and private health insurance. Every citizen pays compulsory income-related premiums for 'catastrophic' long-term care. For acute care, individuals are either publicly insured (36 per cent) through enrollment in a third-party insurer (Sickness Funds) or privately insured (15 per cent). Employers also make contributions for both the privately and publicly insured. The government defines a minimum package of health care services, including outpatient or extramural drugs, to be reimbursed by insurers; private insurers are free to offer extensions on coverage.[3]

Health care delivery in the Netherlands is generally privately delivered. General practitioners (GPs) serve as gatekeepers to the rest of the health care delivery system. GPs receive a uniform capitation payment for each publicly insured patient and a fee-for-service payment for privately insured patients. Payments from insurers to GPs for publicly insured patients are regulated by the government. There is no relationship between prescribing behaviour and GP income, except in the case of the small percentage of GPs who own pharmacies. During the 1990s, the fee-for-service payment system for medical specialists was replaced by fixed budgets for groups of medical specialists. Finally, the hospital sector is heavily regulated through fixed hospital budgets set by a national pricing authority. All services delivered in the hospital setting, including drugs, are accounted for in their budgets.[4]

In 2001, health care expenditure amounted to 9 per cent of the Dutch gross domestic product, as compared to 11 per cent for Germany, 8 per cent for the United Kingdom, and an Organisation for Economic Cooperation and Development (OECD) median of 8 per cent. The drug costs share of total health care costs for 2001 amounted to 10 per cent, which is relatively low as compared to the OECD average of 15 per cent.[5] This is mainly attributed to low rates of drug consumption by the Dutch, which could partly be a reflection of the relatively high drug prices found in the Netherlands.[6] The Netherlands is in the process of implementing major reforms in its financing and organization of health care. In 1987, the Dekker committee proposed that the government promote efficiency in the health care system by implementing regulated competition for health insurance and equity though the payment of income-related premiums to a central financing scheme.[7] Other aspects of these reforms included compulsory basic insurance, allocation of risk-adjusted capitation payments to insurers, and comprehensive uniform benefits package. These reforms have led to two major developments impacting the future of coverage determinations in the Netherlands. First, increased attention has been paid to the method of defining the comprehensive benefits package. Second, as mentioned earlier, the Netherlands is replacing its hospital budgeting system with a Diagnosis and Treatment Combination (DBC) system beginning July 2004. Like the DRG system, the DBC system reimburses providers for the bundled care of a patient by diagnosis. DBCs include the costs of medical technologies used. This change will provide some transparency to policy-makers as to the care that is delivered in hospitals and will offer them greater opportunities to negotiate with hospitals on the quality and price of specific hospital services.

Introduction on areas of coverage

Since the mid-1980s, the Dutch government has developed policies recognizing the need to research new health care programmes (such as breast cancer screening, transplant programmes, and in vitro fertilization (IVF)) prior to deciding on public reimbursement for such programmes.[8] The government has not limited this research to only addressing the uncertainties of a technology's effectiveness, but also sought to address questions of cost effectiveness. For example, the decision to implement a targeted national breast cancer screening programme in the early 1990s was based on an extensive economic evaluation study.[9] The same was true for restricting the number of IVF attempts to three in cases of infertility.

The Dutch government's successful experience with this type of evidence-based decision-making led to the development of a national Investigational Medicine Fund in 1988 to fund prospective research on emerging technologies to inform both clinical guidelines and reimbursement. In addition to being the main source of funding for health technology assessment research in the Netherlands, this fund also increased the capacity of medical academic centres to conduct technology assessment and cost-effectiveness research.[10]

Additionally, a programme exists for the planning of supra-regional, 'high-tech' medical services, formerly referred to as Article 18 of the Hospital Act. These services have included radiation treatment; computer tomography; renal dialysis; and kidney, heart, liver, lung, and pancreatic transplant. The MinVWS provides guidance on the number of facilities and other requirements needed in order for the clinical community to perform these designated procedures. Additional monies are also set aside for their reimbursement. This guidance limits the number of facilities that can perform these procedures and establishes centres of excellence. Competition between hospitals to be one of these facilities is common due to the additional funds provided to perform the procedures. The government has used this programme as a planning instrument to ensure geographic distribution, promote concentration of facilities, enhance expertise and quality, and increase appropriate use.[11; 12; 13; 14]

The most explicit coverage process in the Netherlands, however, is their system for judging which outpatient drugs should be paid for by the public insurance scheme. This process is referred to as the Drug Reimbursement Scheme or GVS. All outpatient drugs are appraised for their therapeutic benefit relative to other drugs already reimbursed before they are reimbursed under the public health insurance. The GVS exists both to contain cost as well as to promote prudent purchasing of pharmaceuticals. Finally, as mentioned, the replacement of the existing global budgeting payment method for hospitals will allow for explicit appraisal of individual technologies for their effectiveness and the development of another coverage determination process in this sector. Because the GVS is the Netherlands's most explicit process for decisions on reimbursement, the experience of policy-makers with its principles, development, and administration will provide the foundation and may illuminate the future of coverage processes in the Netherlands.

THE GVS SCHEME

A brief history of pharmaceutical reimbursement in the Netherlands

Table 6.1 Events in the development of the Netherlands's Drug Reimbursement Scheme (GVS)

1958	Provision of Pharmaceuticals Act (*Wet op de Geneesmiddelenvoorziening* (WGV))
1991	Introduction of the reference price system (*Geneesmiddelen Vergoedingen Systeem* (GVS))
1993	Moratorium on the reimbursement of high-priced new compounds (list 1b) until 1999
1996	Introduction of price law setting the maximum price of a drug at the average price of Belgium, France, Germany, and the UK
8 Sept. 1997	Ministry of Health, Sports, and Welfare asks CVZ to formulate guidelines for pharmoeconomic research for the GVS
10 Feb. 1998	Health Care Committee of CVZ sets up a Preparatory Committee on Guideline Development (*Voorbereidingscommissie Richtlijnontwikkeling*; VBR) for the development of this guideline
23 Mar. 1998	First meeting of VBR to identify key focal areas
30 Nov. 1998	VBR presents draft guidelines to stakeholders at a meeting
25 Mar. 1999	Final publication of the Dutch guidelines on pharmacoeconomic research
2005	Requirement of new drugs seeking premium price (List 1b) to submit pharmacoeconomic studies

The role of the government in financing health care in the Netherlands and their involvement in developing policies aimed at controlling drug expenditures has grown as these costs have increased. Table 6.1 provides a timeline of the events leading to the development of the GVS. Before we get to a detailed discussion of the GVS scheme, it is important to provide a brief description of the context in which it was developed.

Prior to 1991, there was little regulation of pharmaceutical prices. The price of drugs was set by drug companies, and, within the public system, there was little cost-sharing. Concern about the annual rise in drug expenditure from 1987 to 1990 began to increase when the annual growth of pharmaceutical spending exceeded eight per cent.[15] To combat this, the government developed the GVS scheme.

Table 6.2 Categorization of pharmaceuticals under the GVS

Category	Description
List 1a	• Reimbursement limit based on reference category of drugs considered therapeutic equivalents • Evidence to be considered by CHF restricted to general data on product and clinical data supporting manufacturer's claim of which reference category for inclusion • No pharmacoeconomic research necessary • Inclusion for labelled indications
List 1b	• Reimbursement limit based on premium price set by manufacturer • Evidence considered by CHF includes both pharmacoeconomic research (2005) as well as a justification of additional therapeutic value • Inclusion for labelled indications
List 2	• Conditional reimbursement most commonly based on factors such as 1. duty to further undertake research or a treatment protocol and 2. limitations on prescribers or range of indications.

Sources: Health Care Insurance Board (CVZ) (1999), *Dutch Guidelines for Pharmoeconomic Research*. Amstelveen: CVZ; Kruger, Patrick (2004), 'The role of the Ministry of Health, Welfare, and Sports in the GVS Scheme' (Telephone interview by T. Carino). Rotterdam, 26 February 2004.

The GVS is a reference price system for pharmaceutical reimbursement, introduced in 1991 with the intention of limiting public reimbursement without restricting choice. Drugs with comparable pharmaco-therapeutic effect are clustered and reimbursed with a single price per cluster. This price was determined to be the average of the historical prices of the drugs in the cluster. The patient pays the difference between the price and the reimbursement limit. If a new drug does not fit into one of the clusters, it is reimbursed at the price set by the manufacturer or the premium price. The clustered list is referred to as List 1a, while the drugs that receive premium pricing are on List 1b. In addition to this, there is another list of drugs, List 2, where conditions are placed on reimbursement. To date, these conditions have included limits on reimbursement for specific indications narrower than the market approval and limits on who can prescribe the drug.[16] Table 6.2 provides a detailed description of the different lists and criteria for evaluation. In 2004, 10,968 drugs were listed under List 1a, 2519 under 1b, and 37 groups of molecules (such as anti-retrovirals) were included under List 2.[17] The MinVWS relies on the advice of the Health Care Insurance Board (CVZ) and, particularly, their Committee for Pharmaceutical Help (CFH), to make recommendations of a drug's placement on the GVS. Both of these organizations are described in greater detail later in the chapter. It is important to note that because of the former hospital budgeting system, the GVS scheme was only aimed at controlling the cost of outpatient drugs.

Initially after this system was implemented, a convergence of prices towards the reimbursement level was observed and resulted in a reduction of prices by five per cent.[18] However in 1993, another strong increase in expenditures was observed, attributed to the introduction of high-priced compounds. In reaction, the MinVWS decided that the process for inclusion on the premium price list of the GVS was not effective in controlling cost and decided to halt reimbursement for innovative drugs from 1993 to 1999. Only drugs offering the first pharmacological option for a previously intractable condition were exempt. This policy was maintained until 1999 when the wait list for new chemical entities (NCEs) grew too long. As of 1999, new drugs were again paid their premium price after their therapeutic value and the costs were appraised by CVZ. Also in 1999, the MinVWS introduced guidelines for submission by manufacturers of pharmacoeconomics research for drugs to be included on the premium price list. From 2005 onwards, this will be formally required for all new drugs for which List 1b status is requested. Because of these explicit criteria, the GVS is considered one of the world's most rigid reimbursement structures.[19]

Development of 1999 guidelines for pharmacoeconomic research

The development of the MinVWS's 1999 guidelines for pharmacoeconomic research is important both because of their adoption as criteria for reimbursement and as an example of the policy-making environment surrounding the GVS. On 8 September 1997, CVZ was asked by the MinVWS to formulate guidelines for pharmacoeconomic research. The stated goal of these guidelines was for the pharmaceutical industry to provide the MinVWS with 'reliable, reproducible, and verifiable insight into the therapeutic value of a drug, the costs that will result from its use and the possible cost savings compared with other drugs and/or treatments'.[20] This information, as described above, will be required for companies seeking the inclusion of their product onto List 1b as of 2005. Proof will be needed that the new drug offers added value compared to existing treatment options relative to its cost. The industry will be responsible for the financing and conduct of this research.

On 10 February 1998, CVZ, without the formal input of other stakeholders, assembled a Preparatory Committee on Guideline Development (Voorbereidingscommissie Richtlijnontwikkeling (VBR)) to develop these guidelines. CVZ was asked to consider the advice of those in the field as well as international experts, and that 'parties most closely-involved should also be given the opportunity to contribute their expertise in this area'.[21] There were eight members of the VBR as well as observers from the MinVWS and CVZ. The VBR members consisted of experts in epidemiology, medical biology, pharmacy, pharmacology, health economics, public health, and business. Their affiliations were mainly a mix of academia and quasi-government organizations such as the Developmental and Pharmaceutical Committees of CVZ and the Centre of Future Explorations into Public Health and Environment (RIVM). There were no representatives of the pharmaceutical industry or patient groups and only one physician. The development of the guidelines was initially resisted by the pharmaceutical industry, which opposed the additional research and financial burden. However, when its development was perceived to be inevitable, the industry chose to participate rather than resist.

The VBR developed draft guidelines from 23 March to 30 November 1998. It was agreed that the guidances would be applicable to Dutch regulations, be in harmony with the existing system to evaluate drugs, and be applicable to new drugs with expected additional therapeutic value.[22] Most importantly, the goal of the guidelines would be to guarantee transparency and proper execution of research. The VBR chose the Canadian guidelines for the basis of the Dutch guidance both for their scientific standards in pharmacoeconomic research and for their more general scope. Aspects of the Australian guidance on pharmacoeconomic research were also included.[23; 24; 25; 26]

The VBR presented their draft guidance in two meetings at the end of November 1998. The first meeting was exclusively with representatives of the Dutch Organization for Research-oriented

Pharmaceutical Industry (Nefarma). The second meeting was attended by the following organizations:

- Dutch Organization for Research-oriented Pharmaceutical Industry (Nefarma);
- Royal Dutch Association for the Advancement of Pharmacy (KNMP);
- National Organization for General Practitioners (LHV);
- Royal Dutch Association for the Advancement of Medicines (KNMG);
- Order of Medical Specialists (OMS);
- Association for Academic Hospitals (VAZ);
- Dutch Association of Hospital Pharmacists (NVZA);
- Dutch Federation for Patients and Consumers (NP/CF);
- Dutch Organization for Health Care Insurers (ZN);
- Council for Public Health and Care (RVZ);
- Committee for the Evaluations of Medicines (CBG);
- Experts in the field.

During these meetings the draft guidelines were revised to be more flexible in response to protests from commentors. For example, the responsibility to conduct financial analysis of the impact of the inclusion of a new drug on the government list was removed from the responsibility of the applicant and given to CVZ. Also, the initial guidance suggested a strict separation between researchers and the applicant. The industry and others argued, however, that the evidence should be able to speak for itself and that it should be sufficient to disclose the financial and contractual agreement between the applicant and the researchers. The VBR conceded, and the guideline was revised.

The final guidance (a brief description can be found in appendix 6.1) contains 19 separate guidelines and suggestions on the format of submissions. It also states which data should be provided and analytical techniques applied. CVZ and the MinVWS were aware that they and the industry would require some experience before this guidance became compulsory for submission and estimated that this would take only a few years.[27] Full implementation of the guidance, however, was delayed until 2005. The delay has mainly been attributed to the slow growth in capacity at the level of the MinVWS and CFH/CVZ to evaluate this type of research rather than any attempts by the industry to slow the process.

The development of the 1999 guidance demonstrates a general process of policy-making that succeeds in producing explicit criteria.

However, the process by which these guidelines were developed also highlights the absence of key stakeholders in shaping the discussions despite their opportunity to comment on drafts. The following section continues to demonstrate this style of decision-making and further discusses the role of various stakeholders in the process.

The GVS procedure in detail

The GVS refers both to the process for drug reimbursement and to the list of drugs that are paid for under the public scheme. This list contains only drugs used outside the hospital setting because inpatient drugs are included under the hospital budgeting system and within the future DBC system. Inclusion in the GVS is also considered where reimbursement is sought for additional indications for already reimbursed drugs. There are three different lists for which a drug can be included on the GVS: List 1a, 1b, and 2. Which list a drug is included on depends on its therapeutic value relative to other reimbursed drugs, its budgetary impact, and the burden of the disease addressed by the drug, such as its severity and prevalence among the Dutch population. As of 2005, the criteria will also include the results of pharmacoeconomic research. The decisions whether or not to include drugs on the GVS provide a key to understanding how well this system meets the potential goals of coverage decision-making, such as being evidence-based, transparent, and promoting efficiency and the health of a population.

Before continuing with a discussion of the GVS, it is important to address briefly the Dutch marketing approval process. Since the Provision of Pharmaceutical Act of 1958, drugs are restricted from being marketed in the Netherlands until they are approved by the Medical Evaluation Board (College ter Beoordeling van Geneesmiddeken (CBG-MEB)) on the basis of quality, safety, and efficacy. Currently, because the Netherlands is a member of the European Union, pathways for approval for marketing have been broadened.[28] A medicinal product can be registered in the Netherlands when it receives the approval of the central European medicines agency, the European Agency for the Evaluation of Medicinal Products (EMEA), and its advisory committee, the Committee for Proprietary Medicinal Products (CPMP). Their decisions are binding for all member states. Approval can also be gained through a mutual recognition procedure, which involves the Netherlands's acceptance of a market authorization issued by another member state of the EU.[29] For example, if a drug is registered in Sweden, then the Netherlands can accept it. However, mutual recognition is not mandatory and the EMEA is not involved. Formally, applicants to the GVS must wait until marketing approval in the Netherlands is complete to submit their application; however, even before this point they can go ahead and seek advice from the MinVWS and the CFH on their application.

Table 6.3 Summary of the Dutch drug reimbursement system (GVS)

Step	Description
1	Registration holder submits request for inclusion in the GVS to Ministry of Health, Sports, and Welfare.
2	Contents of the dossier are submitted by the claims registrar based on claims of equal to (List 1a) or greater therapeutic value (List 1b).
3	Ministry decides, in consultation with CHF, whether data are sufficient. At this time, additions can be made to the data.
4	Minister hears recommendation on application from CHF, which includes therapeutic value, financial analysis, and possible conditions.
5	Minister makes decision within 90 days of receiving the application. Postponement if applicant is invited to provide new data.
6	Ministry makes decision informs applicant and sends them the assessment by the CFH.
7	Applicant can request a review of decision if information on therapeutic value and efficacy have changed.

Source: Health Care Insurance Board (CVZ) (1999), *Dutch Guidelines for Pharmoeconomic Research*. Amstelveen: CVZ.

A summary of the GVS process can be found as Table 6.3. Only a pharmaceutical manufacturer can request inclusion on the GVS. If a manufacturer decides to pursue reimbursement, it can request that the MinVWS consider the evidence supporting including its drug on either List 1a or 1b. This will depend on whether it claims that its drug has an equivalent therapeutic value as an existing reference cluster, or that its drug provides an additional value over the existing clusters, or has no equivalent. A form must be completed with all relevant information included in a claim. Prior to submission of this information, the applicant can request a meeting with the CFH to get 'scientific advice' with respect to its application.

The MinVWS can decide at this point that there is not enough information and send the application back to the company for more information. If the information is judged to be adequate, the application is sent to CVZ and to the secretary of the CFH. From this point forward, the MinVWS is responsible for assuring that the process is followed appropriately and does not conduct additional review of the evidence submitted separate from CVZ.[30] Although the MinVWS has the final authority for deciding whether a drug is included within the GVS, CVZ and its sub-department, CFH, are responsible for developing recommendations on the therapeutic benefit of the drug for the MinVWS. The CVZ was established in 1999 as an independent administrative authority to advise the MinVWS on health care financing and insurance. CVZ has over 300 employees and is governed by an executive board and managerial staff. The executive board consists of nine independent experts appointed by the Min VWS.[31] The CFH is one of several sub-departments of CVZ and was also established in 1999. The CFH is a standing committee of 19 experts from a variety of backgrounds, including medical professionals (32 per cent), pharmacists (31 per cent), persons with a background in pharmacology (26 per cent), and persons with backgrounds in economics or psychology (11 per cent).

Although the pharmacoeconomic guidelines will be required as of 2005, currently no health economists are members of this committee. Potential committee members are nominated by current CFH members (with help from professional associations) and voted on by the entire committee. Their nomination is based on their expertise and with the goal of retaining the mix of experiences. The CFH, on behalf of the CVZ, evaluates the therapeutic value of a drug requesting reimbursement and its potential budgetary impact for the MinVWS.[32]

At CVZ, the application is reviewed by a member of the secretariat with specific expertise in the type of drug being considered. This staff member develops a concept paper on how the CFH should consider the new drug. This concept paper is shared with the MinVWS and the applicant in order to gather comments and is provided to the CFH during its monthly meeting where the paper is the basis for CFH's discussion.[33; 34] The CFH normally considers between one and two drugs at each meeting and no one except the members of the CFH and a MinVWS representative acting as an observer can be present during the meeting.[35; 36] Excluded from the meeting are the applicant, principal investigators who produced the evidence under consideration, medical professionals, and patient groups. For each drug, the CFH must decide on its therapeutic value relative to other drugs on the list. For each concept paper, the CFH may make modifications based on the evidence presented, review of the literature, and solicited expert opinions. Patient groups and medical expert testimony are not part of this phase of the initial review of application. In fact, the CFH prefers that the evidence come from articles published in peer-reviewed journals and does not normally accept abstracts, posters, or letters from patient groups. For drugs applying under List 1a, only general data on the product and clinical data supporting its substitutability for the other drugs in the requested cluster are needed. For List 1b applications, additional therapeutic value, budgetary impact, and, soon, pharmacoeconomic research must be considered. An important fact about the CFH is that it has currently only two members with training in pharmacoeconomic research (one expert in quality of life analysis and one in modelling), and there is no list of experts to whom the CFH can turn for advice.

This initial CFH meeting and discussion can also raise questions. If that is the case, the applicant is given seven days to respond to the questions of the CFH. This additional information is discussed at a second meeting where supporting letters from other members of the public can also be presented. The most consistent issue raised in CFH is the need for published studies on the new drug compared to existing therapies in the Netherlands rather than other settings.[37] Pharmacoeconomic information regarding a drug is predicted to become more of a focus of the discussion when the guidance becomes compulsory in 2005.[38]

The CFH/CVZ next develops a recommendation to the MinVWS of Health on whether or not the drug should be included as part of a therapeutic cluster (List 1a), receive its premium price (List 1b), be included on the drug list with specific conditions (List 2), or not be included at all. This recommendation is also accompanied by a financial analysis of the new drug's impact on the budget. The CFH recommendations are posted on the CVZ website before the final decision of the MinVWS is reached.[39; 40]

The MinVWS has the final authority to accept the recommendation of the CFH/CVZ. At this stage, the industry can encourage representatives from the medical professions and patient groups to communicate their support for a drug. By law the MinVWS must reach a decision within 90 days of receiving the application, but the decision can be postponed if the applicant is invited to provide new data, which is commonly the case. At this level, the MinVWS weighs the therapeutic value of the drug recommended by CFH as well as the claims of the industry, patient groups, and medical professionals against the drug's budgetary impact and burden of the disease it addresses. The MinVWS sends the applicant and stakeholders who have contacted the MinVWS a letter with the final decision. Positive reimbursement decisions are published in the '*Staatcourant*', a publication by the government on changes to regulation. However, negative reimbursement decisions or withdrawals of coverage are not widely publicized.[41]

There have been very few cases where the MinVWS has gone against the recommendations of the CFH/CVZ. It has happened, however, in cases where the CFH recommends inclusion, but, because of the impact on the budget or appropriateness, the MinVWS rejects the recommendation. On rarer occasions, the CFH does not recommend inclusion and the MinVWS relents to the pressure of patient groups and providers.[42; 43; 44; 45]

The only administrative process available to appeal the decision of the MinVWS deals with the situation where there is new information on the therapeutic value or efficacy of the drug. If additional information on the drug is available, the applicant can ask for a review of the decision. Outside of this, there is no process for an administrative appeal. The applicant is free to go to the Dutch courts to appeal the process by which their decision was made, but not the content of the decision.[46] A court has held that the advice of CFH is essential to the decision-making of the MinVWS on drug reimbursement issues; therefore, there can be no challenge to the content of the decisions of the MinVWS. There is no appeal based on misinterpretation of the evidence, and apart from the published document there is no way to understand the rationale of the CFH for a negative recommendation. Patients can also go to the courts to claim that they are entitled to a particular drug when it is denied to them by their insurer.[47]

The influence of stakeholders on the drug reimbursement process

Table 6.4 provides a summary of the influence that some key stakeholders have on the drug reimbursement process. On the whole, the government and those with perspectives close to the government have very strict control on both the criteria by which drugs are judged for reimbursement as well as the process by which these decisions are made. In the Dutch health care system, private health insurers are limited stakeholders in this debate, as their role

Table 6.4 Summary of stakeholders in the Dutch Drug Reimbursement Scheme

Name	Description	Influence
The Ministry of Health, Welfare, and Sport (MinVWS)	Key decision-maker in decisions on the financing, organization, and what is considered the right of patients to receive as part of the basic insurance package.	Makes the final decision on a drug's inclusion on to the National Health Service's drug list based on the severity to the patient and budget implication.
Health Care Insurance Board (CVZ)	Independent, non-governmental advisory organization to the Ministry for all matters regarding the public insurance scheme, specifically determination of the basic package. Membership appointed by MinVWS.	Advises the government on whether a drug should be included onto the GVS based on its therapeutic value compared to other existing therapies.
Committee on Pharmaceutical Help (CFH)	Standing committee within the CVZ charged with developing recommendations to CVZ on the inclusion of drugs on to the GVS. Membership nominated by fellow CFH members and approved by full committee.	Develop recommendations as requested by the Ministry on the therapeutic value of a drug in relation to other therapies included on the National Health Services drug list.
Pharmaceutical industry	General representation in the Netherlands by the Dutch Organization for Research-oriented Pharmaceutical Industry (Nefarma).	Individual manufacturers must apply for inclusion on to the GVS to the Ministry.
Patient groups	Represented by disease specific patient groups and also by the Dutch Federation for Patients and Consumers (NP/CF).	Cannot apply for the inclusion of a drug on to the GVS. May communicate support for a particular treatment to the Ministry and CVZ/CFH.
Medical professional societies	Represented by various professional societies such as the Order of Medical Specialists (OMS) and the National Organization for General Practitioners (LHV).	Cannot apply for the inclusion of a drug on to the GVS. May communicate support for a particular treatment to the Ministry and CVZ/CFH.

is to implement the decisions of the MinVWS regarding drug reimbursement.[48] Although the CVZ is independent of the government, its members and renewal of its membership body are still within the jurisdiction of the MinVWS. Consequently, the GVS mostly reflects the goals of the government. These goals include being a prudent purchaser of medications for its beneficiaries, but often cost containment is also a goal. Influence of non-governmental stakeholders such as the pharmaceutical industry, patient groups, and medical professionals is limited. Although their formal input is included in the appraisal of individual drugs, they have limited input into the process by which the criteria were formed and, most importantly, no administrative system exists for them to request changes to the process. Although there are cases where the MinVWS decides to have a hearing on a particular drug, there is no way to request that a hearing be done and no criteria for which it is mandatory. Also in the past, the MinVWS has held a meeting with stakeholders to discuss the process in general, but these have been on an ad hoc basis.[49; 50]

The lack of influence of the pharmaceutical industry in these processes has been attributed to many factors, including the small market share that the Netherlands represents.[51; 52] Because of the pharmaceutical industry's lack of strength in the Netherlands, there is very little pressure to change the process by which drugs are appraised, including the industry's representation during discussions of the CFH. The CFH responds to criticisms that it has shut the industry and others out of its discussions by stating that all the evidence it discusses is within the public domain and so there is no need for the meeting to be public.[53] The only way in which the pharmaceutical industry and others can influence the outcome is for the applicant for reimbursement to mobilize patient groups and medical professionals to send letters to CFH or the MinVWS.[54]

In general, the patient movement is not strong in the Netherlands. However, specific disease groups can greatly influence the government although they are usually silent until a drug has been denied. For the most part, patient groups are not involved in individual drug appraisals. One explanation is their lack of knowledge of working of the GVS system and that the pharmaceutical industry is prohibited from direct-to-consumer marketing which might, otherwise, raise awareness of available drugs that are not reimbursed under the GVS system.[55; 56] In addition, there has been little to no outcry by patients regarding whether a particular drug is categorized on either List 1a or 1b. The lack of controversy can mainly be attributed to the convergence of industry prices with the reimbursement amount to avoid losing patients due to increased co-payment and balanced billing. However, this influence and the power of the patient groups may grow as the industry spends more resources and becomes more creative within existing regulations in educating patients on their products.[57]

CONCLUSION

With the coming health reforms, particularly the implementation of the new hospital payment system, the Netherlands is faced with the exciting possibility of extending its long experience in making evidence-based coverage decisions for pharmaceuticals to other health technologies. DBCs require a clear definition of the health services offered and an understanding by both suppliers and financers of what constitutes effectiveness and cost effectiveness. This enhances the opportunity to incorporate knowledge on the effectiveness and efficiency of health services in day-to-day health care provision.

The principles underlying the GVS, including its emphasis on evidence-based medicine, explicit criteria, and independent appraisal, are just a few aspects of the system that may be transferred to a system of looking at technologies delivered within the hospital setting.[58] However, this translation may also highlight some of the criticisms that have been raised of the GVS process.

One of the main goals of the GVS scheme and many other coverage systems world-wide is to make decisions that enhance the lives of the people they serve and promote efficiency within their systems. The Netherlands has long adopted the principles of evidence-based medicine and recognizes the need for good clinical data on a drug's risks, efficacy, and effectiveness. With the full implementation of the 1999 pharmacoeconomic guidelines in 2005, the MinVWS and CVZ/CFH must ensure their capacity to conduct rigorous appraisals of this new data. This will require both staffing within the agency and the development of partnerships with researchers in this area in the field to serve as independent experts in the appraisal process.

Another goal of many coverage determination processes is to ensure that their decisions are transparent and open. The Netherlands has developed a transparent process in that the criteria for inclusion onto the GVS are explicit. Also, in the development of the 1999 guidelines there was some opportunity for stakeholders in the process to comment on the draft guidelines and suggest revisions. However, transparency in the development and availability of criteria are not reflected in the process. The discussions and evidence presented to the CFH are closed to the public, including the applicant, patient groups, and medical professionals. These stakeholders may have obvious biases in terms of how they would like the appraisal to result; however, their input during discussions of the CFH may serve to highlight real-world experiences with the drug such as problems with compliance, patient and provider expectations, or clinical management. Open discussions or publication of CFH meeting minutes can aid the industry in developing stronger applications and make available the rationale supporting recommendations.

Despite these criticisms, the Netherlands, with its long history in health technology assessment, has developed a model system for making coverage determinations. The climate of change with the coming health care reforms provides a catalyst for understanding the success of the GVS scheme and the criticisms it faces. It can be anticipated that the next few years may serve as a watershed in the inclusion of industry, patients, and the medical profession in development and reform of Dutch coverage determination systems.

CASE STUDY 1: GLIVEC®

In 2001, Novartis Europharm Ltd sought approval for marketing for Glivec®, an orphan drug, as a treatment for chronic myeloid leukemia (CML) in the United States and Europe. Glivec offers an example of a drug that received both rapid approval for marketing and reimbursement despite limited evidence of its effectiveness at the time of appraisal. Although this case is not indicative of most drugs that receive inclusion on to the public scheme's drug list, it illustrates the flexibility of the GVS to include expensive drugs for rare conditions expeditiously.

History of marketing approval for Glivec

Novartis pursued concurrent approvals with the US Food and Drug Administration (FDA) and through the European Commission's EMEA. For both processes Glivec was considered an orphan drug and, thus, was given expeditious review and special considerations. On 10 May 2001, the FDA approved Glivec for patients with CML under its 'accelerated approval' regulations, which granted approval in less than three months.[59] This experience was mirrored in Europe where the CPMP agreed to an expedited review 'in view of the quality of the dossier and outstanding activity of the medicinal product'; and on 7 November 2001, the EMEA and, thus, the Dutch MEB, first issued a market authorization for Glivec as a new drug for marketing in the Netherlands. The FDA and EMEA's approval was for the treatment of patients with three stages of CML: CML myeloid blast crisis, CML accelerated phase, or CML in chronic phase after failure of interferon treatment. The approval was based on early clinical studies described earlier.

However, at that time, the long-term benefit of the drug were not yet known.[60; 61; 62] Because of this, the FDA and EMEA recommended further studies to be done as a condition of approval to evaluate whether Glivec provides an actual clinical benefit. These studies would be annually reassessed for the risk/benefit profile.[63; 64; 65] The CPMP stated that the exceptional circumstances that surrounded approval for Glivec were due to the nature of CML and that it is 'encountered so rarely that the applicant cannot reasonably be expected to provide comprehensive evidence/data on the quality, safety, and efficacy of the medicinal product'.[66] In the next few years, additional indications for the use of Glivec were approved for CML patients (both adult and children) where bone marrow transplant is not considered as the first line treatment (9/19/02-CPMP; 19 December 2002) and adults patients with unresectable and/or metastatic malignant gastrointestinal stromal tumors (GIST) (2/21/02- CPMP; 24 May 2002).[67; 68]

Approval for inclusion onto the GVS

Prior to market approval for Glivec, Novartis had already started the process for reimbursement in the Netherlands. Because of its orphan drug and breakthrough status, it was able to apply prior to market approval. On 26 June 2001, Novartis contacted CVZ to begin discussions on the inclusion of Glivec onto List 1b of the GVS and the dossier was submitted on 1 August 2001. The appraisal of Glivec by CFH was rapid and required no additional information from the applicant. Rather than the two meetings needed for appraisal of a drug, the CFH met once on 17 September 2001 to appraise the relevant evidence. Although the existing evidence was from phase II trials and indirect comparisons and no definitive data for effectiveness was available at the time of the decision, the drug was approved as a treatment that would be used by a small population at high risk of mortality without treatment.[69] It was quickly concluded that Glivec should be placed on List 1b because Glivec could not be replaced by another therapeutic with the same functionality, indication area, method of administration, and side effects.[70] Despite the lack of definitive evidence on effectiveness, this approval was fairly clear cut for the CFH whose responsibility was to determine whether Glivec had an additional therapeutic benefit compared to other drugs already within the GVS. The absence of an alternative facilitated this decision and the rapidity of its inclusion.[71]

Based on the premium price of the applicant, CVZ's financial analysis submitted to the MinVWS of the consequences of covering Glivec estimated its cost to be around 5.9 million guilders (2.7 million euros) for an estimated 90 eligible patients per year. The cost consequence to the public insurance scheme was estimated at 4.2 million guilders.[72] Glivec was officially included on to the GVS on 18 December 2001. Novartis Europharma agreed that it would inform the MinVWS of expansions of Glivec's indications and that it would not need to apply formally for additional reimbursement for these.

The Glivec reimbursement process demonstrates the ability of the GVS scheme to work with the applicant to promote the diffusion of a technology with breakthrough potential for a fatal and rare condition. However, this case study is not representative of the process that applicants face in the reimbursement process in general. First, approval for Glivec did not require evidence of its cost effectiveness alongside its added therapeutic effectiveness. As of 2005, this will be required for all drugs seeking List 1b inclusion. Also, because of its orphan drug status, Novartis was allowed to apply before registration and its application was handled with priority. Finally, its appraisal only required one meeting of the CFH which vastly shortened its inclusion to within the 90-day period.[73]

CASE STUDY 2 – RELENZA® (ZANAMIVIR)

One cost-containment policy adopted between 1993 and 1999 by the Netherlands to stem the rising cost of pharmaceutical spending was to limit the reimbursement of innovated drugs. One of the medicines impacted by this policy was Relenza® (zanamivir) manufactured by GlaxoSmithKline (at the time, Glaxo Wellcome Inc.). GlaxoSmithKline requested the inclusion of zanamivir on the Dutch Drug Reimbursement Scheme's List 1b during the 1993–9 waiting list period and concurrent to its submission for marketing approval. However, it was not until February 2000 that the CFH was able to develop a recommendation to the MinVWS when the committee was able to deal with the backlog of several medicines from the waiting list. At that time NICE in the United Kingdom was also preparing their Technology Appraisal Guidance on zanamivir which was published in November 2000.[74] Although no specific reference is made to the NICE guidance, it can be assumed that the discussions in the United Kingdom influenced the thinking of the CFH and, thus, their recommendations to the MinVWS.[75]

Although the standard treatment for influenza is self-care, an orally administered medicine, amantadine, is available for the treatment and prevention of influenza A infections, but it is used in no more than ten per cent of cases. In the evidence reviewed by both NICE and the CFH, no clinical trials compared zanamivir with amantadine. Therefore, the CFH concluded that zanamivir cannot be offered as a substitute for amantadine and cannot be placed on List 1a, as part of a therapeutic cluster.

Next, the CFH considered whether zanamivir offered added therapeutic value compared to standard treatment (in this case self-care). For healthy people, the increased effectiveness was thought to be limited and would not be in balance with the cost of treatment with zanamivir (€16.33) plus the cost of a consultation with a general practitioner (compare the cost of amantadine at €2). It should also be added that the effectiveness was demonstrated to be smaller in those where influenza was not demonstrated through serological and virological tests. So, the use of zanamivir on the basis of symptoms only would offer less benefit than using the drug when influenza is clinically demonstrated. The addition of a test would increase the total cost and delay treatment. Finally, the clinical evidence on the drug's effectiveness for treating influenza B was scarce due to the limited number of these patients in study populations. Therefore, evidence for influenza B was believed to be less rigorous than for those with influenza A. The CFH recognized that for high-risk populations the consequences of influenza are serious. The numbers of high-risk patients represented in patient populations of the studies reviewed at the time were very small. This prevented the CFH from being able to draw conclusions on the (cost) effectiveness of zanamivir for these high-risk groups. The final conclusion of the CFH was that zanamivir does not have sufficient added value to warrant reimbursement and that focusing on vaccination of high-risk groups remains the most cost-effective strategy.[76] This advice was accepted by the Minister, who decided accordingly to not include zanamivir in the GVS and, thus, not provide reimbursement. This remains the policy on zanamivir regardless of the revisions of the original NICE guidance.

APPENDIX 6.1 SUMMARY OF 1999 DUTCH GUIDELINES FOR PHARMACOECONOMIC RESEARCH

Guideline number	Description
1	Target group of the research is MinVWS.
2	Perspective: societal perspective.
3	Timing of studies: research can be performed on any stage (phases II–IV) of development.
4	Perpetrator of the study: transparency between relationship of perpetrators of research and contractor.
5	Analytical technique: either a cost-effectiveness analysis and/or a cost–utility analysis should be presented.
6	Indications: specification of intended patient population should be included.
7	Comparative treatment: should the standard treatment or usual treatment based on treatment regarded in daily practice as the first choice for which effectiveness has been proven.

8   Costs and effects must be reported in terms of both incremental and total values.

9   Analysis period should be sufficient in order to enable 'valid and reliable' statements of costs and outcomes.

10   Preference on reporting effectiveness and efforts should be made to collect data on relevant endpoints in terms or morbidity and mortality under realistic conditions. Modelled data of translated efficacy data to expected practice can be submitted.

11   Quality of life can be measured using generic (recommended SF-36 or EuroQol) or disease-specific questionnaires or using utility instrument (if using cost-utility analysis then this is mandatory).

12   Primary analyses should be based upon quality-adjusted-life-years (QALYs).

13   Direct costs both inside and outside health care must be included. Indirect costs inside the health care system include costs due to illness which are not related to the intervention must be excluded.

14   Deployment of people and resources during treatment must first be described in natural (non-monetary) units (hours, tasks, nursing days, or daily doses).

15   Standard cost list must be used.

16   Future outcomes and costs should both be discounted at 4 per cent.

17   Reliability and validity must be assured by stating all assumptions, major limitations, and inclusion of sensitivity analyses.

18   Reporting must conform to standard form.

19   Modelling of results should be used to obtain effectiveness data from efficacy data.

Source: Health Care Insurance Board (CVZ) (1999), *Dutch Guidelines for Pharmoeconomic Research*. Amstelveen: CVZ.

References

1   M. Bos (2000), 'Health Technology Assessment in the Netherlands', *International Journal of Technology Assessment in Health Care*, 16(2): 485–519.

2   Organisation for Economic Cooperation and Development (OECD) (2004), *OECD Health Data 2003*. Paris: OECD, < www.oecd.org > (accessed 17 Feb. 2004).

3 F. Rutten (2003), 'The Impact of Health Care Reform in the Netherlands' (accepted for publication).
4 Rutten (2003).
5 OECD (2004).
6 Rutten (2003).
7 Committee on the Structuring and Finance of Health Care (1987), *Preparing for Change*. The Hague: DOP.
8 Bos (2000), pp. 494–6.
9 P.J. van der Maas, H.J. de Koning, B. van Ineveld, et al. (1989), 'The Cost-Effectiveness of Breast Cancer Screening', *International Journal of Cancer*, 43: 1055–60.
10 Bos (2000), pp. 502–3.
11 Bos (2000), p. 502.
12 M. Bos (2004), 'Clarification of Article 18' (Digitally recorded interview by T. Carino). Den Haag, 5 February.
13 B. Hermans (2003), 'Clarification of Article 18' (Digitally recorded interview by T. Carino). Rotterdam, 29 October.
14 M. Buijsen (2003), 'Clarification of Article 18' (Digitally recorded interview by T. Carino). Rotterdam, 20 October.
15 M. Dickson and H. Redwood (1998), 'Pharmaceutical Reference Prices. How Do They Work in Practice?', *Pharmacoeconomics*, 14(5): 471–9.
16 A. Steenhoek (2004), 'The GVS Process and Membership on the CFH' (Digitally recorded interview by T. Carino). Alkmaar, 11 February.
17 P. Kruger (2004a), 'Informal Analysis of the Number of Drugs in the GVS' (Email communication to T. Carino). Rotterdam, 1 March.
18 M. Dickson and H. Redwood (1998), p. 473.
19 P. Spoorendonk (2003), 'Drug Reimbursement in the Netherlands' (Digitally recorded interview by T. Carino). Haarlem, 14 November.
20 Health Care Insurance Board (CVZ) (1999), *Dutch Guidelines for Farmoeconomic Research*. Amstelveen: CVZ, p. 3.
21 CVZ (1999), pp. 3–7.
22 CVZ (1999), p. 4.
23 Commonwealth of Australia, Department of Health, Housing, Local Government and Community Services (1993), *Manual of Resource Items and their Associated Costs, for use in Submissions to the Pharmaceutical Benefits Advisory Committee Involving Economic Analyses*. Canberra: Australian Government Publishing Service.
24 Commonwealth of Australia, Department of Human Services and Health (1995), *Guidelines for the Pharmaceutical Industry on Preparation of Submissions to the Pharmaceutical Benefits Advisory Committee, Including Economic Analyses*. Canberra: Australian Government Publishing Service.
25 Canadian Coordinating Office for Health Technology Assessment

(CCOHTA) (1996), *A Guidance Document for the Costing Process*, Version 1.0. Ottawa: CCOHTA.

26 Canadian Coordinating Office for Health Technology Assessment (CCOHTA) (1997), *Guidelines for Economic Evaluation of Pharmaceuticals: Canada*, 2nd edn. Ottawa: CCOHTA.

27 CVZ (1999), p. 2.

28 Medicine Evaluation Board (CBG) (2003b), *The Medicines Evaluation Board (Agency) in 2002: Changes consolidated*. Den Haag: CBG.

29 CBG (2003b), pp. 1–2.

30 P. Kruger (2004b), 'The Role of the Ministry of Health, Welfare, and Sports in the GVS System' (Telephone interview by T. Carino). Rotterdam, 26 February.

31 Health Care Insurance Board (CVZ) (2004), *Forerunner at the Heart of the Health Care System*. Amstelveen: CVZ. p. 2.

32 Steenhoek (2004).

33 Kruger (2004b).

34 Steenhoek (2004).

35 Steenhoek (2004).

36 Kruger (2004b).

37 Steenhoek (2004).

38 Steenhoek (2004).

39 Kruger (2004b).

40 Steenhoek (2004).

41 Kruger (2004b).

42 A. Boer (2003), 'Technology Reimbursement in the Netherlands' (Digitally recorded interview with T. Carino). Daimen, 3 November.

43 Kruger (2004b).

44 Spoorendonk (2003).

45 Steenhoek (2004).

46 Spoorendonk (2003).

47 J. Schouten (2004), 'Insurers and Technology Assessment in the Netherlands' (Telephone interview by T. Carino). Rotterdam, 17 February.

48 Schouten (2004).

49 Kruger (2004b).

50 Steenhoek (2004).

51 Spoorendonk (2003).

52 Spoorendonk (2003).

53 Steenhoek (2004).

54 Steenhoek (2004).

55 Spoorendonk (2003).

56 Steenhoek (2004).

57 Spoorendonk (2003).

58 Boer (2003).

59 Food and Drug Administration (FDA) (2001), 'FDA Approves Gleevec for Leukemia Treatment', *FDA Consumer Magazine*, 35.

< www.fda.gov/bbs/topics/NEWS/2003/NEW00909.html > (accessed 25 Jan. 2004).

60 B.J. Druker, C.L. Sawyers, H. Kantarjian, et al. (2001a), 'Activity of a Specific Inhibitor of the BCR-ABL Tyrosine Kinase in the Blast Crisis of Chronic Myeloid Leukemia and Acute Lymphoblastic Leukemia with the Philadelphia Chromosome', *New England Journal of Medicine*, 344(14): 1038–42.

61 B.J. Druker, M. Resta, D.J. Peng, B. Buchdunger, et al. (2001b), 'Efficacy and Safety of a Specific Inhibitor of the BCR-ABL Tyrosine Kinase in Chronic Myeloid Leukemia', *New England Journal of Medicine*, (14): 1031–7.

62 The European Agency for the Evaluation of Medicinal Products (EMEA) (2001), *Committee for Proprietary Medicinal Products European Public Assessment Report (EPAR) on Glivec*. London: EMEA

63 FDA (2001).

64 EMEA (2001), p. 1.

65 Medicine Evaluation Board (CBG) (2003), *Glivec, 100 mg*. EU/1/01/198/007. < www.cbg.nl > (accessed 6 Jan. 2004).

66 EMEA (2001), p. 2.

67 EMEA (2001).

68 CBG (2003).

69 Health Care Insurance Board (CVZ) (2001a), *Committee on Pharmaceutical Help Recommendation for Celebrex, Climodien, Glivec, and Menopur*. Amstelveen: CVZ, p. 2.

70 CVZ (2001a), p. 1.

71 Steenhoek (2004).

72 Health Care Insurance Board (CVZ) (2001b), *Cost Consequences of Glivec*. CVZ, October 26.

73 Guido van den Boom (2004), 'Approval of Glivec in the Netherlands' (Email communication to T. Carino). Rotterdam, 19 February.

74 National Institute for Clinical Excellence (NICE) (1999), *Old Guidance – Zanamivir (Relenza)*. London: NICE.

75 Health Care Insurance Board (CVZ) (2000), *Committee on Pharmaceutical Help Recommendation for Cisapride (Prepulsid) and Zanamivir (Relenza)*. Amstelveen: CVZ, pp. 2–5.

76 CVZ (2000), p. 5.

7

HEALTH CARE COVERAGE DETERMINATIONS IN SPAIN

Anna García-Altés[1]

INTRODUCTION

The Spanish Constitution, passed in 1978, establishes Spain as a social and democratic state, governed by a parliamentary monarchy. The government is ruled through a bicameral parliament, composed of the House of Commons and the Senate, whose members are elected every four years by the Spanish people. The president of the Spanish government is elected by the members of the House of Commons. The state is territorially organized into municipalities, provinces, and Autonomous Regions (ARs) that manage their own interests. The creation of 17 ARs began a decentralization process of different public management powers, including authority over health care, which was completed in 2003.

The Spanish Constitution also established a health care system, available to everyone and free at point of service. The General Health Law of 1986 defined the framework for a National Health System (NHS), which included universal coverage.[2] The law's guiding principles include priority for promotion of health and prevention, equity of access to services, and community participation. The Constitution and the General Health Law form the regulatory framework for the devolution of health care services to the ARs. All 17 ARs have complete authority regarding public health and planning. Responsibilities for health care financing, organization, provision, and management have been completely devolved to all ARs as of 2003 through the Law of Cohesion and Quality of the NHS.[3] The Ministry of Health guarantees the effective right of all citizens to health care protection. It co-ordinates public health and health care services, sets health policy, drafts any basic enabling legislation, and ensures co-ordination of health and social services with the Ministry of Labor and Social Affairs. It also regulates postgraduate training for medical professionals (together with the Ministry of Education), establishes pharmaceutical policy, standardizes medical and health products in general, and is the highest authority in consumer affairs.

The Ministry of Labor and Social Affairs defines the financial structure of the social security system, establishes the guaranteed package of health care benefits, and authorizes payments made within the NHS. The Ministry of Labor and Social Affairs is also responsible for social and community care, although these have been progressively transferred to the ARs.

Until 1995, there was no clearly defined package of benefits guaranteed under the social security health care system. The extension of available treatments was a gradual process, which often responded to advances in technology and medical developments without any prior attempt to assess effectiveness or efficiency. This failure to evaluate new interventions threatened both the quality of health care and efforts to control rising costs. In addition, the absence of a systematic response to technological innovations in a decentralized environment increasingly gave rise to inequalities in the benefits offered by the different regional health care services.

For all these reasons, the Royal Decree 63/1995 was passed to define services covered by the NHS.[4] The proposal for this decree was based on technical criteria, and underwent parliamentary debate. The two main objectives of this regulation were to complement the portfolio of citizens' rights with an explicit list of benefits guaranteed by the public health care system and to regulate the introduction of new services and technologies. Benefits covered by the NHS include: primary health care, which includes medical and pediatric health care, prevention of disease, and health promotion and rehabilitation; specialized health care in the form of outpatient and inpatient care, including all medical and surgical specialties in acute care; pharmaceutical benefits; and complementary benefits such as prostheses or orthopedic products. The package does not include social and community care. The main benefit historically excluded is dental care.

Regional governments of ARs possess health planning powers as well as the capacity to organize their own health services. The role of local governments in the system has decreased because the Constitution allocated most of the former local responsibilities to regional governments, though they still have some authority over sanitation policies and environmental health activities.

Although the bulk of health care assistance is provided through the public health care system (hospitals, primary care, specialized health care, and long-term care centres), private insurance companies have a minor but increasing role. Private voluntary schemes cover 10 per cent of the population. Three publicly funded mutual funds also exist which exclusively cover civil servants, who are free to choose between public or private provision. There are also other providers such as military health services or prison services. Traditionally, the public system has contracted out approximately 15 to 20 per cent of hospital provision with private, non-profit providers.[5]

Responsibility for planning and regulation of the health system are shared between the central and regional governments. Central and regional top management institutions in general continue to integrate the functions of financing, purchasing, and provision. However, since 1990, legislation has been adopted aimed at gradually separating provider and purchaser functions through the use of contracts with funding attached to the achievement of objectives.[6]

Financing for public health insurance comes from taxes, social compulsory contributions, and other sources. The health care system is financed out of general revenue taxation, which has replaced a more insurance-oriented system. Most taxes are centrally raised, since regional and local governments have limited fiscal autonomy. Civil servants' mutual funds are funded approximately 70 per cent by the state and 30 per cent through contributions from civil servants to their own funds.[7] The General Health Law of 1986 established the distribution of the Spanish global budget for health care among the ARs,[8] based on criteria that were modified by the 21/2001 Act.[9]

The self-employed and liberal professionals, who constitute less than 1 per cent of the population, are not covered by the NHS. Of the remaining Spaniards covered by the statutory system, 94.6 per cent are covered by obligatory membership in the social security system and the remaining 4.6 per cent are civil servants and their dependants, mostly covered by mutual funds. A special means-tested, non-contributory scheme is in place for the disadvantaged.

The extension of health care rights to the adult immigrant population was approved recently, but its future remains unclear.[10] Citizens' participation in decision-making about their health care system was incorporated into the General Health Law, and participatory committees were introduced at all levels of the managerial structure of the health care system. These mostly consist, however, of representatives of local governments and professional groups, with only a small percentage of membership reserved to local civic associations. In practical terms, this participation has not been wholly effective because these committees lack direct responsibility for health care expenditure, and because Spanish consumer associations are weak and not entirely representative of the wider community.[11]

REGULATION OF PHARMACEUTICALS

The Medicines Act of 1990 forms the basis for pharmaceutical policy in Spain, and most legislation regulating the pharmaceutical market has been updated since 1990 in line with this Act's requirements.[12] Governmental authority over pharmaceuticals is again divided into three levels (among the state, ARs, and local health services) with the relevant health authority taking charge at the appropriate level. The state is empowered to carry on the following activities:

- to regulate and authorize clinical trials;
- to issue marketing authorizations for pharmaceuticals;
- to control the advertising of drugs and health care products directed toward the general population;
- to license pharmaceutical laboratories;
- to regulate the quality and manufacture of pharmaceutical products; and
- to fix the price of drugs, set co-payments, and decide on the inclusion or exclusion of pharmaceuticals on or from the list of publicly-financed medicines.

ARs undertake the planning of pharmacies and fixing the criteria for the opening or relocation of pharmaceutical outlets, while local health services are in charge of the day-to-day administration of pharmaceutical benefits, setting the conditions of the agreements with pharmacies, and implementing cost-containment programmes.

By law, local health services hold wide powers over the implementation of centrally issued legislation in the pharmaceutical field. Prices of drugs are established at the national level based on technical criteria, and are then negotiated between the Ministry of Health and the pharmaceutical industry. After that, the Ministry of Health issues a positive list of drugs covered at 100 per cent by the NHS. For some other listed medicines, the patient must pay a copayment of 40 per cent, or in some instances 10 per cent (which is the case for drugs for the treatment of chronic diseases).

Significant year-by-year growth in pharmaceutical expenditures during the 1980s and early 1990s led to the adoption of a number of cost-containment measures from 1993 onwards, which were targeted at different areas of the pharmaceutical sector. The most important policy change has been the introduction of a negative list of pharmaceuticals excluded from public funding by the 83/1993 Royal Decree on selective pharmaceutical financing,[13] which was enlarged and updated through the 1663/1998 Royal Decree.[14] The combined effect of both decrees led to the exclusion from public funding of 29 per cent of all pharmaceutical brands registered on the market.

Additionally, in 1993, a reduction in the value added tax (VAT) rate from 6 per cent to 3 per cent was applied to medicines, while in 1995 the rate was fixed at 4 per cent. Also, an agreement with the pharmaceutical industry to reduce the commercial prices of drugs by 3 per cent on average annually was reached this same year, which remained in force until November 1999. This reduction was scaled differently for drugs in different price intervals in a way that did not permit pharmaceutical companies to choose which type of drugs would be subject to sharper reductions. In addition, in July 1995, a further agreement was reached with the pharmaceutical industry, which set down a system of profit reduction in sales to the public sector with an annual growth ceiling (7 per cent for the next three years) and committed *Farmaindustria* (the national employers' association in the pharmaceutical sector) to encourage the use of generic products.[15]

The 1990 Medicines Act was modified through the 13/1996 and 66/1997 Acts,[16; 17] opening the way for the introduction of generic drugs and global reference pricing within the Spanish health care market. In particular, the first generic brands were registered for commercial distribution in July 1997, while reference prices were effectively introduced through the 1035/1999 Royal Decree.[18] Between July 1997 and November 1999, 343 generic brands were authorized, which yielded sales of 260 million pesetas in 1998, a figure which rose to 1585 million in total sales by October 1999. The creation of the National Medicines Agency in 1997, and its effective implementation in 1999, promotes the diffusion and implementation of guidelines and protocols.[19] The agency is the governmental organization that assesses, authorizes, registers, and controls the use of drugs for humans and animals, as well as for cosmetic and personal hygiene purposes, according to the Spanish and European laws. It also has the competence to rule on the imports of foreign drugs, to administer the compassionate use of drugs, to control the state reserve of strategic drugs, and to disseminate information about drugs.

The 1990 Medicine Act established the criteria to be followed for controlling the quality, safety, efficacy, prices, marketing, and advertising of medicines.[20] As in other European countries, the introduction of new drugs is thoroughly regulated. The Ministry of Health approves drugs after examining the scientific evidence of their safety and efficacy. There are also special regulations for clinical trials. Spain participates in the EU regulatory programme concerning pharmaceuticals.

REGULATION OF MEDICAL DEVICES

Compared with pharmaceuticals, the control of medical equipment and devices has been minimal until recently, as has also been the case in many other European countries. Most regulation has been related to technical safety and good manufacturing practices.[21] Up to now, the Ministry of Industry has had the task of authorizing the introduction and installation of some types of medical equipment (x-rays, ionizing radiation equipment, and portable radio surgical equipment), taking into account its technical efficacy, quality, reliability, and mechanical and electrical safety for the patient and operator. Additionally, in collaboration with the ARs, the Ministry of Industry is in charge of guaranteeing the safety of electrical equipment used for medical purposes (such as electroencephalograph) before introduction in the market. The evaluation procedures and protection requirements for any equipment that may create electromagnetic disturbances have been regulated since 1994.

With respect to active implantable medical devices, the 90/385 and the 93/42 Economic European Community Directives have been adapted to the Spanish national legislation.[22] These directives require evidence of an adequate risk–benefit calculus, which can be established through a bibliographic review or through clinical trials. As with most pre-marketing approval rules, the type of information required to guarantee safety is focused on short-term consequences of the medical device, and not on long-term consequences, so the EC mark does not necessarily guarantee that a device is 100 per cent safe. There have also been unequal applications of the rule, which have led to the marketing of some types of equipment based on its technical safety and efficacy, performance, and operating instructions, but with minimal analysis of its actual clinical safety and effectiveness.

The acquisition of medium- and low-level health technology (products that result from intensive technological development that can be used without an elaborate and complex support system and whose adoption does not require mobilization of many financial and human resources) is controlled mainly through hospital budgets. High health technologies (products that can not be used without an elaborate and complex support system and whose adoption require mobilization of many financial and human resources) require formal prior approval. There are specific rules for specific technologies, such as transplants or breast cancer screening.

HEALTH TECHNOLOGY ASSESSMENT IN SPAIN

The previously mentioned Royal Decree 63/1995 establishes a list of health care services directly offered to users by the NHS and financed by the social security or by state funds dedicated to health care, as well as the criteria to be fulfilled by these services.[23] Among the criteria used to exclude a health service from financing with public funds are lack of sufficient scientific evidence establishing clinical safety and efficacy for conserving or improving life expectancy or self-sufficiency, or for the elimination or reduction of physical pain.

Any mechanism for controlling health technology must aim at promoting the introduction and diffusion of those health technologies that will improve the population's health status and quality of life, while restricting or avoiding those technologies whose health benefit is unknown or that impose an economic burden on society that is not justified by the health benefits obtained. The introduction and diffusion of health technologies can be controlled directly or indirectly.[24] Both types of mechanisms are represented in Spain through specific laws, and through differing financing or payment methods and research strategies.

The creation and development of organizations and formal activities in the health technology assessment field have occurred at different speeds among the Spanish ARs.[25] The first institutional initiative for the promotion of the rational introduction and diffusion of health technology dates from 1984, when the Advisory Board for High Technology was created in Catalonia. As a consequence of evolving scientific knowledge and the need to undertake a more comprehensive analysis, the Catalan Office for Health Technology Assessment (CAHTA) was created as an administrative unit inside the Catalan Department of Health. Some time later, CAHTA became a not-for-profit public company.[26]

In 1992, the Basque Country was the next AR to create an organization devoted to health technology assessment – Osteba.[27] After the creation of several administrative units within the Central Government Department of Health, aimed primarily at regulating health technologies rather than evaluating them, the *Agencia de Evaluación de Tecnologías Sanitarias* (AETS) was formed in 1994.[28] Finally, during 1996, the Andalusian agency appeared (AETSA). Similar organizations developed later in Galicia (1999) and Valencia (2000). It should be noted that all of these health technology assessment organizations have begun co-ordinating their evaluative efforts in order to avoid duplications and to strengthen and promote dissemination of health technology assessment results.

The main objective of all health technology assessment organizations is to support decision-making processes so that the introduction, adoption, diffusion, and utilization of health technology can be made according to scientifically proven criteria of efficacy, safety, effectiveness, and efficiency. All health technology assessment organizations in Spain are consultative: none of them have a decision-making role with respect to the coverage of assessed technologies. They just make recommendations regarding the use of health technologies. Decisions, if any, are made at the AR or state level by health authorities, without an explicit process, and taking into account the recommendations of the assessment organization, and any other legal, economic, and third-party pressures. There is no process to appeal those decisions.

As is true with other health technology assessment organizations, assessment methods include systematic reviews of the scientific evidence, meta-analysis, economic analysis, and analysis of the legal and social implications of technologies. Identification of technologies or technology/indication combinations needing assessment may be done proactively, reactively, or in a mixed manner. Identification of health technology assessment priorities differs among institutions both in the emphasis given to different approaches, and in the process of needs identification itself.[29]

The Central Government health assessment agency (AETS) sets priorities in two ways. Working proactively, AETS issues a list of health technologies to be assessed, following the criteria of safety, efficacy, effectiveness, level of uncertainty, level of controversy, variations in clinical practice, innovation capacity, cost, and consideration of ethical and social issues. The resulting list is evaluated by the Ministry of Health, which determines the health technologies that will be assessed. AETS also uses a reactive approach, under which health care professionals may identify a health technology to be assessed in terms of the above-mentioned criteria.

Osteba relies on the Health Minister, the Directorate Council, and health care professionals to identify health technology assessment priorities. Additionally, Osteba has developed an explicit priority-setting process based on the one proposed by the US Institute of Health in 1992. This process is co-ordinated by Osteba and carried out by a multidisciplinary panel of experts using established criteria and creating a prioritized health technology list through consensus techniques. The criteria used, in order of importance, are: variation in rate of use; disease burden; prevalence of disease; the possibility that an evaluation will change clinical outcomes; the possibility that an evaluation will help with resolving ethical and legal issues; the possibility that an evaluation will change costs; and finally, costs themselves.[30]

Since its creation, AETSA has been working on topics directly selected by the Andalusian Department of Health, and identified as needs in the Andalusian Health Plan. AETSA is designing a prioritization process using Osteba's process as a model. CAHTA has also developed a prioritization process for their biennial research call following the criteria of the US Institute of Medicine.[31]

Finally, a working group on health technology assessment has been recently created as an advisory committee for the Interregional Council of the NHS. This group consists of the directors of the different Spanish agencies for health technology assessment and representatives of all ARs. Its duties are: to identify a list of health technologies that have to be assessed within the framework of the NHS; to create an information system to detect emerging technologies; to establish a schedule of assessment activities and deadlines; and to define criteria for trials of new technologies before their inclusion in the NHS. All Spanish agencies are members of the International Network of Agencies of Health Technology Assessment (INAHTA). CAHTA and Osteba were two of the founding members and have been part of the working group of the first INAHTA collaborative project.[32] Dissemination activities involve active processes to spread information to defined target groups by use of the media. This process is aimed primarily at enhancing awareness, and may or may not lead to behaviour change.[33] Dissemination activities carried out by Spanish health technology assessment organizations do not differ substantially in type but differ in their level of sophistication. Health technology assessment reports are published and distributed in formats adapted to and aimed at target groups. Reports include an executive summary that facilitates a quick and comprehensive understanding of the key points addressed by the report. Additionally, some of the organizations send reports to key policy makers, offer report abstracts, or produce press releases.

The organizations also edit their own newsletters. The aim of these newsletters is to inform readers about controversial health technology assessment issues, the results of assessment activities, papers published in scientific journals, and academic activities. These organizations also present lectures and seminars, and offer many forms of training activities. They also have their own webpages.

One of the main differentiating characteristics among the assessment organizations is their legal framework. While Osteba is an administrative unit within the Basque Department of Health, and AETS is a branch of a research organization within the Spanish Ministry of Health, CAHTA is a not-for-profit public company affiliated with the Catalan Department of Health. This quasi-independent status answers the need to adapt CAHTA's evaluation process to the changing decentralized health care system in Catalonia, which requires information for decision-making, both at different health care levels and in the research and development arena. This legal framework has allowed CAHTA to work for all the providers of the Catalan health care system, public and private health care centres, and other health administrations and organizations, national and international.[34]

CAHTA's structure consists of an executive board, a scientific committee, a director, and a multidisciplinary staff, covering the areas of projects, research, academic activities, documentation, and communication. CAHTA identifies health technologies that need assessment through the priorities contained in the Health Plan of Catalonia, the appraisal of assessment needs made by members of its scientific committee, and the selection made by CAHTA's own staff. A proposal is then prioritized and approved by the executive board, which in turn must take into account criteria with respect to the uncertainty of this technology, its epidemiologic and economic impact, variability of clinical practice, and social expectations, among other critical priority parameters. Because CAHTA is a public not-for-profit agency, the process may also be initiated by a request from health policy makers working in public organizations, such as the Catalan Department of Health, managers and physicians from public and private health care centres, scientific societies, insurance companies, and biomedical manufacturers.[35]

The assessment method chosen by the CAHTA is influenced by several factors including the policy question, the time available to perform the assessment, and the characteristics of the scientific evidence available. Although the CAHTA at first operated primarily by performing syntheses of the scientific evidence, its range of methods has widened. Primary and secondary research is carried out, both in-house or in collaboration with scientific societies. Research methods are also varied, including economic evaluation, meta-analysis, and synthesis of the scientific evidence graded by design quality. An analysis of the Catalan health care also includes different degrees of consideration for the legal, ethical, and social implications of the health technology studied, whenever this is possible and required.[36]

In a number of instances, implementation activities have put into effect recommendations based on CAHTA's assessments. These activities have been advised by CAHTA and developed by the Catalan Department of Health. Some examples include the creation of specific regulations to improve the prescription of long-term home oxygen therapy, the development of quality of care guidelines for stem-cell transplants, and changes in the payment system for some technologies to improve their effectiveness and increase their use whenever needed, as was done for ambulatory surgery and for low osmolarity contrast.[37]

Table 7.1 Description of the reviews of PET done by the Spanish HTA organizations

Org., year	Indications studied	Assessment type	Conclusions/Recommendations
AETS, 1995	■ Myocardial perfusion ■ Myocardial viability	Synthesis of reports from ECRI and AHCPR	1. PET and SPECT appear to perform similarly for diagnosing coronary perfusion in coronary disease and for making subsequent management decisions (AHCPR). 2. Substituting PET for SPECT or vice versa for determining myocardial viability depends on which is more cost-effective to use (ECRI).
AETS, 1997	■ Head and neck ■ Recurrent colorectal ■ Breast cancer ■ Lung cancer ■ SPN ■ Pancreatic ■ Metastasic melanoma ■ Ovarian cancer	Systematic review	1. No definitive conclusions can be reached relative to the contribution of PET in the management of the oncological patient. 2. PET seems to offer a good alternative for lung cancer staging and SPN diagnosis. 3. As no controlled clinical trials exist, PET is deemed an investigative technology. 4. Rigorous, clinical trials are needed to assess the clinical benefit of PET in all clinical indications.
AETS, 1999	■ Alzheimer disease ■ Parkinsonism ■ Epilepsy ■ Brain tumors ■ Other less frequent indications	Systematic review	1. FDG-PET has proven clinical utility in the management of: ■ Refractory complex partial seizures and temporal epilepsy candidates for surgery, as a complementary diagnostic and prognostic tool. ■ FDG-PET does not preclude invasive methods in most cases. ■ Differential diagnosis between radionecrosis and residual or relapsing tumoral lesions. ■ FDG-PET aids in the early diagnosis of AD. This fact does not modify the current clinical management of this disorder.

Org., year	Indications studied	Assessment type	Conclusions/Recommendations
			2. There is a remarkable lack of studies of adequate methodological quality to establish PET's utility in handling of specific clinical situations, and its contribution to improving therapeutic results. 3. Recommend developing appropriately designed prospective studies mainly to answer questions of great interest for the National Health System in order to use PET most effectively. 10. PET use should be controlled according to a research protocol.
CAHTA, 1993	■ Myocardial perfusion ■ Myocardial viability ■ Brain tumor recurrence vs. necrosis ■ Alzheimer's diagnosis ■ Oncology	Literature review	1. For myocardial perfusion, differences in sensitivity and specificity between PET and SPECT (using new isotopes) are negligible. 2. FDG18-PET can be a support technology to identify myocardial viability and to assess the feasibility for a revascularization procedure for those patients with an inconclusive diagnosis using conventional technologies (Thallium-201 reinjection after 4 hours). 3. PET has been shown to be superior to diagnostic conventional techniques (CT, MRI) in the differential diagnosis between post-radiation tissue necrosis and tumor recurrence. 4. PET is useful in the differential diagnosis between Alzheimer's and other dementias. However, the therapeutic approach of the Alzheimer patient does not change with the information. This indication is still considered experimental. 5. PET seems to have a great potential in the early detection of cancer. However, its use is still in the experimental stage.

Org., year	Indications studied	Assessment type	Conclusions/Recommendations
CAHTA, 1996	■ Autism	Synthesis of the evidence	1. The scientific evidence shows a lack of a consistent anatomical or metabolic image which can be associated with the presence of autism. The available studies have a low methodological quality. PET is still an experimental technology for this clinical indication. 2. No conclusive scientific evidence has shown a consistent PET brain image pattern associated with different neuropsychiatric disorders. Study results are questioned due to their methodological limitations. PET is still an experimental technology.
OSTEBA, 1998	■ Head and neck ■ Colorectal ■ Breast ■ Lung ■ SPN ■ Brain ■ Pancreatic ■ Melanoma ■ Soft tissue ■ Myocardial perfusion ■ Myocardial viability ■ Epilepsy ■ West infantile spasms ■ Lennox-Gastaut syndrome ■ Alzheimer's disease	Literature synthesis, utilization survey	1. Studies of good methodological quality are needed to establish PET's role in routine clinical practice. 2. In certain situations PET may have complementary utility, and possibly a future with hybrid or fusion imaging. 3. PET could be appropriate on a case by case basis, taking into account characteristics of the disease, patient conditions, the diagnostic problem, the quality of the complementary information that can be obtained and its possible influence in clinical decision-making. 4. It may be appropriate to initiate a registry of all cases in which the problem occurs to advance knowledge of the practical value of PET. 5. There is agreement regarding PET's utility for the following: ■ Diagnosing SPNs when other diagnostic tests are inconclusive; ■ Staging lung cancer;

Org., year	Indications studied	Assessment type	Conclusions/Recommendations
			■ Localizing epileptic foci in medically refractory temporal lobe epilepsy.
			6. Although PET seems to help in the diagnosis of patients with Alzheimer's disease, no therapy exists that can cure or improve the prognosis. The information that can be obtained is not relevant from the clinical-therapeutic point of view.
			7. For the remaining indications in light of the existing discrepancies, it is appropriate to await the results of new studies.
			8. Gamma cameras with coincidence detection capability that offer diagnostic ability and advantages (lower cost and simpler technology) with respect to PET are now marketed. They are being studied and may hold the future of emission tomography.

Source: E.J. Adams, J. Asua, J.G. Conde Olasagasti, et al. (1999), *Positron Emission Tomography: Experience with PET and Synthesis of the Evidence.* Stockholm: International Network of Agencies for Health Technology Assessment.

CASE STUDY: POSITRON EMISSION TOMOGRAPHY IN SPAIN

Positron emission tomography (PET) is a non-invasive image technology developed in the field of nuclear medicine. In contrast to other image diagnosis techniques, such as computed tomography (CT) or magnetic resonance imaging (MRI), which provide anatomic information (morphology), PET provides biochemical and metabolic information from the tissues (function). This information can be obtained from the administration of different radio-labelled drugs. In the current clinical applications, the most common radio-labelled drugs are 18FDG (18 fluor-deoxi-glucose).[38] At present PET is used as a research and clinical diagnosis tool in three main fields of medicine: cardiology, oncology, and neurology/psychiatry; but it is in oncology where it has most clinical indications. The degree of application of PET in each of these specialties varies both among countries and among the different centres that use this type of image technology worldwide.

Several health technology assessment agencies around the world have carried out reviews of the available scientific knowledge of PET in different clinical specialties.[39] Most of the available studies on the diagnostic ability of PET seem to be of low methodological quality, and their results may be questioned. The studies with the most rigorous design are found in the field of cardiology, but these also show methodological limitations, and thus their results have to be considered carefully, as must be the alternative functional image technology available in this field. In Table 7.1 a description of the reviews done by the Spanish health technology organizations regarding PET are shown.

The introduction of PET in Spain started in 1996, when the first two PET devices became available, in Madrid (*Universidad Complutense de Madrid*) and Pamplona (*Universidad de Navarra*), for research purposes. As soon as the devices were available, clinical cases started to appear. The first cases involved oncology – or more specifically the differential diagnosis between radionecrosis and residual or relapsing tumoral lesions. Those cases were channelled through a Coverage Commission and were based on favourable reports from health technology assessment agencies. If the

Commission agreed that those cases needed the diagnostic device, the patient was sent to any of the non-public centres that offered PET. The NHS paid for both transportation and diagnostic procedures. PET was then one of the first technologies to be included in a register. AETS, the Central Government health assessment agency, started a registry of cases. They also developed and produced list of indications through consensus. Patients meeting those criteria were candidates for PET diagnosis. The use of the registry was to monitor the characteristics of the patients that received the diagnosis and the contribution of PET inpatient management. In 2001, Andalusia became the first AR to have a PET available in public hospitals for diagnostic purposes. Andalusia also developed a list of indications that were considered appropriate for PET.

Catalonia was the next AR to have a PET, also in 2001. The first centre to have it, CETIR, a private company with some services contracted with the public health sector, also bought a cyclotron, which was necessary to prepare the drugs for the PET diagnosis. The second PET in Catalonia was bought in 2003, also by a public company with services contracted with the public health sector. They bought a PET-CT. Since they did not buy a cyclotron, they must buy supplies from the other private centres.

Currently, there are a total of 16 PET scanners in Spain, four in public and 12 in private facilities. In public centres, the introduction of this type of technology depends on the approval by the regional Department of Health since it involves a big investment. It also depends on the estimated demand. Moreover, since PET is a diagnostic device based on nuclear drugs, any PET purchase requires the approval of the Spanish Counsel of Nuclear Safety. This technology is still an expensive one. The cost per examination is around €1072. The registry of cases is proving helpful to understand the characteristics of the demand. The number of examinations requested in the public sector in 2003 was 532; the most frequent reason for requesting PET examinations was cancer; the most frequent cancers were lung and colorectal.[40]

The potential applications of PET for types of cancer involve:

• differentiation between malignant and benign tumors

- staging
- control or response to treatment
- identification of relapses
- localization of the primary tumor in the presence of a metastasis

The technologies to which the diagnostic accuracy of PET is usually compared are CT, MRI and, occasionally, biopsy histological diagnoses. It should be noted that despite the fact that reviews of the evidence often include the appraisal of additional issues that must be considered in the assessment of diagnosis tests – such as the evaluation of therapeutic impact, changes in the treatment attributable to the information provided by the examination, the measure of the health outcomes in the patient, or the cost effectiveness of PET compared to other diagnostic measures – this information is often absent or is based on flawed studies.[41]

The role of PET in relation to other diagnostic techniques is yet to be determined, and thus, until further knowledge is provided with respect to its clinical utility, PET joins the set of available diagnostic tests and it is not a substitute for any one in particular. In a recently published meta-analysis on the application of PET for the staging of melanoma (one of the frequent applications of PET), it was found that even although PET may have a high validity for this application, the methodological limitations of the studies prevent the establishment of guidelines for its use. This is also true with respect to most of the other indications for PET. This background will probably make the evolution of PET resemble that of other previously introduced image diagnosis technologies, such as CT (in the 80s) and MRI (in the 90s).[42]

In view of the uncertainty regarding the scientific knowledge of the application, the incremental benefit, and the cost effectiveness of the current image diagnosis technologies, as well as the expected increase of demand and expenditure, CAHTA recommends monitoring the use of PET and the rationality of its utilization in its first diffusion stages in Catalonia. The recommendations included in CAHTA's proposal involve:[43]

- creation of an experts' committee to define the clinical or pathologic conditions for which PET examinations would be authorized after review of the scientific evidence;

- establishment of requirements that professionals and centres must comply with to be allowed to request examinations;
- designation of a standard request form for all PET examinations;
- registration of all PET examinations, individualized for each examination request, with the objectives of: 1. assessing the use of PET and its variability (geographical, type of requester, clinical condition), and 2. determining the diagnostic and therapeutic impact of this technology;
- fostering research related to the clinical application of PET, which must be financed independently from the health care budget. This research should be open to public contributions and respond to quality standards.

Recently, the first recommendation has been put into place. With the collaboration of a group of experts, the CAHTA and the Catalan Department of Health defined a list of indications to be included under public coverage. This list was drafted on the basis of systematic reviews of the evidence on the diagnostic validity (sensitivity, specificity, and predictive value) of the applications of PET, and will be used as a reference to guide funding policies of this technology in other health care contexts. It will be submitted to and agreed upon by the relevant Catalan experts. Basically, the indications identified were those in which PET might have an impact on the therapeutic treatment of the patient. The list of indications drawn up will be applicable for one year, and will be subsequently revised by the experts and the CAHTA according to the results of the monitoring on the use of PET in the Catalan AR, as well as any other new data that may arise in the medical literature. The fourth recommendation is also in place, since the CAHTA is continuously monitoring the use of PET, the characteristics of patients on whom PET is used, their follow-up, and the results obtained.[44] All of this should bring a more effective and efficient use of this health technology.

References

1 The author is grateful to Joan M.V. Pons and Cari Almazán, former colleagues of the author at the Catalan Agency for Health Technology

Assessment, for their helpful comments on the paper, and for providing data about PET use in Spain.

2 Ley 14/1986, de 25 de Abril, General de Sanidad.
3 Ley 16/2003, de 28 de Mayo, de Cohesión y Calidad del Sistema Nacional de Salud.
4 Real Decreto 63/1995, de 20 de Enero, sobre ordenación de prestaciones sanitarias del Sistema Nacional de Salud.
5 European Observatory on Health Care Systems (EOHCS) (2000), *Health Care Systems in Transition: Spain.* Copenhagen: European Observatory on Health Care Systems.
6 EOHCS (2000).
7 EOHCS (2000).
8 Ley 14/1986.
9 Ley 21/2001, de 27 de Diciembre, por la que se regulan las medidas fiscales y administrativas del nuevo sistema de financiación de las Comunidades Autónomas de régimen común y Ciudades con Estatuto de Autonomía.
10 EOHCS (2000).
11 EOHCS (2000).
12 Ley 25/1990, de 20 de Diciembre, del medicamento.
13 Real Decreto 83/1993, de 22 de Enero, por el que se regula la selección de los medicamentos a efectos de su financiación por el Sistema Nacional de Salud.
14 Real Decreto 1663/1998, de 24 de Julio, por el que se amplía la relación de medicamentos a efectos de su financiación con cargo a fondos de la Seguridad Social o a fondos estatales afectos a la sanidad.
15 EOHCS (2000).
16 Ley 13/1996, de 30 de Diciembre de 1996, de medidas fiscales, administrativas y del orden social.
17 Ley 66/1997, de 30 de Diciembre de 1997, de medidas fiscales, administrativas y del orden social.
18 Real Decreto 1035/1999, de 18 de Junio, por el que se regula el sistema de precios de referencia en la financiación de medicamentos con cargo a fondos de la Seguridad Social o a fondos estatales afectos a la sanidad.
19 Real Decreto 520/1999, de 26 de Marzo, por el que se aprueba el Estatuto de la Agencia Española del Medicamento.
20 Ley 25/1990.
21 Real Decreto 414/1996, de 1 de Marzo, por el que se regulan los productos sanitarios. BOE núm. 72, 24/4/1996.
22 Real Decreto 634/1997, de 3 de Mayo, sobre productos sanitarios implantables activos. BOE núm. 126, 27/5/1997.
23 Real Decreto 63/1995.
24 R. Cranovsky, Y. Matillon, and D. Banta (1997), 'EUR-ASSESS

Project Subgroup Report on Coverage', *International Journal of Technology Assessment in Health Care*, 13(2): 287–332.

25 A. Granados, L. Sampietro-Colom, J. Asua, et al. (2000), 'Health Technology Assessment in Spain', *International Journal of Technology Assessment in Health Care*, 16(2): 532–59.

26 International Network of Agencies for Health Technology Assessment (1997), 'This is CAHTA', Catalan Agency for Health Technology Assessment. INAHTA Newsletter, May.

27 International Network of Agencies for Health Technology Assessment (1997), 'This is Osteba', Basque Office for Health Technology Assessment. INAHTA Newsletter, January.

28 International Network of Agencies for Health Technology Assessment (1997), This is AETS', Agencia de Evaluación de Tecnologías Sanitarias. INAHTA Newsletter, April.

29 C. Henshall, W. Oortwijn, A. Stevens, et al. (1997), 'Priority Setting for Health Technology Assessment. Theoretical Considerations and Practical Approaches. Priority Setting Subgroup of the EUR-ASSESS Project', *International Journal of Technology Assessment in Health Care*, 13(2): 144–85.

30 Osteba (1996), *Priorización de los temas a evaluar*. Vitoria-Gasteiz: Osteba.

31 M. Aymerich (2001), 'Priority Setting for Research and Assessment in Health Services', CAHTA Informatiu, 22: 18–20.

32 D. Hailey, L. Sampietro-Colom, D. Marshal, et al. (1998), 'The Effectiveness of Bone Density Measurement and Associated Treatments for Prevention of Fractures: An International Collaborative Review', *International Journal of Technology Assessment in Health Care*, 14(2): 237–54.

33 A. Granados, E. Jonsson, H.D. Banta, et al. (1997), 'EUR-ASSESS Project Subgroup Report on Dissemination and Impact'. *International Journal Technology Assessment in Health Care*, 13(2): 220–86.

34 Granados, Sampietro-Colom, and Asua (2000).

35 Granados, Sampietro-Colom and Asua (2000).

36 A. Granados (1995). [The evaluation of medical technologies]. *Medicinia Clinica* (Barcelona), 22;104(15): 581–5.

37 Granados, Sampietro-Colom, and Asua (2000).

38 L. Sampietro-Colom (1997), 'Financing of Emerging Technologies. Positron Emission Tomography', CAHTA Informatiu, 11: 5–7.

39 E.J. Adams, J. Asua, J.G. Conde Olasagasti, et al. (1999), *Positron Emission Tomography: Experience with PET and Synthesis of the Evidence*. Stockholm: International Network of Agencies for Health Technology Assessment.

40 C. Almazán (2001), 'Positron Emission Tomography (PET) in Oncology in Catalonia: Current State and Proposal for Monitorisation', CAHTA Informatiu, 23: 5–7.

41 Almazán (2001).

42 Almazán (2001).
43 Almazán (2001).
44 C. Almazán (2002), 'Proposal for the Indication of PET in Oncology with Public Coverage in Catalonia', CAHTA Informatiu, 25: 8–9.

8

HEALTH CARE COVERAGE DETERMINATIONS IN SWITZERLAND

Dominique Sprumont, Felix Gurtner and Guillaume Roduit[1]

INTRODUCTION

Basic elements

The Swiss health care system incorporates a mix of the various approaches to health care financing identified by the OECD.[2] Switzerland relies on compulsory social insurance for basic health care and private insurance coverage for other types of health care. Yet, even the compulsory part of the system remains very liberal, as it encourages competition among the sickness funds and, to a certain extent, among health care providers. Thus, the system can be described as being based on compulsory social insurance, but incorporating contracting with health care providers and freedom to choose among insurers, while permitting both indemnity reimbursement of the insured or direct payment of health care providers.

In contrast with some countries of northern Europe, which have a central body administering and financing the health care system under the Beveridge model, the Swiss system, inspired by the Bismark model, is based on sickness funds supervised by the State.[3]

The Accident and Sickness Insurance Unit of the Federal Office of Public Health (FOPH) (which was attached to the Federal Social Insurance Office (FSIO) until 2003) is responsible for the control of the sickness funds that provide compulsory social insurance[4] and the Federal Office of Private Insurance is in charge of the supervision of all other supplementary insurance coverages.[5] The Swiss health care system is particularly complex due to the federal structure of the political system. The various regulatory and administrative authorities are distributed between the federal, the cantonal, and the communal governments.[6; 7]

The first federal law on sickness insurance was adopted in 1911. It also covered injuries caused by accidents. This was the Federal Law on Sickness and Accident Law.[8] It has been one of the key elements in the building of the Swiss health care system and one of the most important tools for the definition of the public health policies of the federal government. This law also created the Federal Social Insurance Office (FSIO) and the Federal Supreme Court for Social Insurance (TFA).

In 1994, there was a major revision of the legislation, with the adoption of the new Federal Law on Sickness Insurance.[9] The Swiss health care system has been strongly influenced by this law and the ordinances that apply it.[10] It should also be noted that in 1981 the Federal Law on Accident Insurance abrogated the chapters on professional accident and illness that were in place under the 1911 Federal Law on Sickness and Accident Law.

The major change introduced by the 1994 legislation is that everyone living in Switzerland for at least three months is obligated to be insured for illness. The new law is based on the principle of solidarity: solidarity between rich and poor, healthy and sick, older and younger, women and men.[11] In return, the law guarantees reimbursement for a rather comprehensive set of health goods and services. In principle, a health care product or service deemed effective, appropriate, and efficient will be reimbursed by the compulsory social sickness insurance. The law also encourages competition, both among health care providers and among sickness funds. With the 1994 law, the role of private insurance is limited to the coverage of extra services that are not evaluated for medical necessity but are provided mainly for the comfort of the patients, such as the use of a private room at a hospital.

The sickness funds accredited by the FOPH compete with each other. Their premiums have to be approved by the FOPH. Each fund must treat equally all its insureds under the principle of solidarity. There are only limited exceptions based on the age of the insured – premiums are divided into three separate categories for persons under 18, between 18 and 25, and above 25 – and on the canton where the insured lives. In each canton, the FOPH can define two or more regions, and premiums may vary according to the effective cost of health care coverage in the different regions. Cost differences due to variation in the age and sex structures of the insured population among the sickness funds are compensated through the use of a risk adjustment scheme. This scheme, however, does not take into account health indicators reflecting differences in the burden of disease (as it does, for instance, in Germany).

The principle of solidarity is reinforced through the use of federal and cantonal subsidies for those with limited revenues who cannot afford health insurance premiums.[12] On average, about one third of all residents in Switzerland benefit from this programme.[13] Although everyone living in Switzerland for a least three months has an obligation to be insured, insureds have the freedom to choose their insurer, and can change freely from one insurer to another. On the other hand, insurers have an obligation to accept any new member who applies for insurance, without applying selection criteria.[14] Insured persons are also free to choose among any health care providers licensed to exercise their profession according to the cantonal regulation.[15]

Health care coverage

The Federal Law on Sickness Insurance defines all medical services that must be covered by insurance.[16] Article 32 specifies that these procedures 'ought to be effective, appropriate and efficient'.[17] This means that all health care products and services, in order to be reimbursed by a sickness fund, must be scientifically evaluated to verify whether they are medically necessary. A distinction must be drawn, therefore, between covered health care products and services, and other products and services that provide personal comfort to the patient, but that must be covered at the patient's own expenses or by a private or supplementary insurance.[18]

In principle, health care is accepted as medically necessary when it is prescribed by a doctor or by a limited number of other authorized health care providers. Thus, in Switzerland the decision of a sickness fund not to cover a health care product or service remains the exception, the rule being that most medical care is reimbursed. This explains why the Swiss health care system remains one of the most generous in comparison to other national systems.[19] In principle, all sickness insurance funds are expected to cover the same types of preventive, diagnostic, or therapeutic measures. This means that they must review the medical bills presented for reimbursement by the insured.[20] According to Article 42, Paragraph 4 of the law, the sickness funds have the right to request more diagnostic or treatment information from health care providers in order to control these bills. This is done through medical advisers working for the funds. This review is conducted randomly, but review can also be initiated if the bills of a given provider appear to be higher on average than the bills of other providers in the same region. Article 56 of the law also imposes on health care providers the obligation and responsibility to provide only those treatments that are essential in a particular case. Procedures have been negotiated between providers and insurers on how to identify and sanction outliers. Article 59 of the Federal Law on Sickness Insurance allows the exclusion of a provider who fails to comply with these provisions.

Since 1996, the sickness funds have not had the legal competency either to refuse to pay for a necessary health care product or service that is covered under the criteria provided by Article 32 of the Federal Law on Sickness Insurance, or to cover a product or service that does not meet these criteria. One can, however, still notice some differences in practice among the sickness funds. Although these differences remain rather limited, they may have a dramatic impact on individual patients. These discrepancies are explained primarily by lack of information (on the part of the insured, health care providers, and even insurers) but also by inconsistencies in the various control systems set up by the insurers and, in some cases, by different interpretations of the law.[21]

When the coverage of a specific product or service is contested either by the medical profession or, most often, by the sickness funds, it is submitted to an evaluation by an expert commission nominated by the Federal Government pursuant to the Ordinance on Sickness Insurance.[22] This and four other advisory commissions on reimbursement issues (see Table 8.1) are composed of representatives from the medical profession, the sickness funds, the federal administration, and patients' organizations. It should be emphasized that, as in other countries, most medical products (drugs, medical devices) go through a specific evaluation of safety and effectiveness leading to marketing approval. The mere fact a drug or device has been authorized for marketing by the Swiss Institute of Therapeutic

Table 8.1 Decisions on sickness insurance benefits

Category	Nature of the list	Decision taken by	Advised by
Providers (e.g., dieticians)	Positive list	Federal Council (Federal government)	Federal Commission for General Health Insurance Benefits
New and/or contested medical procedures	Negative / conditional list	Federal Department of Home Affairs	Federal Commission for General Health Insurance Benefits
Laboratory analyses	Positive list	Federal Department of Home Affairs	Federal Commission for Analyses
Devices for use by patients	Positive list	Federal Department of Home Affairs	Federal Commission for Devices
Drugs	Positive list	Federal Office of Public health	Federal Pharmaceuticals Commission
Guidance on issues involving more than one commission on principles			Federal Commission on the Basic Principles in the Sickness Insurance

Product (Swissmedic) or is accredited for marketing, however, does not guarantee its reimbursement by the sickness funds.

The ordinance concerning the sickness covered by Basic Health Insurance – the ordinance that sets out the procedures for basic health insurance coverage[23] – contains a list of all the medical procedures that have been evaluated for coverage, therefore facilitating the reimbursement procedure applied by the sickness funds.[24] We will describe this process of evaluation in details. When a insurer refuses to cover a specific care, the insured may also obtain judicial review, a process that we will describe as well.

ADMINISTRATIVE PROCEDURE

Coverage determinations at the national level

Article 33 of the Federal Law gives the government – the Federal Council – the authority to designate which interventions provided by a physician are either not eligible for reimbursement, or may be reimbursed only under certain conditions by the sickness funds. Interventions that are subject to such limitations, as well as those not recognized for reimbursement, appear on a specific list. By contrast, all drugs and laboratory analysis covered by health insurance must be evaluated. They are listed on separate lists.

As we noted before, these decisions are based on the principle stated in Article 32 of the Federal law that all procedures 'ought to be effective, appropriate, and efficient'.[25] Article 33 of the Federal Law on Sickness Insurance also provides that the Federal Council may authorize the reimbursement of procedures, whether new or contested, that are under evaluation with respect to their effectiveness, appropriateness and efficacy. It can create advisory bodies or expert commissions to fulfil this responsibility, among which is the Federal Commission for General Health Insurance Benefits, instituted by the Articles 33, Paragraph 3 of the Federal Sickness Insurance Law and 37d of the Ordinance on Sickness Insurance. According to Article 33 of the Ordinance on Sickness Insurance, the Federal Council has delegated its authority concerning the definition of the procedures that may be reimbursed by the sickness fund to the Federal Department of Home Affairs. This explains why the Ordinance Concerning the Services Covered by Basic Health Insurance[26] is adopted by the Federal Department of Home Affairs pursuant to proposals from the FOPH after a scientific evaluation by an expert commission.

The Federal Commission for General Health Insurance Benefits and other Related Commissions

The composition of the Federal Commission is specified at Paragraph 2 of Article 37d of the Ordinance on Sickness Insurance. The Commission includes 20 members representing the medical profession (seven members including two representatives of complementary medicines), hospitals (two members), pharmacists (one member), sickness funds (six members), insureds (two members), cantonal health authorities (one member) and the Swiss Federal

Office of Social Insurance (one member). The group is divided in half between the health care providers and the other interested parties, with strong representation of the sickness funds. The health care providers are mainly represented by physicians, their number in the Commission being even greater as some representatives of other groups, such as the sickness funds, are also physicians. This is consistent with the fact that the first condition for reimbursement of a specific care by the sickness fund is that it has been prescribed by a doctor or, in some instances, a chiropractor. The representation of patients and insureds remains rather symbolic, partly due to the weakness of the insured and patients' organizations, which are not well co-ordinated, and the lack of necessary resources for patients and insureds to build an effective political presence.

There are three other federal commissions that define the services covered by the social sickness insurance, covering the fields of drugs (Article 37e of the Ordinance on Sickness Insurance), medical materials and devices that are used by patients themselves (such as inhalation equipment or incontinence pads) (Article 37g of the Ordinance on Sickness Insurance) and laboratory analysis (Article 37f of the Ordinance on Sickness Insurance). Again, the medical profession as well as other health care providers and public health experts constitute half of the members of each commission. The pharmaceutical industry has two representatives on the Federal Commission for Drugs. It should be pointed out that Article 90 of the Federal Law on Sickness Insurance provides a specific procedure for appeals against the decision to include or exclude a drug from the list of the reimbursed drugs. The formulary is adapted directly by the FOPH, not by the Department of Home Affairs, in contrast to the Ordinance Concerning the Services Covered by Basic Health Insurance.[27]

In 2002, there were 6933 drugs authorized for marketing by Swissmedic in Switzerland, while only 2588 were listed in the formulary, around 85 per cent of which were under prescription and 15 per cent over the counter.[28] The pharmaceutical companies do not systematically request that their drugs be included in the formulary, one main reason being the fact that their products are, if listed, subject to stricter price controls and cannot be advertised. Yet, a pharmaceutical company whose product is not accepted for reimbursement can appeal directly to a specific commission. There is no such appeal procedure for other types of health care. As we will see, there is also available a judicial review procedure, but it is more complex and time consuming.

Finally Article 37c of the Ordinance on Sickness Insurance establishes the Federal Commission on the Basic Principles in the Sickness Insurance. This Commission does not assess specific services, but rather provides guidance and advice to the other above-mentioned commissions. It is, in particular, in charge of defining under which criteria – both scientific and ethical – services should be evaluated.[29] For instance, this Commission has issued recommendations regarding medically assisted reproduction, living donor transplants and the allocation of preventive services between individual medical care and public health.

Evaluation process

In order to assist the Commission for General Health Insurance Benefits in carrying out its tasks, the Federal Social Insurance Office created the *Manual for the Standardisation of Clinical and Economic Evaluation of Medical Technology*.[30] This manual provides directives on the procedures that must be followed to submit an application to the Commission for evaluation. It also clarifies the criteria used by the Commission to assess a new or contested procedure as follows:

> Effectiveness: term used to describe the clinical value of a medical procedure in practical use. 'Clinical effectiveness' refers to the extent to which objectives are reached under particular conditions in clinical practice, taking into account indications and contraindications.

> Appropriateness: reflects an assessment comparing the relative medical value of a procedure to the patient, and the risks associated with it. Procedures are considered to be appropriate where the benefit is greater than the risks of the procedure itself, and outweigh the risks attaching to other, alternative procedures or approaches. [. . .]

> Efficiency: reflects an assessment comparing the use of resources for the procedure with the value outcome.

The Commission determines whether a new or contested product or service meets these three criteria on the basis of a report submitted by a sponsor of the technology (provider or manufacturer). The Commission rarely conducts its own evaluation. It primarily analyses the existing evidence as presented by the provider seeking reimbursement from the sickness funds and/or evidence provided by the sickness funds themselves that contest the treatment. The evidence has to be presented by the applicant according to the directives given in the 'manual' mentioned above. The Commission has very few resources to conduct its own research to complete the information provided by the applicant. Yet, the Commission tends to refer to existing data from other national or international health technology assessments (HTAs).

HTA has evolved as the major tool supporting decisions evaluating health care technologies on the macro level in developed countries. It consists of the assessment of the literature concerning a technology (that is, the systematic search, evaluation and synthesis of medical and economic literature regarding the specific technology) as well as an appraisal of the technology itself (that is, a discussion of the social, ethical, organizational and professional implications of the use and diffusion of this technology).[31]

The procedure of evaluation can be summarized as follows (see Figure 8.1):

1. The stakeholders (health care providers, sickness funds, health authorities, or patients' organizations) can, if there are doubts about the effectiveness, appropriateness, or efficiency of a given product or service, demand that the FOPH initiate an evaluation procedure.
2. Prior to initiating such an evaluation procedure, the FOPH requests the opinion of the Swiss Medical Association (FMH) and of the Swiss Association of the Sickness Funds (Santé-Suisse). It also conducts an initial review of the scientific literature to assess whether the given technology is controversial. If this review or the requested opinions suggest that the technology is controversial, the FOPH opens an evaluation procedure. The case becomes, that is, a 'contested' care. If a technology is not contested, it remains reimbursable, usually without being mentioned in the Ordinance. Where a technology is obviously controversial, there is no need for this 'pre-evaluation' step.
3. If a technology is contested, the FOPH informs providers and the sickness funds that the technology should not be reimbursable until the evaluation procedure is completed. The FOPH also at this point invites the provider or industry sponsors of a technology to submit an application for an evaluation of the technology. As the commission does not conduct its own evaluation, the applicant should be a health care provider who can

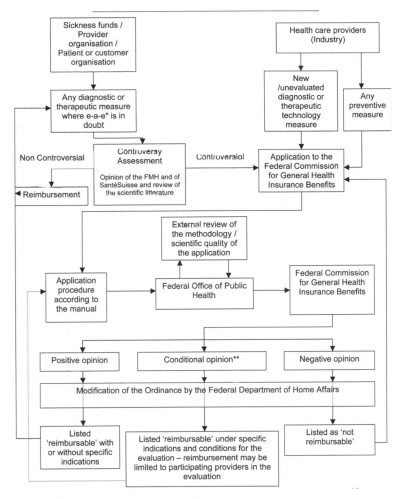

*e-a-e: efficacy, appropriateness and efficiency
**conditional meaning limited in time and subject to re-evaluation by the Commission

Figure 8.1 Evaluation Procedure

take upon itself the burden of collecting all existing scientific evidences in favour of the reimbursement of the contested technology, and who is in the position to identify the professional implications (such as quality issues) related to the broader introduction of a technology following a positive reimbursement decision.

4. The applicant, with the support of the Accident and Sickness Insurance Unit of the FOPH, prepares a file following the directives of the 'manual'. The applicant submits this application, when it is completed, to the FOPH.

5. The FOPH requests an expert opinion or external review of the methodology and quality of the application.

6. The FOPH transmits the application together with the results of the external review to the commission.

7. The Commission reviews the application and the external review during a regular meeting. It formulates its opinion to the Federal Department of Home Affairs recommending that it:

   a. refuse reimbursement of the contested technology by the sickness funds;

   b. accept complete coverage of the evaluated technology;

   c. accept coverage only for a specific indication,[32] or for a limited number of indications;[33] or

   d. direct that reimbursement be limited for a given period of time during which the technology will be under continuing evaluation.

In this last case of conditional reimbursement, the evaluation process will be prepared, conducted, and paid for by the providers or the industry or, occasionally, by the sickness funds. Yet the technology itself is covered by the sickness funds. Depending on the nature of the product or service, reimbursement for it can be limited to health care centres and providers collaborating in the evaluation procedure. All the technologies that have been contested and, thus, evaluated by the Commission are listed in the annex 1 of the Ordinance Concerning the Services Covered by Basic Health Insurance.[34]

Depending on the number of requests and re-evaluations that need to be handled, the Commission meets between two and four times a year. Applications must be submitted approximately ten weeks before a meeting. A recommendation from the Commission to the Federal Department of Home Affairs normally leads to a revision of the Ordinance Concerning the Services Covered by Basic Health Insurance. Usually such a revision is implemented 1 January of the following year to allow the sickness funds to readjust their premiums taking into consideration reimbursement of the new procedure. The whole process can take up to two years including the time necessary to prepare the application.[35]

In principle, inpatient and outpatient care are treated equally. In practice, different reimbursement principles have resulted in slightly different evaluation practices: outpatient care is reimbursed by health insurance alone (minus co-payment) on a fee-for-service basis, while inpatient care is financed half by insurance reimbursement and half by cantonal hospital financing, which until the late 1990s was on a fee-per-day basis. Previously new inpatient procedures and technologies tended to be introduced gradually and almost never became apparent to the authorities, while outpatient procedures were more prone to be subjected to the evaluation process. This has changed in recent years, since fees per day are gradually being replaced by other schemes (such as fee per stay or DRG-like systems). In these new schemes, certain expensive procedures (like PET) or implants (like third generation heart pacemakers or coated stents) are often not included into the overall fees, but billed separately. This development has increased transparency with respect to technological innovations in the hospital sector and resulted in an increasing number of evaluations of such technologies through the processes described above. This has also resulted in the building of a cantonal evaluation process that we describe next.

Coverage determinations at the cantonal level

The 1994 Federal Law on Sickness Insurance introduced the need for the cantons to plan their health care resources according to the needs of their populations. Article 39 of the Law requires in particular that each canton establish a list of the hospitals and clinics where patients can be treated at the expense of the sickness funds. As the cantons also contribute more than 50 per cent of the coverage of inpatient care in the hospitals[36] planning is an important programme for controlling health care expenditures. The contribution of the cantons to hospital care can be either direct, in the sense that the cantons are the owner of public hospitals, or indirect, through subsidies allocated to hospitals that offer services of public interest (such as emergency units, specialized care not provided in a public hospital). In both cases, the cantonal contribution is directly integrated into the budget of the hospital.

At one point, several cantons intended to extend this principle of health care planning beyond hospital services to include also a broader range of new and expensive technologies.[37] This attempt provoked a heated debate, as it implied the limitation of business freedom currently enjoyed by health care providers. In the end, this form of regulation was only introduced in the Canton of Neuchâtel.[38]

The legislation in Neuchâtel was adopted at a time when health care costs in the canton had increased more than 7 per cent over the previous two years. Members of the cantonal Parliament expressed a concern that the opening of a new MRI centre under a private initiative would worsen this situation even more. Two centres were already in operation, while according to the health care planning of the canton, only one was needed. The opening of a third centre was perceived as a potential risk in terms of the protection of public health and cost control. The government prepared a revision of the Cantonal Health Law[39] which gave authority to the cantonal government to limit the introduction of new technologies that are expensive or for which maintenance is expensive, which are not part of 'ordinary' medicine, which have a regional or cantonal impact, or which require the support of particularly qualified technicians.[40] The purpose of that legislation was to grant the health authorities the competency to limit or prohibit the introduction of 'big ticket technologies' that could induce an increase of public health care cost in the canton.

The draft law was adopted by the parliament with an important amendment requiring the government to regularly update the list of equipment targeted by the law and stipulating that the final authorization to introduce such equipment should be based on an agreement between the public and private health care sectors of the canton. This last requirement was included to cover cases where there is competition between a public hospital and a private company to exploit a new technology that is subject to authorization. A provider working in the private sector could be given priority over a public hospital if he or she offers appropriate guarantees in terms of quality and proves to be more efficient. The private provider must, however, guarantee access to his or her equipment for all of the population.

Though PET scanners are on the list of high technology equipment identified by the government in an ordinance, the legislation has so far only been applied in one case concerning an MRI centre.[41] A provider planning to open a PET scanner in Neuchâtel would have first to comply with the cantonal law, which can block the installation of such equipment regardless of whether or not such care is covered at the federal level. The technology will also have to comply with the requirements of the Federal Law on Sickness Insurance we described in the previous section.

In concluding this section on coverage determinations at the cantonal level, it should also be mentioned that there is an attempt at the intercantonal level to co-ordinate 'big ticket technology' in health care through a distribution scheme involving the major public hospitals. This is an initiative of the Swiss Conference of the Directors of Health Care Authorities. This conference was founded in 1919 and includes all ministries of health at the cantonal level. It has created a task force for the co-ordination and planning of 'highly specialized medicine', the main purpose of which is to rationalize the provision of such highly specialized care by co-ordinating among the university hospitals and creating specialty-specific centres of competency. So far, about ten domains have been identified as candidates for greater co-ordination. This is the case with PET, but also with organ transplantation, highly infectious diseases, and cardiac surgery. Thus, 'big ticket technology' will be available for Swiss patients but not in every hospital. Under this programme, there will be an Intercantonal Convention on the Coordination and Concentration of Highly Specialized Medicine, which will institute a commission whose task it will be to define which care should be co-ordinated and under what conditions. It will then be the duty of the cantons to introduce these recommendations in their own health care planning. This should have both an impact on the quality and the cost of expensive health care technologies.[42]

JUDICIAL REVIEW

As mentioned above, most health care products and services that are deemed medically necessary are reimbursed by the social sickness funds. Only a minority of new or contested technologies are subject to the evaluation process we described in the previous section. Yet, it is a duty of the sickness funds to verify that the health care products and services that they cover fulfil the legal criteria of effectiveness, appropriateness, and efficiency. According the Article 42 of the Federal Law on Sickness Insurance, a sickness fund can, for the purpose of establishing compliance with these criteria, request precise diagnostic information from the treating physician or health care professional or demand detailed information regarding the health status of the insured or his or her treatment. If the requirements of Article 32 are not met in a given case, the sickness fund should deny reimbursement. If, for instance, a patient seeks coverage for hyperbaric oxygen therapy for an indication that is not specified in Annex 1 of the Ordinance Concerning the Services Covered by Basic Health Insurance, the claim should be denied.[43] If this should happen, however, the insured patient is granted judicial review against the decision of the sickness fund. The procedure for judicial review is found in the new Federal Law on the General Part of Social Insurance Laws that came into force on 1 January 2003.[44] Basically, the insured is entitled to the right to contest a decision of the sickness fund, first directly to the sickness fund, then to the competent administrative tribunal at the cantonal level and, finally, to the Federal Supreme Court for Social Insurance.[45] It should be pointed out that cases where the manufacturer or the provider will pay for patient appeals are rare. Indeed, we have no evidence of such cases.

A recent research study financed by the Federal Office of Social Insurance analysed the case law in this field between 1997 and 1999.[46] At the cantonal level, there were 852 court decisions in 1998, of which 247 concerned health care coverage, and 827 court decisions in 1999, of which 254 concerned health care coverage. At the federal level, the Federal Supreme Court for Social Insurance issued 26 decisions between 1985 and 1997 concerning disputes involving health care coverage based on the previous Federal Sickness and Accident Law. Between 1997 and 1999, 25 decisions were published applying the new Federal Law on Sickness Insurance. A very small percentage of these cases concerned coverage determinations involving technologies. We will comment briefly on two major decisions concerning in vitro fertilization (IVF) and magnetic resonance imagery (MRI).

One key issue in this case law is the extent to which the Federal Supreme Court for Social Insurance can evaluate the legality of the Ordinance Concerning the Services Covered by Basic Health Insurance. In a decision concerning an IVF procedure, the Court limited drastically its power to review decisions involving the ordinance.[47] It argued that the list contained in the Annex 1 of the ordinance can easily be revised and that the mere existence of this list limits the authority of the court to extend the list. The Court seemed reluctant to overturn the expert opinion of the Commission, concluding that the establishment of the Annex 1 of the ordinance is primarily a scientific process not a legal one. This decision raised concerns as it dramatically restricted the rights of insureds to contest the decision of a sickness fund.

Fortunately, the court has since adopted a more interventionist position in a later case concerning a MRI intervention that was not included in the ordinance.[48] Contrary to the case involving the IVF intervention, the Court concluded that the limitation of the ordinance was neither justified medically nor economically and, therefore, was contrary to the Federal Law on Sickness Insurance. To reach this conclusion, the Court requested the expert opinion of specialists as well as that of the medical staff of the Federal Office for Social Insurance. Based on this expertise, the Court considered the ordinance as discriminatory and, thus, void.[49]

The Federal Law on Sickness Insurance does not create any direct link between the process through which the Commission for General Health Insurance Benefits evaluates health care technologies under the ordinance to determine whether services are covered by basic health insurance under the auspices of the Federal Department of Home Affairs and the judicial review procedure. For instance, the Commission is not obligated to evaluate health care services that have been challenged in courts. The fact that there has been a court decision is not *per se* a sufficient condition to open an evaluation procedure. Theoretically, it is still up to the Commission to decide whether or not to start such a procedure. Of course, in practice, the Ordinance Concerning the Services Covered by Basic Health Insurance will be modified if the Federal Supreme Court adopts a decision concerning a given product or service. Yet, the decision from the Federal Supreme Court for Social Insurance to reimburse a given product or service in a given case does not apply automatically in other cases. The ordinance remains valid and the insurers are not obliged to follow the decision of the Court if they are not specifically requested to do so by an insured seeking reimbursement of the same type of care. In practice, it would not be uncommon for insureds to fail to refer to a court decision, both because of ignorance of the cases and ignorance of their rights. This creates a discrepancy in coverage among insured patients.

DISCUSSION

Health care coverage determination in Switzerland is a complex process including both formal and informal elements. The Federal Law on Sickness Insurance seems primarily to be founded on an evidence based or scientific approach. The law defines the criteria that limit the scope of care that can be covered by the sickness funds. The primary result of this policy is the Ordinance

Concerning the Services Covered by Basic Health Insurance,[50] which contains a list of products and services that have been contested by health care providers or by the sickness funds based on a contention that they failed to meet the legal criteria of effectiveness, appropriateness, and efficiency. As we saw, the Federal Commission for General Health Insurance Benefits usually does not conduct its own health technology assessment but rather refers to existing evidence provided by health care professionals or by the sickness funds, as well as to the results of international or foreign evaluations. The Commission also takes into consideration ethical and political concerns. Several elements in this process raise serious concerns.

Lack of transparency

First, the evaluation process lacks transparency. Neither the minutes of the meetings, the reports on which the Commission bases its opinions, nor the conclusions of the Commission transmitted to the Federal Department of Home Affairs are published or can be consulted. The applicants, however, receive a written summary of the arguments behind the FDHA decision. This lack of transparency is particularly problematic when the technology at stake raises ethical or political concerns. In such case, decisions are based on value judgements in addition to hard evidence, and are thus prone to political pressures. There remain uncertainties as to the nature and importance of each argument in this process. This may lead to arbitrary and discriminatory decisions. The risk of discrimination is also increased by the reluctance of the courts, including the Federal Supreme Court for Social Insurance to analyse more in depth the legitimacy of the ordinance concerning the services in basic health insurance coverage.[51]

Difficulties with issuing coverage recommendations when important values are at stake

The manual specifies that

> a newly introduced procedure should improve social welfare in general. Thus the ideal assessment of a medical procedure would consider both its direct and indirect consequences for society. Such comprehensive analyses clearly go far beyond the

sort of economic assessment of medical procedures set out in this manual.

This last sentence reminds that the final decision is after all a political one taken by the Federal Department of Home Affairs.

In vitro fertilization intervention

The decision not to reimburse in vitro fertilization with the transfer of the embryo seems to have been partly based on political arguments rather than scientific ones. Under a scientific view, IVF cannot be considered as 'experimental' at this point. It has been rather thoroughly evaluated. It is in fact reimbursed in many countries by social insurance. Yet, there remains a controversy in Switzerland. Some argue that infertility is not a sickness under the social insurance laws, thus treatment of infertility should not be financed by the solidarity-based social insurance system. It is a matter of personal choice of the couple. Others are opposed by principle to all form of medically assisted reproduction.

The Federal Supreme Court has rejected the first conclusion for more than two decades. It has constantly recognized the fact that infertility is a sickness according to the social insurance laws, and thus that treatment of this sickness should be covered as far as the treatment is efficacious, appropriate, and efficient. As we saw above, the Court's position concerning the non-reimbursement of IVF is based only on the fact that it considers IVF as experimental, but this is inconsistent with the present scientific reality. Concerning the second argument, a new Federal Law on Medically Assisted Reproduction, which came into force on 1 January 2001, defines the conditions under which such assisted reproduction is lawful, especially in regards of the protection of the embryo and the unborn child.

Nevertheless, the Federal Department of Home Affairs organized a public consultation on the general acceptability by the population of IVF being covered by social insurance. There were doubts whether the mere fact that infertility is a sickness according to the Federal Supreme Court justifies the full coverage of all measures available to cure it. There may be societal limits to the solidarity-based assistance that a couple suffering from infertility is entitled to. The consultation organized by the Centre for Technology Assessment (TA-SWISS) provided an answer to this value question. This consultation was conducted through five public discussions in the various regions of Switzerland in which samples of the population reflecting different attitudes and values concerning IVF were represented (such as couples without children, couples with adopted children, churches). In each case, about 15 participants were invited to react to a given list of questions. This remains the first and only public consultation on social insurance coverage in Switzerland.

It is interesting to note that the Commission is now expected to review its position on IVF based on the globally positive results of this consultation, showing that there is a broad acceptance of IVF.[52] Thus IVF procedures could be included in the ordinance by the year 2006.

Complementary medicine

Some types of complementary medicine – namely acupuncture, anthroposophic medicine, traditional Chinese medicine, homeopathy, neural therapy, and phytotherapy – are reimbursed by the sickness funds according to point 10 of annex 1 of the Ordinance Concerning the Services Covered by Basic Health Insurance unless they are prescribed and provided by a physician with a specific training.[53] With the exception of acupuncture, all of these procedures remain under evaluation until 30 June 2005. An evaluation programme consisting of HTAs, analysis of the Swiss Health Survey (in order to describe demand for the procedures), and a health services research type study (aiming at describing in detail the provision of complementary care) is under way. One may argue that this conflicts with the principle of evidence-based medicine as provided by Article 32 of the Federal Law on Sickness Insurance. Yet complementary medicines have always enjoyed a broad recognition in the Swiss population, especially in the eastern, German-speaking part of Switzerland. Even more, the coverage of some types of complementary medicines can also be seen as a gesture favouring the medical profession, as complementary medicine is reimbursed only if provided by a trained physician. Thus, all of the budget for complementary medicines goes to the MDs and not to the traditional therapists.

It will be interesting to see how the authorities will decide on further coverage when the results of this broad evaluation – incorporating mainstream international scientific evidence (which, not surprisingly, will remain very limited), insight into local provision, and information regarding demand by the population – will be available.

CONCLUSION

It is to be noted that the making of reimbursement or major investment decisions in health care is, in general, rarely based on hard scientific evidence alone. It is a universal challenge to design and adapt decision processes regarding reimbursement and major investments in health care so that they best reflect both scientific evidence on efficacy (which is, in principle, universally valid and internationally exchangeable) and ethical, societal, and professional implications (which require national or local appraisals and often value judgements). Economic evaluations lie between, insofar as they should be based on scientifically sound cost-effectiveness studies, but their results need to be adapted to local circumstances (such as prices and reimbursement schemes) and – in the case of cost–utility studies – to local value tables. The evidence needed for full evaluation of technologies for national coverage decisions (including scientific evidence on effectiveness and cost effectiveness in the local health service and societal and ethical considerations based on qualitative research methods) will never be available.

In the processes described above, the Commission takes the role of an appraisal committee, which integrates hard quantitative evidence on efficacy and cost effectiveness with qualitative evidence – as far as it is available – with respect to local implications. Almost no resources, however, are available for commissioned research either to conduct reviews of the evidence or qualitative studies regarding ethical, societal or professional impacts. Only in sensitive areas (such as IVF or complementary medicine) has such research been initiated and funded by the administration.

In parallel, it should be underlined that most products and services do not go through any evaluation process since these services have never been contested. The administration, so far, has not taken an active role in searching internationally and nationally for procedures that are about to be introduced into everyday practice, and to check whether these procedures have gone through evaluation procedures in other countries. New technologies are covered based on the mere fact that they are prescribed by physicians and provided by authorized health care professionals. There are in fact very few health care systems that strictly limit the scope of care covered by social insurance or public health care services by the means of a fixed catalogue.[54] This is due in part to the difficulty of defining the criteria under which to establish such a catalogue, but also to the fact that medicine is not only a science but also an art.

There will always remain a grey zone where the physician is left alone to decide what treatment would be best for his or her patient.

It is interesting to see that the Swiss health care system gives rather substantial independence to health care providers, especially the medical profession, at least concerning the determination of the nature of health care covered by the sickness funds. This is certainly a legitimate policy in view of the nature of modern medicine. The status of complementary medicine raises serious concerns here because, by definition, such practices are not evidence-based, or at least hardly meet scientific criteria. One can also argue, however, that complementary medicine represents replacement of one largely unevaluated approach – the conventional medical approach dealing with chronic disease and chronic pain or unclear symptoms – by another unevaluated approach, the complementary one.

The listed shortcomings (lack of transparency; insufficient local appraisal of ethical, societal, and professional implications; almost no active programme for horizon scanning for new, unevaluated procedures about to be introduced) reflects the underfunding of evaluation processes in general and decision processes in particular in Switzerland.

CASE STUDIES: POSITRON EMISSION TOMOGRAPHY (PET), HYPERBARIC OXYGEN THERAPY (HBOT), GLIVEC ®, AND INFLUENZA ANTIVIRALS

To better understand the functioning of the Swiss legal procedures for making healthcare coverage policy, we will analyse in more detail the case of positron emission tomography (PET) and hyperbaric oxygen therapy (HBOT). According to the Ordinance Concerning the Services in Basic Health Insurance Coverage,[55] both of these procedures are reimbursed by the sickness funds under specific conditions.

Hyperbaric oxygen therapy was evaluated twice. It was first accepted for reimbursement by social sickness insurance in 1988 in case of chronic 'osteomyelitis (any localization)' and 'mandibular osteomyelitis (acute and chronic)', then in 1994 the coverage was extended also to cases of 'late or chronic actinic lesions'.[56] There have been no requests since then from providers to consider the reimbursement of HBOT for other indications or from the health insurance to review the adequacy of the existing reimbursement indications. Positron Emission Tomography (PET), on the other hand, has been under constant evaluation since 1994. The list of indications for which coverage is granted is regularly updated.[57] The Federal Commission for General Health Insurance Benefits established in 1999 the PET Study Group with the objective of defining a new PET-concept for Switzerland. This group published its report in May 2000.[58] The first reimbursement decision round was prepared by a national consensus conference. Subsequent requests from providers for extending the list of reimbursable indications were weighed against the findings and recommendations of various international health technology assessments published at the time, notably those from the INAHTA and the Veterans administration. The extension of the indications was attached to several requirements, in particular for:

• An evaluation registry created under the auspices of the Swiss Society for Nuclear Medicine (SSNM), for selected indications outcome studies (in order to document changes in clinical pathways and decision-making, resource use and outcomes in patients evaluated with and without PET).

• Accreditation of new PET centres for reimbursement by SSNM.

In 2000, SSNM published directives with respect to the quality of PET. These directives cover infrastructure and processes (including a patient registry). Only PET centres fulfilling these directives are entitled to be reimbursed by compulsory health insurance. Mobile PET scanners do not fulfill these directives. The SSNM is still struggling to establish the outcome studies (setting up collaboration among referring oncologists, cardiologists, and neurologists was difficult and time consuming).

The fact that PET scans have been reimbursed for more than ten years did not guarantee at the beginning that this new technology would be widely available. By the end of 2000, just before the new indications were added to the Ordinance, increasing the total number of potential reimbursable patients to about 8000 patients per year, only two PET scanners were operational with a capacity of 1500 patients per year each (at best). Today, there are six PET scanners working according to the directives of the SSNM. This demonstrates that reimbursement by social health insurance was, in Switzerland, the main factor for diffusion of this technology.

The transparency of the coverage decision-making process remains rather limited even if communication is improving. While at the time of the first PET decisions even the applicants received only limited information, by now applicants receive a summary information of the evidence used and the rationale for the decisions. But this information is not routinely made publicly available.

Glivec received marketing approval in June 2001 for the treatment of chronic myeloid leukaemia in the blast, accelerated or chronic phase in cases of failure of the treatment with Interferon alpha. In July 2001, the Federal Commission for Drugs decided to include Glivec (with reference to these indications) into the formulary of compulsory health insurance at a price of $25 per 100 mg tablet (ex factory price / exchange rate: $1 = 1.3 SFr). In April 2002, the indications with marketing approval were extended to metastatic and/or not resectable gastrointestinal stroma tumors (GIST). With the marketing approval of new indications, the reimbursable indications were automatically extended.

Out of the antiviral drugs used in case of influenza, only amantadine is reimbursed by compulsory health insurance since 1971, while the new antiviral drugs zanamavir and oseltamir are not. Requests for reimbursement of both drugs have been submitted to the Federal Commission for Drugs in 1999, but rejected by the Commission. No new reimbursement requests have been submitted since. The reasons for approval, limited approval or rejection from reimbursement are communicated to the companies who submit reimbursement requests only, and cannot, therefore, be explained here.

References

1 The authors wish to thank Timothy Jost for editing this paper and Severine Boillat for her support in collecting references and material.

2 OCDE (1992), *La réforme des systèmes de santé, Analyse comparée de 7 pays de l'OCDE*. Paris: OCDE, p. 19.

3 M. Duriez (1998), *Les systèmes de santé en Europe*. Paris: Presses universitaires de France, p. 3.

4 Loi fédérale du 18 mars 1994 sur l'assurance-maladie (LAMal), RS 832.10, art. 21. < www.admin.ch/ch/f/rs/832_10/a21.html > (accessed 24 Feb., 2004).

5 Loi fédérale du 2 avril 1908 sur le contrat d'assurance (LCA), RS 221.229.1. < www.admin.ch/ch/f/rs/c221_229_1.html > (accessed 24 Feb., 2004).

6 OMS (2000), *European Health Care Systems in Transition: Switzerland*. Copenhagen: European Observatory on Health Care Systems; B. Berger and T. Poledna (2002), *Öffentliches Gesundheitsrecht*. Berne: Stämpfli, p. 11.

7 Berger and Poledna (2002), p. 11.

8 See FF 1906, VI 213 and FF 1912, I 473.

9 LAMal, < www.admin.ch/ch/f/rs/c832_10.html > (accessed 24 Feb., 2004).

10 Berger and Poledna (2002), p. 223.

11 LAMal, art. 61. < www.admin.ch/ch/f/rs/832_10/a61.html > (accessed 24 Feb., 2004).

12 LAMal, art. 65–66a. < www.admin.ch/ch/f/rs/832_10/a65.html > (accessed 24 Feb., 2004).

13 In 2001, 32.7 per cent of all insured in Switzerland received such subsidies from the authorities. See OFAS (2003), *Statistique des assurances sociales suisses 2003*. Berne: OFAS, p. 159. < www.bsv.admin.ch/publikat/svs/f/svs_2003_f.pdf > (accessed 24 Feb., 2004).

14 LAMal, art. 7. < www.admin.ch/ch/f/rs/832_10/a7.html > (accessed 24 Feb., 2004).

15 LAMal, art. 35–41. < www.admin.ch/ch/f/rs/832_10/a35.html > (accessed 24 Feb., 2004).

16 J. Berra (2000), *La structure des systèmes de sécurité sociale*. Lausanne: IRAL, p. 362.

17 LAMal, art. 32 al. 1 < www.admin.ch/ch/f/rs/832_10/a32.html > (accessed 24 Feb., 2004).

18 F. Colombo (2001), *Toward More Choice in Social Protection? Individual Choice of Insurer in Basic Mandatory Health Insurance in Switzerland*. Paris: OCED, p. 15. < www.olis.oecd.org/OLIS/2001DOC.NSF/43bb6130e5e86e5fc12569fa005d004c/c1256985004c66e3c1256acb00548723/$FILE/JT00112830.PDF > (accessed 24 Feb., 2004).

19 See M. Polikowski and B. Santos-Eggimann (2002), 'How Comprehensive Are the Basic Packages of Health Services? An International Comparison of Six Health Insurance Systems', *Journal of Health Services Research and Policy*, 7(3): 133–42.

20 See for instance G. Eugster (2003), *Wirtschaftlichkeitskontrolle ambulanter ärztlicher Leistungen mit statistischen Methoden*. Berne: P. Haupt.

21 For a detailed analysis of this problem, see D. Hornung, T. Röthlisberger, and A. Stiefel (2001), *Wirkungsanalyse KVG: Praxis der Versicherer bei der Vergütung von Leistungen nach KVG.* Berne: OFAS.

22 Ordonnance du 27 juin 1995 sur l'assurance-maladie (OAMal), RS 832.102. < www.admin.ch/ch/f/rs/c832_102.html > (accessed 24 Feb., 2004).

23 Ordonnance du 29 septembre 1995 sur les prestations dans l'assurance obligatoire des soins en cas de maladie (OPAS), RS 832.112.31. < www.admin.ch/ch/f/rs/c832_112_31.html > (accessed 24 Feb., 2004).

24 A. Maurer (1996), *Das neue Krankenversicherungsrecht.* Bâle: Helbing & Lichtenhahn, p. 44.

25 LAMal, art. 32 al. 1. < www.admin.ch/ch/f/rs/c832_10.html > (accessed 24 Feb., 2004).

26 OPAS, < www.admin.ch/ch/f/rs/c832_112_31.html > (accessed 24 Feb., 2004).

27 OPAS, < www.admin.ch/ch/f/rs/c832_112_31.html > (accessed 24 Feb., 2004).

28 Pharma Markt Schweiz (2003), *Pharma Information.* Bâle. < www.interpharma.ch/de/pdf/gb03-d-download.pdf > (accessed March 23, 2004).

29 OAMal, art. 37 c paragraph 2 lit. e. < www.admin.ch/ch/f/rs/ 832_102/a37c.html > (accessed 24 Feb., 2004).

30 The English version of this manual was published in 1998. It has since been revised in 2000 and is again under revision. A new version should be published in 2004 according to the Federal Social Insurance Office (personal communication of Helena Kottmann, Federal Social Insurance Office).

31 E. Jonsson, D. Banta, C. Henshall, and L. Sampietro-Colom (2002), 'Summary Report of the ECHTA/ECAHI Project', *International Journal of Technology Assessment in Health Care*, 18(2): 218–37.

32 An example of this is Xenical, which can be prescribed only for some specific types of obesity.

33 The number and frequency of appointments for psychotherapy is limited (two appointments of one hour per week during the three first years, one appointment of one hour per week during the next three years and one appointment of one hour every two weeks afterward. (Art. 3 of the Ordinance Concerning the Services Covered in Basic Health Insurance.)

34 OPAS, art. 1. < www.admin.ch/ch/f/rs/c832_112_31.html > (accessed 24 Feb., 2004).

35 See A. Ayer, et al. (2000), *Analyse juridique des effets de la LAMal: catalogue des prestations et procédures* (Rapport de recherche n° 14/ 00), p.14. Berne: OFAS.

36 LAMal, art. 49 paragraph 1. < www.admin.ch/ch/f/rs/832_10/a49.html > (accessed 24 Feb., 2004).

37 In the mid-1990s, proposals to introduce a limitation of expensive and new technologies were made in the following cantons: Ticino, Geneva, Vaud, Fribourg, and Neuchâtel.

38 Loi portant révision de la loi de santé (clause du besoin concernant les équipements lourds), FO 1998, n° 12; Arrêté du 1er avril 1998 concernant la mise en services d'équipements techniques lourds et d'autres équipements de médecine de pointe, RSN 800.100.02. < www.ne.ch/neat/site/jsp/rubrique/rubrique.jsp?StyleType = blcu& CatId = 2151 > (accessed 24 Feb., 2004).

39 Loi de santé du 6 février 1995, RSN 800.1. < www.ne.ch/neat/site/jsp/rubrique/rubrique.jsp?StyleType = bleu&CatId = 2151 > (accessed 24 Feb., 2004).

40 Arrêté du 1 cr avril 1998 concernant la mise en services d'équipements techniques lourds et d'autres équipements de médecine de pointe, RSN 800.100.02, article 1. < www.nc.ch/ncat/site/jsp/rubrique/rubrique.jsp?StyleType = bleu&CatId = 2151 > (accessed 24 Feb., 2004).

41 Arrêté du 29 octobre 2003 approuvant une demande d'acquisition d'équipement technique lourd des Hôpitaux de la ville de Neuchâtel, Cadolles/Pourtalès, FO 2003, n° 84 < www.ne.ch/neat/site/jsp/rubrique/rubrique.jsp?StyleType = bleu&DocId = 7281 > (accessed 24 Feb., 2004).

42 See Rapport final du groupe de travail « Médecine de pointe » à l'intention du comité directeur de la Conférence des directeurs cantonaux des affaires sanitaires (CDS) (2003), *Coordination et concentration de la médecine hautement spécialisée*, 29 avril. < www.gdk-cds.ch/fr/ges-politik-f.html > (accessed March 23, 2004).

43 OPAS, < www.admin.ch/ch/f/rs/c832_112_31.html > (accessed 24 Feb., 2004).

44 Loi fédérale du 6 octobre 2000 sur la partie générale du droit des assurances sociales (LPGA), RS 830.1. < www.admin.ch/ch/f/rs/c830_1.html > (accessed 24 Feb., 2004).

45 See B. Kahil-Wolf, et al. (2003), *La partie générale des assurances sociales*. Lausanne: IRAL.

46 See A. Ayer, et al. (2000).

47 ATF 125 V 21. < www.bger.ch/fr/index/juridiction/jurisdiction-inherit-template/jurisdiction-recht/jurisdiction-recht-leitentscheide 1954.htm > (accessed 24 Feb., 2004).

48 See J.-M. Frésard (2000), 'Examen de la constitutionnalité et de la légalité d'une règle figurant dans l'annexe à l'ordonnance sur les prestations dans l'assurance obligatoire des soins en cas de maladie (OPAS)', *Revue suisse des assurances sociales*, 44: 89.

49 Arrêt du TFA du 8 septembre 1999, *RAMA*, 1999, 6: 498 < www.bsv.admin.ch/publikat/rkuv/d/rkuv9906.pdf > (accessed 24 Feb., 2004).

50 OPAS, <www.admin.ch/ch/f/rs/c832_112_31.html> (accessed 24 Feb., 2004).

51 OPAS <www.admin.ch/ch/f/rs/c832_112_31.html> (accessed 24 Feb., 2004).

52 See Publifocus sur la fécondation in vitro (2003), rapport d'une méthode participative. TA P4/2003. <www.ta-swiss.ch/www-remain/reports_archive/publications/2003/pf_Bericht_IVF_f.pdf> (accessed February 10, 2004).

53 See S. Maddalena (1999), *The Legal Status of Complementary Medicines in Europe*. Berne: Stämpfli.

54 See Polikowski and Santos-Eggimann (2002), p. 133.

55 OPAS, <www.admin.ch/ch/f/rs/c832_112_31.html> (accessed 24 Feb., 2004).

56 OPAS, annexe 1, ch. 2.1. <www.admin.ch/ch/f/rs/832_112_31/appl.html> (accessed 24 Feb., 2004).

57 OPAS, annexe 1, ch. 9.2. <www.admin.ch/ch/f/rs/832_112_31/appl.html> (accessed 24 Feb., 2004). There has been a revision of the indications for PET in 1.1.1994, 1.4.1994, 1.1.1997, 1.1.1999, 1.1.2001 and 1.1.2004.

58 OFAS (Medical Technology Unit) (2000), *New PET-Concept for Switzerland, Report of the PET Study Group prepared on behalf of the Federal Commission for General Health Insurance Benefits*. Berne: OFAS.

9

THE MEDICARE COVERAGE DETERMINATION PROCESS IN THE UNITED STATES

Timothy Stoltzfus Jost

INTRODUCTION: COVERAGE POLICY IN THE AMERICAN HEALTH CARE SYSTEM

Unlike other developed countries, the United States depends primarily on private health insurance to insure its population. Most Americans (about 63 per cent[1]) belong to group health insurance plans sponsored by their employers and subsidized by federal and state tax subsidies. A much smaller number (about 8 per cent) purchase individual insurance policies. Because private insurance coverage depends on willingness and ability to pay (and is often risk-rated), many Americans, about 43 million currently, are simply uninsured. They must pay for their health care out of pocket, or go without.

Despite our basic reliance on private insurance coverage, however, the United States spends as much public money as a percentage of gross domestic product as the average OECD country, while only three other countries spend more public money per capita.[2] Two massive government programmes provide health care services for the elderly and disabled (Medicare) and for poor elderly and disabled people and poor children and their families (Medicaid). Because the populations that are covered by these programmes are often those most in need of health care services, they together account for 45 per cent of health spending.[3]

All insurers, public and private, must decide which categories of services they will cover and which they will not. Medicare covers hospital care, short-term skilled nursing care, home health services, the services of physicians and some other professionals, durable medical equipment, and a limited amount of preventive care. It does not cover dental, optical, or long-term care, and does not yet cover outpatient pharmaceuticals, though it will after 1 January 2006. Coverage decisions must also be made within categories of services. Historically, most insurers, including Medicare, have simply stated that they covered only 'medically necessary' services, and usually excluded experimental treatments.[4] These provisions were rarely invoked to limit coverage, however, except to exclude the services of charlatans or cosmetic treatments. With the coming of managed care, however, private insurers have become much more serious about reviewing coverage of services, both by examining individual cases through utilization review, and by assessing technologies to decide whether or not to cover them.

At this point in time, private insurers in the United States are probably further along than public insurers in assessing technology for coverage policy.[5; 6; 7] The largest and most advanced technology assessment body in the country is probably the Technology Evaluation Center (TEC), a Blue Cross/Blue Shield Association programme, administered in partnership with Kaiser Permanente. The nation's 42, generally non-profit, Blue Cross and Blue Shield plans cover about one quarter of the American population. The TEC does not make coverage determinations, which are made by local plans.[8] It does, however, evaluate technologies, and advise local plans, as well as other entities that subscribe to its services, as to whether technologies improve health outcomes. The TEC evaluates about 30 new technologies a year. Several other private technology assessment services offer technology assessments to their subscribers, while large insurers and managed care organizations or consortia of managed plan organizations or health centres also have their own technology assessment units.[9] Insurers and managed care organizations use these assessments for setting coverage policy, although it is perhaps more common for insurers and managed care organizations to make coverage decisions on a case by case basis rather than across the board, especially when end of life treatment is involved.

Technology assessment for coverage policy also occurs in the public sector, in particular in the federal Medicare, Medicaid, and

Veterans Administration programmes. This chapter will focus on the federal Medicare programme. Medicare was chosen for several reasons. First, Medicare coverage determinations are made through publicly transparent and accountable procedures. Second, Medicare is a public social insurance programme, and thus resembles more closely the public insurance programmes of the other countries that we are studying here. Finally, between Medicare and Medicaid we chose Medicare because it is a national programme with a more or less unitary approach to coverage policy, while Medicaid is a federal/state programme, in which most coverage decisions are made at the state level and each programme has different procedures.

TECHNOLOGY ASSESSMENT FOR COVERAGE POLICY IN MEDICARE

The Medicare programme is currently divided into three components, Parts A, B, and C. A fourth component, Part D, covering outpatient prescription drugs, will begin in 2006. Part A is a traditional social insurance programme, financed through payroll taxes imposed on employers and employees. It covers institutional services – primarily inpatient hospital services, skilled nursing services, home health care, and hospice care. Part B covers the services of physicians and other professionals, some home health services, durable medical equipment, and some preventive services, and is funded through general revenue taxes and premiums. Part C provides Part A and B services through Medicare Advantage managed care organizations to those Medicare beneficiaries who choose to join these plans (currently about 12 per cent). Part C managed care organizations must cover all services covered by Part A and B.[10]

Though the focus of this chapter is coverage policy, the primary concern of Medicare providers is payment. Medicare will only pay a provider for an item or service if the item or service falls within one of the 55 categories of services covered by Medicare and if it is not subject to an explicit exclusion, such as that for cosmetic services.[11] The Medicare statute further provides that the programme may only pay for services that are 'reasonable and necessary'.[12] Medicare coverage determinations specify which services meet, or fail to meet, these standards, and in particular which services are 'reasonable and necessary'.

The Medicare programme is a national programme of the federal government, but it is administered by private contractors, currently called carriers in the Part B programme and fiscal intermediaries in the Part A programme. Each state has a Part B carrier, though a number of carriers operate in several different states, and there are currently only a total of 20 carriers in the programme. Each hospital can choose a fiscal intermediary, and there are currently 28 intermediaries participating in the Medicare programme, some limited to particular states and regions, while others operate at the national level. Four special regional carriers process durable medical equipment claims. Under recently adopted legislation, the functions of carriers and intermediaries will be taken over by unified Medicare contractors, but this change will not be fully implemented until 2012.

Medicare contractors are responsible for receiving, screening, and paying about 900 million provider and professional claims a year.[13] Each contractor is authorized under procedures described below to establish local medical review policies (LMRPs) (including local coverage determinations (LCDs)) and 9000 coverage policies were posted on the local coverage website of the Center for Medicare and Medicaid Services (CMS) in 2001.[14; 15] CMS itself, however, also makes national coverage determinations, and where such coverage determinations exist they take precedence over local coverage determinations. The vast majority of coverage determinations are local, and thus Medicare coverage varies from place to place throughout the country.

Most Medicare items and services, however, are not subject to an explicit coverage determination. This is certainly true for currently covered items and services, but it is also true for many new items and services as well. Medicare currently pays for virtually all Part A institutional services on a prospective or per diem basis. Prospective payments are generally unrelated to individual costs or charges. Inpatient hospital services are paid for on the basis of diagnosis related groups, or DRGs.[16] DRG-PPS payments are in the first instance based on an admitting diagnosis, and are further broken down by age, sex, discharge status, additional diagnoses, and whether or not a particular procedure, usually a major surgical intervention, was performed during the stay.[17] As long as a patient was admitted to a hospital for a covered purpose, however, nothing turns on whether, for example, the patient received a particular drug or was screened by a particular diagnostic device. Of course, if a patient receives a drug, device, or procedure not covered by

Medicare, the physician or professional who administered it may not be paid for his or her services under Part B. Also, since the payment for the DRG will be based on traditional treatment for the diagnosis, the hospital may not be paid enough to cover its costs if it has substituted an expensive new technology for a less costly old one.[18] Except in the fairly unusual circumstance where an admission is itself for an uncovered service (such as sex reassignment surgery), the hospital's payment is not likely to turn on a coverage issue.

Payment for outpatient services is based on prospectively established ambulatory payment classifications (APCs), based on clinical and cost similarity.[19] In general, the provider is not paid more just because it uses a more expensive technology. This general rule, however, is subject to limited exceptions for new technologies.

Because Part A services are paid for by and large on a prospective basis, coverage policy is primarily an issue for Part B. Medicare pays for part B professional services on a fee-for-service basis, generally using prospectively established fee schedules. Medicare will only pay for a Part B service if an appropriate code exists for the service. Services are coded using HCPCS codes (Healthcare Common Procedure Code System).[20] For most services provided by physicians and other health care professionals, HCPCS codes are based on the CPT-4 codes provided by the American Medical Association (HCPCS level I). For other Part B services, however, such as durable medical equipment or prosthetics, orthotics, or supplies, the HCPCS codes are established by the HCPCS National Panel, which is composed of representatives from the national Blue Cross/Blue Shield Association, the Center for Medicare and Medicaid Services, and America's Health Insurance Plans (HCPCS level II codes).

If a manufacturer, provider, or physician creates a new technology for which it hopes to get paid under Part B, it must obtain a billing code. To do this, it must either fit the technology under an existing HCPCS code (and accept the payment currently available for that code); bill under a miscellaneous code, which will mean that the service will be processed manually; or apply for a new code, either to AMA or to the HCPCS panel or by applying for a coverage determination, as appropriate.[21] If a CPT-4 or other HCPCS code is applied to a procedure, CMS must determine whether the code is for one of the 55 categories of items or services covered under Medicare, and then, if it is, assign a payment level to the code. This may or may not happen through a coverage determination. In fact, only about a quarter of new codes are subject to national coverage determinations.[22] Another half are subject to local coverage determinations, but most by only a few Part B carriers. Many new codes are simply covered without an explicit coverage determination, though a coverage determination is presumably much more likely if the item or service presents significant cost, safety, or efficacy issues.

MEDICARE LOCAL COVERAGE DETERMINATIONS

As already noted, the vast majority of coverage determinations are local. Carriers and intermediaries, including Durable Medical Equipment Regional Carriers (DMERCs), set local medical review policies (LMRPs) in accordance with the procedures set out in chapter 13 of the Medicare Program Integrity Manual.[23] To the extent that LMRPs address the question of whether the service is reasonable or necessary under section 1862(a)(1)(A) of the Social Security Act, they are considered to be local coverage determinations (LCDs).[24]

LCDs can be initiated by providers, manufacturers, patients, or by others seeking coverage of a new item or service. LCDs can also be initiated by internal carrier or intermediary staff.[25] To determine that an item or service meets the reasonable or necessary test, the contractor must find that it is:

1. safe and effective;
2. not experimental or investigational (except for the routine costs of clinical investigations, which can be covered under a national coverage determination); and
3. appropriate, that is, it is
   • furnished in accordance with accepted standards of medical practice,
   • furnished in an appropriate setting,
   • ordered or furnished by qualified personnel
   • able to meet, but does not exceed, the patient's medical needs
   • at least as beneficial as an existing and available medically appropriate alternative.[26]

LCDs are supposed to be based, if possible, on published authoritative studies using randomized controlled trials or other definitive study methodologies.[27] When authoritative studies are not available, LCDs must be based on the standard of care in the medical community, as evidenced by scientific data or research studies; the consensus of medical expert opinion; or advice from medical associations or health care experts.

Upon receiving a request for a LMRP (including an LCD), contractors usually begin by gathering and reviewing information about the policy. They are encouraged to adopt LMRPs from other contractors if these are available. If, as is often the case, a contractor covers several states, it is encouraged to maintain consistent policies. If a contractor must devise a new policy, it will gather and review relevant information by conducting literature reviews, contacting other carriers or intermediaries, consulting advisory committees, or contacting medical societies or local experts. Under recently adopted legislation, CMS is supposed to strive for greater consistency among LCDs and disseminate information among contractors about LCDs to reduce duplication of effort, while contractors operating within the same area are supposed to consult regarding new LCDs within a particular area.[28]

Once a contractor develops a draft policy, it must determine whether the policy has to be made available for comment or not. Generally new policies or policies that restrict or substantially change existing policies require comment, while policies that make insubstantial changes, that liberalize existing coverage, that are necessary to implement NCDs, or that make emergency-type changes do not.[29] If a policy requires comment, it must be made available for a 45-day comment period.[30] During this period, the contractor must circulate the policy to a list of specified recipients, including health professionals, specialty societies, other carriers and intermediaries, CMS regional administrators, and the general public. It must also provide an open meeting at which comments on the draft LMRP may be offered and then present the draft to its contractor advisory committee, as well as posting the draft on its website for comment.

Once a final LMRP is written, it must be posted at the contractors website for at least 45 days (the notice period) before it becomes effective.[31] The contractor must also post a summary of comments received, and its response to those comments. All final policies must also be posted on the national LRMP website.

MEDICARE NATIONAL COVERAGE DETERMINATIONS

Procedures

Alternatively, the proponent of a new technology may apply for a national coverage determination (NCD). The procedures for making national coverage determinations have evolved over the past decade and a half as NCDs have become more common. In particular, they have become more formal.[32; 33; 34] CMS currently follows a procedure that it published in September 2003 for creating NCDs.[35] In May 2000, HCFA published a notice of intent to also publish a proposed rule establishing substantive criteria for making NCDs.[36] A proposed rule has not been published in the three years that have followed, and CMS appears to have decided to rather follow a 'case law' approach to developing policy criteria.[37] Recently adopted legislation, however, directs HHS to 'make available to the public the factors considered in making' NCDs and to 'develop guidance documents' to carry out this function.[38]

Under the 2003 procedure, an NCD can be initiated either by an internal CMS decision or by an external formal request.[39] Internal initiation may occur when (a) there are conflicting local policies or (b) the service represents a significant medical advance not otherwise available under Medicare, is medically controversial, is currently covered but widely considered to be ineffective, or presents programme integrity issues surrounding significant over- or under-utilization. Formal requests can be made either by any party (including beneficiaries, manufacturers, providers or suppliers), or by an 'aggrieved party' defined as a beneficiary who is in need of the items and services covered by the NCD. While special procedures exist for 'aggrieved parties', most NCDs are initiated by formal requests from manufacturers, providers, provider groups, or, less commonly, patients.[40] Formal requests must be submitted in writing and electronically, and include a full and complete description of the service in question and a compilation of medical and scientific information relevant to the item or service, including a description of clinical trials underway that might be relevant to it. Generally, CMS will accept a request for coverage for a drug or device subject to Food and Drug Administration (FDA) approval only once FDA approval is obtained, though an exception is made for certain investigational devices which FDA concludes do not pose a significant risk.[41]

Once a request is complete, CMS notifies the requester and posts the request on its tracking website.[42] This posting initiates a 30-day comment period, during which the public may submit evidence or otherwise comment on the proposal. If the request has been submitted by an 'aggrieved party' CMS must review it within 90 days. By the conclusion of that period CMS must:

1. issue a national coverage determination with or without limitations;
2. issue a national non-coverage determination;
3. issue a determination that no national coverage determination is appropriate (in which case the issue remains open for local coverage determinations);
4. or issue a notice that it has not yet completed its review, identifying steps that remain, and setting a deadline for completion of these steps.[43]

If CMS fails to take any action within 90 days on an application from an 'aggrieved party', it is deemed to have issued a determination that no national coverage decision is appropriate.[44] If the request is submitted by a manufacturer, or by someone else other than an 'aggrieved party', CMS will attempt to act within 90 days, but the time frame is not binding. As a practical matter, most complex issues will result in a determination that the review cannot be completed in 90 days, accompanied by a referral to the CMS Medicare Coverage Advisory Committee (MCAC), a referral for a technology assessment (HTA), or both. If CMS does not refer a coverage determination to the MCAC, it must nonetheless consult with 'appropriate clinical experts'.[45]

The MCAC consists of a maximum of 100 members with expertise relevant to coverage policy. It meets in panels of 13 to 15 members to consider coverage issues.[46] Each panel contains two non-voting members representing consumers and manufacturers. Non-voting members can participate fully in the deliberations of the committee and have full access to information that voting members have access to, except where information is protected as trade secrets, or participation would constitute a conflict of interest. CMS will refer a coverage issue to the MCAC if it has the potential to have a major impact on the Medicare programme or if it is subject to a substantial medical or public controversy.[47]

Once an issue has been referred to it, the MCAC will hold a public meeting at which interested individuals may present their views. The public is given 30 days' notice of these meetings, and all evidentiary presentations must be submitted at least 20 days before the meeting. The MCAC then makes a recommendation to CMS. CMS may accept or reject the MCAC recommendation, but if it rejects it, it must explain why and make available to the public the information on which the decision was based.[48] Though CMS itself does not currently have published criteria for evaluating technologies, the MCAC does.[49] The MCAC begins by asking whether the evidence is sufficient to evaluate the effectiveness of the technology for clinical use with Medicare populations. Second, it must consider how the effectiveness of the proposed technology compares to that of existing technologies. In particular, it attempts to place the technology in one of seven categories:

1. *Breakthrough technology*: the improvement in health outcomes is so large that the intervention becomes the standard of care.
2. *More effective*: the new intervention improves health outcomes by a significant, albeit small, margin as compared with established services or medical items.
3. *As effective, but with advantages*: the intervention has the same effect on health outcomes as established services or medical items but has some advantages (convenience, rapidity of effect, fewer side effects, other advantages) that some patients will prefer.
4. *As effective and with no advantage*: the intervention has the same effect on health outcomes as established alternatives but with no advantages.
5. *Less effective but with advantages*: although the intervention is less effective than established alternatives (but more effective than doing nothing), it has some advantages (such as convenience, tolerability).
6. *Less effective and with no advantages*: the intervention is less effective than established alternatives (but more effective than doing nothing) and has no significant advantages.
7. *Not effective*: the intervention has no effect or has deleterious effects on health outcomes when compared with 'doing nothing'.

When the MCAC determines that evidence is inadequate to make a determination, it will advise CMS as to the possibility and potential benefits of developing better evidence. It will also consider whether it is possible otherwise to reach a conclusion about a technology if high-quality studies are lacking.

Either CMS or the MCAC may also request a technology

assessment where the complexity of the issue presented by the medical and scientific literature exceeds the capacity or expertise of CMS staff.[50] CMS either requests an HTA from the federal Agency for Health Care Research and Quality (AHRQ), which in turn works through a network of about a dozen evidence-based practice centres, or purchases a commercial off-the-shelf assessment.[51] CMS may also, in less complex cases, assess the clinical evidence itself without MCAC assistance or an HTA. HTAs can take a year or more to complete.

Within 90 days of receiving a formal request, or within 60 days of receiving an MCAC recommendation or a technology assessment, whichever is later, CMS will publish and provide to an NCD requester a decision memorandum, discussing the evidence presented and reviewed, and the conclusions of the technology assessment or the MCAC recommendation. Under a recently adopted law, CMS is supposed to make such a recommendation within nine months if a technology assessment or MCAC recommendation is needed, and otherwise within six months.[52] Under the new law CMS is supposed to post the draft proposed decision and accept comments for 30 days, then promulgate a final decision within 60 days thereafter, responding to the comments.[53] If a decision is positive, codes must be assigned (if they have not already been), and payment levels determined. This generally takes an additional 180 days from the beginning of the first day of the next full calendar quarter following the decision, but in cases involving a formal request from an aggrieved party, CMS will attempt to complete the whole process within the 90-day period. The new law seems to direct that coding change (temporary if necessary) be made immediately.[54] Currently, however, the whole process can take almost three years to complete, and it will be difficult to cut it down to as short as period as is required by the new statute. Each pending national coverage determination is tracked at CMS's coverage determination homepage on the internet.[55]

Criteria

As noted already, CMS does not follow explicit written criteria in making NCDs, other than the statutory requirement that Medicare must cover all technologies that are 'reasonable and necessary'. The Medicare programme has twice proposed coverage decision criteria that would have included within this determination an explicit consideration of cost effectiveness. In 1989, the Health Care

Financing Administration, which then administered the Medicare programme, published a notice of proposed rule-making proposing to specify explicit criteria for making NCDs, including cost-effectiveness.[56] This proposal was vigorously opposed by the technology industry, and was abandoned in 1992.[57] The Medicare programme tried again to promulgate explicit coverage criteria in May of 2000, when it published a notice of intent to develop a regulation.[58] This notice proposed a process for making coverage determinations applying the following four steps:

1. Determine whether there is sufficient evidence that the technology is medically beneficial to a defined population;
2. if so, determine whether it offers a new clinical modality not currently covered by Medicare, in which case it will be covered;
3. if the item offers no new modality, ask whether it is substantially more beneficial than existing treatments (in which case it is covered) or substantially less beneficial (in which case it will not be); and
4. if it is neither substantially less nor more beneficial, determine whether it will result in equivalent or lower costs, in which case it will be covered but not otherwise.

In other words, cost would be considered, but only for technologies that offered no new modality or additional benefit. This proposal met with significant opposition, and CMS has stated that it will instead apply implicit criteria on a case-by-case basis.[59] Medicare reform legislation adopted late in 2003, however, directs the Medicare programme to articulate explicit criteria for coverage policy decisions, forcing Medicare explicitly to confront the coverage issue.[60]

It does seem clear that Medicare currently pays more attention to high-cost technologies than it does to technologies that impose minimal financial burdens on the programme. Sean Tunis, director of Medicare's coverage programme, was quoted in 2003 as stating, 'If you have a technology . . . and you are talking about potentially spending in the $1 billion range, then we're going to be much more careful about analyzing and being certain that we've got it right.'[61] This means that approval of high-cost technologies may take longer, and that they are likely to be scrutinized more closely for effectiveness. It has also meant targeting high-cost procedures more carefully. A recent NCD covering lung volume reduction surgery, for example, only approved it for patients in certain categories for which the surgery was proved effective through clinical trials.[62] Another NCD approving coverage for left ventricular assist devices was limited only to certain categories of patients and to a limited number of medical centres with experience in implanting the devices. As the Medicare drug benefit programme is implemented, it is also likely that the private health plans administering the programme will attempt to steer their members toward lower-cost generics, and may exclude from their formularies high-cost drugs that do not offer significant additional benefits. At this point, however, there is little evidence that Medicare denies coverage of effective technologies solely on the basis of cost.

RECONSIDERATIONS AND APPEALS OF COVERAGE DETERMINATIONS

A number of routes exist for challenging Medicare coverage decisions. First, the proponent of a new technology can request that an initial national coverage decision be revisited.[63] Such a request must include additional medical or scientific information not considered in the initial coverage decision, or an 'analysis of how [CMS] materially misinterpreted original information submitted by the requester'.[64] CMS essentially treats a request for reconsideration as a new request.

Alternatively, section 522 of the Medicare, Medicaid, and SCHIP Benefits Improvement and Protection Act of 2000 (BIPA) provides mechanisms for appealing both local and national coverage determinations.[65] Under Section 522 of BIPA, a national coverage determination may be appealed to the HHS Departmental Appeals Board (DAB), while a local coverage decision may be appealed to an administrative law judge (ALJ), and then further to the DAB.[66] An appeal may be brought to challenge a coverage determination, but may also be brought when CMS fails to take any action within 90 days of a formal request for a NCD, and thus is deemed to have made a decision that no coverage determination is appropriate.[67]

The only persons with standing to appeal a coverage determination under BIPA, however, are Medicare beneficiaries who need or have received the items or services that are the subject of the coverage determination.[68] Moreover, contrary to the normal practice with Medicare appeals, a beneficiary appealing a coverage determination may not assign his or her rights to appeal to a provider.[69] CMS gives public notice of each complaint, and allow 'interested parties' to submit written or brief oral statements as amici.[70] In actual practice, most coverage appeals are probably sponsored by manufacturers or providers with a stake in the particular technology, but the appeal has to be brought in the name of a particular beneficiary, who is the identified party of interest in the case. ALJs reviewing local coverage determinations and the DAB reviewing national coverage must apply a standard of reasonableness.[71] ALJs and the DAB must, therefore, defer to reasonable findings of fact, reasonable interpretations of law, and reasonable applications of fact to law by CMS and its contractors. They must also follow applicable provisions of the Social Security Act and CMS regulations and rulings, and treat as precendential any prior Board decisions.[72] The ALJ or the DAB may, however, consult with appropriate scientific and clinical experts if the record is incomplete or lacks adequate information to support the validity of the determination.[73] The ALJ or DAB may also permit discovery, and conduct a hearing. Privileged or proprietary information, however, cannot be disclosed without consent of the party who claims a right to protection of the information, and must be kept under seal if accepted as evidence.[74]

The proposed rules limit the relief that ALJs may grant in reviewing LCDs or the DAB in reviewing NCDs. All an ALJ or the DAB may do is to hold the determination to be invalid, at which point CMS will ask its contractors to readjudicate the claim without consideration of the LCD or NCD, and to review future claims without using the LCD or NCD.[75] A final decision of the DAB on a coverage appeal is a final agency action, and is subject to judicial review.[76]

A third route through which NCDs or LCDs can be challenged is by appealing discrete individual claim determinations. Historically, separate beneficiary appeal provisions existed for Part A and Part B claims.[77] BIPA created a common process for appealing both Part A and B claims, though Part C managed care determinations are still handled separately, and though the new process has not yet been fully implemented. The process involves five steps, that must each be exhausted before moving on to the next, beginning with a contractor redetermination, followed by review by a qualified independent contractor (QIC), an ALJ, the DAB, and, finally, judicial review.[78] For most purposes only a beneficiary has the right to appeal,[79] but a provider, physician or supplier may undertake an appeal as an assignee of the representative.[80]

The QIC and ALJs are bound by national coverage determinations, but not by local coverage determinations.[81] The DAB is bound by neither. BIPA requires, however, that QICs consider LCDs in making their decisions,[82] and proposed regulations require the QICs to give deference to LCDs, and state their rationale if their decision conflicts with an LCD. Although the appeals process provides a means for providers to challenge a coverage decision directly, it only decides an individual case, and has no necessary effect on other applications of a coverage policy.

All appeals must be exhausted before judicial review may be sought,[83] and there are few reported cases reviewing national and local coverage determinations. In general, the courts give considerable deference to HHS and its contractors in their coverage decisions.[84] If there is substantial evidence to support a coverage determination it will be upheld, even though the beneficiary's treating physician believes that the technology would be of benefit to the beneficiary. Local Medical review policies will be upheld, even though they vary from the LMRPs of other contractors.[85] Non-provider manufacturers may not even have standing to challenge Medicare decisions.[86; 87] Where a court believes, however, that the record simply does not support a non-coverage determination, the court may reverse the decision of HHS.[88]

CASE STUDY 1: HYPERBARIC OXYGEN THERAPY COVERAGE

Medicare currently covers hyperbaric oxygen therapy (HBOT) for 15 indications, including gas embolism, crush injuries and suturing of severed limbs, progressive necrotizing infections, preparation and preservation of compromised skin grants, and diabetic wounds of the lower extremities.[89] For several of these indications, HBOT is only covered as an adjunct to conventional therapy and/or when the disease is refractory to other forms of treatment. Medicare does not cover HBOT for 22 other listed indications, nor does it cover it for topical application. Thirty-three contractors also have local medical review policies dealing with HBOT.[90] Medicare allowed charges of approximately $76 million, and paid about $47 million for HBOT in 1998, including payments to hospitals, skilled nursing facilities, and physicians.[91]

Medicare's HBOT coverage determination has been revised several times, most recently in December 2002, effective April of 2003. In October 2000 the Office of Inspector General of HHS issued a report on the use of HBOT.[92] The report concluded that 32 per cent of beneficiaries who had received HBOT in the last six months of 1997 and the first six of 1998 received it for non-covered indications or in situations where documentation did not support the use of HBOT. An additional 11 per cent received treatments not medically necessary and 37 per cent received treatments of questionable quality. The Report was also critical of the lack of medical supervision of HBOT. The OIG recommended, inter alia, that HCFA initiate a new national coverage determination, improve policy guidance, and improve contractor oversight of HBOT.

HCFA (now CMS), more or less simultaneously received formal requests in October 2000 from the Undersea & Hyperbaric Medical Society, American College of Hyperbaric Medicine, and International Hyperbaric Medical Association for a national coverage determination. After further negotiations, this request was accepted in November of 2000.[93] In February 2001, HCFA asked the AHRQ to commission a health technology assessment (HTA) examining the appropriate use of HBOT in wound care. This HTA was received at the end of November 2001, but during the second half of 2001 and early 2002, the focus of the NCD was evolving beyond the general questions addressed by the HTA.[94] In particular HCFA came to focus on three issues: 1. whether a category of 'hypoxic' wounds could be identified that would benefit from HBOT, 2. whether indications for HBOT should be expanded to include treatment of diabetic wounds in the lower extremities, and 3. whether physician and supervision requirements should be strengthened in light of the OIG's report.[95] HCFA met with the requesters twice during the review, and requested public comment on the issues raised by the request in February of 2002.[96] It received no comments other than those of the requesters on the issue of hypoxic wounds, received one supportive comment from a physician who used HBOT on the issue of diabetic wounds, and received nine comments from physicians on the question of supervision, all supportive of the position of one of the requesters.[97]

The HTA requested of AHRQ was provided by the New England Medical Center's Evidence-Based Practice Center (NEMC EPC).[98] It reviewed earlier HTAs conducted by the Blue Cross and Blue Shield Association, and in Australia, Canada and England, and also reviewed a number of original clinical studies. The HTA concluded that evidence supported the use of HBOT for five of the ten wound indications covered by the then-current policy, and possibly supported a sixth. It found insufficient evidence to support the concept of hypoxic wounds. HCFA's final decision memo, posted in August 2002, reviewed many of the same studies and technology assessments reviewed by the NEMC EPC TA. It concluded that there was insufficient evidence supporting the notion of hypoxic wounds, but extended HBOT coverage to diabetic wounds of the lower extremities under some circumstances, and rejected additional physician supervision requirements.[99] CMS's final NCD, published in December 2002, effective April 2003, adopted these recommendations.[100]

Several observations on this process are in order. First, the CMS seems to have been in close contact with the requesters, organizations that support HBOT, throughout the process. Second, the only other participants in the process were physicians who provide HBOT services. Third, the CMS process focused closely on the available scientific evidence, extending coverage for a new indication where available studies supported coverage, rejecting a new approach (the 'hypoxic' wound approach) advocated by the requesters because of lack of evidence. Fourth, CMS did not reduce the indications currently covered by its coverage policy, even though the HTA it commissioned indicated that there was insufficient evidence to support coverage for several of these. Finally, it did not address the concerns about excessive use or inadequate supervision raised by the OIG.

CASE STUDY 2: POSITRON EMISSION TOMOGRAPHY (PET) COVERAGE

Positron emission tomography (PET) is a non-invasive diagnostic imaging procedure. A positron camera (tomograph) is used to produce cross-sectional images of the human body, which are obtained from positron emitting radioactive tracer substances (radiopharmaceuticals) that are administered intravenously to the patient.[101] Medicare has covered PET scans for some indications since 1995, and for some cancer indications since 1998. In addition to the PET NCD, two dozen local coverage determinations covering PET are currently in place.

Medicare currently covers PET scans for a dozen indications, including solitary pulmonary nodules, lung cancer, oesophageal cancer, colorectal cancer, lymphoma, melanoma, breast cancer, head and neck cancers, certain kinds of thyroid cancer, myocardial viability, refractory seizures, and perfusion of the heart. It has also issued coverage analysis recommending non-coverage for diagnosis of Alzheimers, soft-tissue sarcoma, and other types of thyroid cancer. CMS is currently considering extension of PET scan coverage for brain, cervical, ovarian, pancreatic, small-cell lung, and testicular cancers. In each case, PET is covered for only certain purposes (such as diagnosis, staging, or treatment monitoring) and subject to certain limitations, including frequency limitations. PET scanning is covered for diagnostic purposes only when it would help avoid an invasive procedure or assist in determining the optimal anatomical location for an invasive procedure, and it cannot be used for asymptomatic screening purposes, or, in most instances, for monitoring treatment. Only PET scanners with certain design characteristics are covered, and only FDA approved drugs and devices may be used.

Medicare PET scan coverage is in a state of continual evolution. Between December of 2000 and April 2003, CMS issued eight National Coverage Analyses, six of which were based on commissioned HTAs, and five of which involved MCAC review. Four were internally generated in response to a broad-based request from two doctors at the UCLA Medical Centre, one was initiated by a private party, one by a specialty society, one by a physician at Duke Medical Center, and one by HCFA. Five coverage analyses resulted in expanded coverage, three did not, though some of the recommended coverage expansions were not as broad as those initially requested.

We focus here on three of the PET scan processes: the initial general PET scan national coverage analysis process, the process dealing with breast cancer, and the process dealing with thyroid cancer. CMS initial proceeding dealing with PET scanning began in July 2000 in response to a broad-based request from two doctors at the UCLA medical centre that CMS consider coverage of PET scans for a wide variety of indications.[102] HCFA requested an HTA from AHRQ, which referred the matter to the NEMC EPC. HCFA also met to discuss the matter with the National Cancer Institute. The

EPC HTA found significant limitations in studies with respect to indications for which PET was not currently covered.[103] This HTA was referred to the MCAC Executive Committee, which considered it at its November 2000 meeting.[104] The MCAC heard from nine speakers, including four advocates of PET technology, a representative of the FDA, and representatives of entities that had performed technology assessments on PET, including the BC/BS TEC, the Veterans Administration, and EPC. In the discussion that followed, the MCAC did not take any formal votes on PET coverage, though the minutes of the meeting reflect a general consensus that PET could be useful for diagnosing local recurrence of colorectal cancer.

On 15 December 2000, CMS published a lengthy decision memorandum on PET scan coverage, based on the HTAs it had received.[105] This decision memorandum authorized extending PET scan coverage under some circumstances for diagnosis, staging, or monitoring of esophageal cancer, colorectal cancer, malignant melanoma, head and neck cancers; for determining myocardial viability for coronary revascularization; and for managing recurrent seizures.

The breast cancer process was initiated by CMS in response to the same general request from two doctors for PET coverage expansion.[106] CMS referred the request to AHRQ for a technology assessment in March of 2001. The HTA was again conducted by the BC/BS TEC. The technology assessment focused on whether the use of PET could improve health outcomes for:

• initial diagnosis of breast cancer;
• initial staging of axillary lymph nodes;
• detection of locoregional recurrence or distant metastasis/ recurrence; and
• evaluating response to treatment.[107]

As to each of these issues, the TEC HTA concluded that there was insufficient evidence to support coverage.

The HTA was next considered by the MCAC Diagnostic Imaging Panel at its June 2001 meeting. The panel ultimately voted on a somewhat different series of six questions:

1. Is there adequate evidence that PET can improve health outcomes when used to decide whether to perform a

biopsy in patients with an abnormal mammogram or palpable mass?

2. Is there adequate evidence that PET can improve health outcomes by leading to earlier and more accurate diagnosis of breast cancer compared to mammography and other routine imaging procedures?

3. Is there adequate evidence that PET improves health outcomes when used to decide whether to perform axillary lymph node dissection?

4. Is there adequate evidence that PET improves health outcomes as an adjunct to standard staging tests in detecting locoregional recurrence or distant metastasises/ recurrence when results from other tests are inconclusive?

5. Is there adequate evidence that PET improves health outcomes as a replacement for standard staging tests in detecting locoregional recurrence or distant metastasises recurrence?

6. Is there adequate evidence that PET can improve health outcomes by providing either a more accurate or earlier determination of tumor response to treatment compared to the use of conventional response criteria which may rely upon clinical exam and/or standard imaging tests, such as CT, MRI or bone scan?[108]

The MCAC panel was led by a radiologist, but was composed primarily of physicians from other specialties and health services researchers. The panel received a report on the HTA, and then heard testimony from one of the physician requesters, a manufacturer spokesman, a representative of the American Society of Clinical Oncology, a representative of the Society of Nuclear Medicine of the American College of Radiology, a breast cancer survivor and member of the National Breast Cancer Coalition (who brought a petition with over 1000 signatures), a physician-president of a technology company, and a professor of nuclear medicine, all of whom spoke in favour of coverage expansion. The panel voted negatively and unanimously on questions 1, 2, 3, 5, and 6, voting positively only on question 4, with five votes in favour and one abstention.[109] The position of the panel was upheld by the MCAC executive committee.

In its final coverage analysis decision memorandum, CMS rejected PET scans for initial diagnosis of breast cancer and for initial staging of axillary lymph nodes, consistent with the HTA and MCAC recommendation.[110] It also concluded, consistent with the MCAC recommendation but contrary to the HTA, that PET is reasonable and necessary when used as an adjunct to other conventional anatomical imaging modalities in the detection of locoregional recurrence or distant metastasis. Finally, CMS concluded, contrary to both the HTA and the MCAC recommendation, that PET scanning should be covered for monitoring tumor response during therapy.

The third coverage analysis was initiated by a request for reconsideration from the American Thyroid Association, which asked that CMS reconsider its earlier refusal to cover FDG PET scans for the management of thyroid cancer.[111] CMS referred the matter to the AHRQ for a TA, which was provided by the NEMC EPC. The EPC was asked to address several questions:

• What is the test performance of FDG PET for localization or staging of previously treated thyroid cancer suspected to be metastatic for which standard imaging modalities have failed to localize metastatic lesions or are thought not to be helpful to locate metastatic disease?
• In the same population, what is the evidence that FDG PET affects health outcomes or alters management?
• What is the test performance and effect on clinical management of FDG PET for initial, pre-treatment, staging of patients with differentiated thyroid cancer types that commonly do not take up radioiodine?[112]

The EPC performed a literature search, and concluded that studies of the use of PET for thyroid cancer were small and of poor quality, and did not support extension of coverage.[113] The HTA was referred to the MCAC, which apparently also did not make any recommendations, other than that coverage decisions should be made on solid evidence.[114] After reviewing additional meta-analyses, guidelines from specialty organizations, and the expert opinions of three physicians who reviewed the HTA, CMS reached its own conclusions:

After reviewing the TA and our literature review, CMS was unable to find studies of sufficient quality in design and sample size to define the diagnostic characteristics of FDG PET in identifying metastatic disease in patients with treated differentiated thyroid cancer of follicular cell origin, elevated Tg and negative I-131 WBS. However, though studies on the effects of FDG PET in altering clinical management were also not optimal, they did demonstrate definite trends in prompting providers to modify therapy and, in a few studies, reported cure. In addition, guidelines from AACE/AAES [specialty societies], though not critically appraising the evidence, do support the use of FDG PET for this indication, as do the experts we polled. In addition, in this group of patients with elevated tumor markers and negative standard imaging tests, there are no other options for identifying disease.[115]

CMS decided to cover PET for restaging of recurrent or residual thyroid cancer of follicular cell origin in patients with serum thyroglobulin levels above 10 ng/ml, where standard imaging tests have failed to localize metastatic or recurrent disease. It decided not to cover PET for the other thyroid cancers that it was considering, including cancer of medullary cell origin.

Some observations can be drawn from this partial exploration of CMS experience with PET scanning. First, as a major diagnostic imaging technology matures, and increasing evidence accumulates as to its use in various circumstances, continual pressure will be applied to CMS to expand Medicare coverage for the technology. Second, in each instance, the initial technology assessment commissioned by CMS through AHRQ concluded that there was insufficient evidence to support expansion of coverage, evidencing a serious attempt to discern whether an evidence-base in fact existed for expanding coverage. Third, in each instance, all speakers who appeared before the MCAC (other than presenters of commissioned technology analyses) were advocates of expansion of coverage, including representatives of manufacturers, specialty societies, professionals who offered the service, or, in one instance, patient groups. No one appeared to advocate restriction on coverage. This supports the notion that all the interest-group pressure is on CMS to expand, not to limit coverage. Finally, in each instance CMS expanded coverage beyond that recommended by the HTA, or even the MCAC, suggesting that CMS was sensitive to this pressure.

CONCLUSIONS

When one views the medicare coverage process as a whole through our public choice lens, several characteristics of the process become clear. First, there are multiple entry points into the process: a manufacturer may seek an NCD, an LCD, or both simultaneously, or may sometimes get the technology covered without any explicit coverage decision at all. A manufacturer may obtain a new HCPCS code, seek an LCD in high-volume markets, simply encourage providers to bill for the technology without an LCD in low-volume markets, and eventually, once the technology begins to become accepted, apply for an NCD to assure national coverage. The proponent of a technology used in a hospital setting may seek a technology pass through (an additional payment for a new technology), or may simply attempt to price and market the technology within the framework of existing payment categories. These multiple points of entry give those who produce technologies tremendous flexibility, and many opportunities to game the system. Conversely, they make it very difficult for CMS to control technology diffusion.

A second characteristic of the system is that it is very transparent. At every step of the coverage determination process, it can be tracked on the internet. At different points, drafts must be made available to the public, including technology advocates. This allows proponents of a new technology to intervene more aggressively when they see things going badly. Because of the flexibility that proponents gain from multiple processes, moreover, proponents can attempt to stall or speed up the process at one level, depending on whether it seems to be proceeding better or worse than at another level.[116]

Third, the process is porous and participatory. Hearings are held, opportunities are given for public comment, and, if technology proponents fail at one level, multiple routes are available for reconsideration and appeal. In the end, coverage decisions are made by CMS, which is a federal agency open to pressure both from the Secretary of Health and Human Services (and, ultimately the White House), and from Congress. Only ALJs and the DAB are protected from *ex parte* comments during appeals; CMS is not, and in relation to the technologies we studied meetings with the industry were common. Thus proponents of technologies can not only track the progress of a decision because of the transparency of the process, they also have multiple levers to take action if they see the process going astray.

Of course, the process is open to opponents as well as proponents of new technologies, to those who want to hold the line on spending as well as those who oppose it. But they seem to be silent. There was no evidence of participation of non-advocates in the processes we studied. Persons whom I interviewed at CMS did not remember receiving comments from those opposed to coverage. Even competitors seem to be silent.

Finally, the Medicare coverage system has not proved amenable to controlling programme costs. In 1989, HCFA articulated a belief that the statutory 'reasonable and necessary' standard granted HCFA authority to consider the fiscal impact of a technology on the Medicare programme. The opposition this statement provoked from technology advocates stalled attempts to articulate coverage criteria for a decade,[117] but in the late 1990s technology advocates began to conclude that they would be better off with articulated criteria, and pushed HCFA again for publishing proposed rules.[118] When HCFA in 2000 published criteria that contained the somewhat vaguer concept of 'added value', it again faced opposition from the industry.[119] In the end, CMS (replacing HCFA) seems to have decided to proceed with technology assessment without published criteria, though the recent Medicare Modernization Act may change this. The processes that we studied here, however, seem to be entirely focused on evidence of efficacy, and not to consider cost, except to the extent that they are focused on high-cost technologies.

In the end, therefore, the Medicare process, like much of the rest of the health care system of the United States, seems well suited for maximizing technological innovation and providing access to new technology, and seems poorly suited for making cost–benefit calculi with respect to new technologies.

References

1 United States Census Bureau (2002), *Health Insurance Coverage, 2001.* < landview.census.gov/hhes/hlthins/hlthin01/hlth01asc.html > (accessed 6 Mar. 2004).
2 G.F. Anderson, et al. (2003), It's the Prices Stupid: Why the United States is So Different from Other Countries, *Health Affairs*, 22(3): 89–105.
3 S. Heffler, et al. (2004), 'Health spending projections, 2003–2013', *Health Affairs Web Exclusive*. < content.healthaffairs.org/cgi/reprint/hlthaff.w4.79v1.pdf > (accessed 6 Mar. 2004).
4 M.A. Hall and G.F. Anderson (1992), 'Health Insurer's Assessment

of Medical Necessity', *University of Pennsylvania Law Review*, 140(5): 1637–712.
5 P.E. Morh, P.J. Neumann, and S. Bausch (2003), *Paying for New Medical Technology: Lessons for the Medicare Program from Other Large Health Care Purchasers*. Washington: MedPac.
6 R.A. Rettig (1997), *Health Care in Transition: Technology Assessment in the Private Sector*. Santa Monica: Rand.
7 A.M. Garber (2001), 'Evidence-Based Coverage Policy', *Health Affairs*, 20(5): 62–82.
8 Garber (2001), pp. 69–70.
9 Rettig (1997), chapter 3.
10 42 U.S.C. § 1395w-22(a)(1).
11 General Accounting Office (2003), *Divided Authority for Policies on Coverage of Procedures and Devices Results in Inequities*. Washington: GAO.
12 42 U.S.C. § 13905y(a)(1)(A).
13 General Accounting Office (2003), p. 6.
14 S.B. Foote (2003), 'Focus on Locus: Evolution of Medicare's Local Coverage Policy', *Health Affairs*, 22(4), 137–46.
15 Local coverage determinations can be found at < www.cms.gov/mcd/search.asp > (assessed 6 Mar. 2004).
16 42 U.S.C. § 1396ww(d).
17 Center for Medicare and Medicaid Services (CMS) (2003a), 'Final rule for 2003, PPS for inpatient hospital services', 67 *Fed. Reg.* 49982, 49985.
18 DRG weights and definitions are adjusted over time to accommodate technological advances. See GAO, 'Technology Assessment and Medical Coverage Decisions', Fact Sheet, GAO/HEHS-94-195FS. Also, a special pass-through payment system has been created for dealing in the short-term with extraordinarily expensive technologies.
19 42 U.S.C. § 1395l(t)(2)(B).
20 CMS (2002a), *Procedures for Coding and Payment Determinations for Clinical Laboratory Tests and for Durable Medical Equipment*. < www.cms.hhs.gov/medicare/hcpcs/codpayproc.asp > (accessed 6 Mar. 2004). Codes can be temporary or permanent and existing codes can also be revised.
21 Lewin Group (2000), *The Medicare Payment Process and Patient Access to Technology*. Washington: AdvaMed.
22 General Accounting Office (2003), pp. 11–22.
23 CMS (2003b), *Medicare Program Integrity Manual: Local Medical Review Policy*. < www.cms.hhs.gov/manuals/108_pim/pim83c13. pdf > (accessed 6 Mar. 2004).
24 42 C.F.R. § 400.202.
25 General Accounting Office (2003), p. 40.
26 CMS (2003b), sec. 5.1.C.
27 CMS (2003b), sec. 7.1.

28　42 U.S.C. § 1395y(l)(5).
29　CMS (2003b), secs. 7.2 and 7.3.
30　CMS (2003b), sec. 7.4.1.
31　CMS (2003b), sec. 7.4.3.
32　D.J. Grinstead (2002), 'Evolution of Medicare's Coverage Policy-Making Process', in E.D. Kinney (ed.), *Guide to Medicare Coverage Decision-Making and Appeals*. Chicago: American Bar Association.
33　E.D. Kinney (2004), Medicare Coverage Decision Making and Appeal Procedures: Can Process Meet the Challenge of New Medical Technology? *Washington and Lee Law Review*, 60(4): 1461–512.
34　S.B. Foote (2002), 'Why Medicare Cannot Promulgate a National Coverage Rule: A Case of Regula Mortis', *Journal of Health Politics, Policy and Law*, 27(5): 707–30.
35　CMS (2003c), 'Notice, Revised Process for Making National Coverage Determinations', 68 *Fed. Reg.* 55634.
36　CMS (2000a), 'Notice of Intent to Publish a Proposed Rule, Criteria for Making Coverage Decisions', 65 *Fed. Reg.* 31124.
37　General Accounting Office (2003), pp. 28–9.
38　42 U.S.C. § 1395y(l)(1)(1).
39　CMS (2003c).
40　G. Bagley (2002), 'Current Procedures and Standards for Making National Coverage Decisions', in E.D. Kinney (ed.), *Guide to Medicare Coverage Decision-Making and Appeals*. Chicago: American Bar Association, p. 22.
41　The CMS policy on investigational devices is found at 42 C.F.R. § 405.205. Under recent legislation, Medicare also covers routine cousts associated with clinical trials for certain medical devices. 42 U.S.C. § 1395y(m).
42　CMS (2003c), p. 55637.
43　42 U.S.C. § 1395ff(f)(4)(A).
44　42 U.S.C. § 1395ff(f))(4)(B).
45　42 U.S.C. § 1395y(l)(4).
46　CMS (2002b), 'Notice, Renewal and Amendment of the Charter for the Medicare Coverage Advisory Committee', 67 *Fed. Reg.* 79109.
47　CMS (2003c), p. 55640.
48　42 U.S.C. § 1395y(l)(3)(C)(iv).
49　MCAC Executive Committee (2001), *Recommendations for Evaluating Effectiveness*. < www.cms.gov/mcac/8b1-i9.asp > (accessed 6 Mar. 2004).
50　CMS (2003c), p. 55639.
51　Bagley (2002), pp. 26–7.
52　42 U.S.C. § 1395y(l)(2).
53　42 U.S.C. § 1395y(l)(3).
54　42 U.S.C. § 1395y(l)(3)(C)(iv).
55　CMS (2004), *National Coverage Determinations Index*. < www.cms. gov/ncd/ncdindexlist.asp > (accessed 6 Mar. 2004).

56 Health Care Financing Administration (1989), 'Criteria and Procedures for Making Medical Services Coverage Decisions That Relate to Health Care Technology', 54 *Fed. Reg.* 4302.
57 Foote (2002), pp. 712–20.
58 65 *Fed. Reg.* 31,124 (16 May 2000).
59 General Accounting Office (2003).
60 See, discussing the difficult of coming up with criteria, S.R. Tunis (2004), 'Why Medicare Has Not Established Criteria for Coverage Decisions', *New England Journal of Medicine*, 340(21): 2197–8.
61 L. McGinley and T.M. Burton (2003), 'Medicare Panel to Debate Use of Defribillator', *Wall Street Journal*, 12 Feb., at B1.
62 See M.R. Gillick (2004), 'Medicare Coverage for Technological Interventions – Time for New Criteria?' *New England Journal of Medicine*, 350(21): 2199–203.
63 CMS (2003c), pp. 55638–9.
64 CMS (2003c), pp. 55638–9.
65 42 U.S.C. § 1395ff(f).
66 42 U.S.C. § 1395ff(f)(1) & (2).
67 42 U.S.C. § 1395ff(f)(4)(B).
68 42 C.F.R. § 426.110.
69 42 C.F.R. § 426.320 (b).
70 42 C.F.R. §§ 426.510(f), 426.513.
71 42 C.F.R. §§ 426.431, 426.531.
72 42 C.F.R. §§ 426.431(a)(4), (c), 426.531 (a)(4), (c).
73 42 C.F.R. §§ 426.405(c)(6), 426.505(c)(6).
74 42 C.F.R. §§ 426.432(f), 426.440(c), 426.532(f), 426.540(c).
75 42 C.F.R. §§ 426.455, 426.460, 426.555, 426.560.
76 42 C.F.R. § 426.560(a).
77 E.D. Kinney (2002), 'Medicare Beneficiary Appeals Processes', in E.D. Kinney (ed.), *Guide to Medicare Coverage Decision-Making and Appeals*. Chicago: American Bar Association, pp. 65–8.
78 42 U.S.C. § 1395ff(b)(1), (c) & (d).
79 42 U.S.C. § 1395ff(b)(1)(B).
80 42 U.S.C. § 1395ff(b)(1)(C).
81 See CMS (2002), Proposed Rules, Changes to the Medicare Claims Appeal Procedures, 67 *Fed. Reg.* 69312, 69325 (2002).
82 42 U.S.C. § 1395ff(c)(B)(ii).
83 *Heckler* v. *Ringer*, 466 U.S. 602 (1984).
84 *Bosko* v. *Shalala*, 995 F.Supp. 580 (W.D. Pa. 1996).
85 *Arruejo* v. *Thompson*, 2001 WL 1563699 (E.D.N.Y. 2001).
86 *TAP Pharmaceuticals* v. *U.S. Dept. of Health & Human Servs.*, 163 F.2d 199 (4th Cir. 1998).
87 But see *Amgen* v. *Smith*, 357 F.3d 103 (D.C.Cir. 2004) (Holding that manufacturers do have standing to challenge a CMS action affecting payments under the Outpatient Prospective Payment System, but that

the CMS decision was not subject to judicial review because of statutory preclusion).

88 *Aitkin* v. *Shalala*, 986 F.Supp. 57 (D. Mass. 1997).

89 CMS (2002d), *Medicare Coverage Issues Manual*, sec, 35.10. < www.cms.hhs.gov/manuals/06_cim/ci35.asp#_35_10 > (accessed 6 Mar. 2004).

90 < www.cms.gov/mcd/results.asp?show = all&t = 200372153015 >

91 DHHS (2000), Office of Inspector General, *Hyperbaric Oxygen Therapy: Its Use and Appropriateness.* Washington: OIG.

92 DHHS (2000).

93 CMS (2003d), *National Coverage Analysis, Hyperbaric Oxygen Therapy for Hypoxic Wounds and Diabetic Wounds of the Lower Extremities, Tracking Sheet.* < www.cms.gov/ncdr/memo.asp?id = 37 > (accessed 6 Mar. 2004).

94 C. Wang (2001), *Medicare Coverage Policy – NCDs, Hyperbaric Oxygen Therapy in Treatment of Hypoxic Wounds and Diabetic Wounds of the Lower Extremities, Technology Assessment.* < www.cms.gov/coverage/download/8b3-mm2.pdf > (accessed 6 Mar. 2004).

95 CMS (2002e), *National Coverage Analysis, Hyperbaric Oxygen Therapy for Hypoxic Wounds and Diabetic Wounds of the Lower Extremities, Decision Memorandum.* < www.cms.gov/ncdr/memo.asp?id = 37 > (accessed 6 Mar. 2004).

96 CMS (2003d).

97 CMS (2002e).

98 Wang (2001).

99 CMS (2002e).

100 CMS (2003e), *National Coverage Determination, Hyperbaric Oxygen Therapy.* < www.cms.hhs.gov/ncdr/memo.asp?id = 37 > (accessed 6 Mar. 2004)

101 CMS (2003f), *National Coverage Determination, Positron Emission Tomography (PET) Scans.* < www.cms.gov/ncd/searchdisplay. asp? NCD_ID = 211&NCD_vrsn_num = 2 > (accessed 6 Mar. 2004).

102 CMS (2003g), *National Coverage Analysis, Positron Emission Tomography (FDG), Tracking Sheet.* < www.cms.gov/ncdr/tracking sheet. asp?id = 85 > (accessed 6 Mar. 2004).

103 CMS (2000b), *National Coverage Analysis, Positron Emission Tomography, Decision Memorandum,* < www.cms.gov/ncdr/memo.asp?id = 85 > (accessed 6 Mar. 2004).

104 MCAC, Executive Committee (2000), *Positron Emission Tomography (FDG), Minutes of 7 November 2000 Meeting.* < www.cms.gov/mcac/ 8b1-i21.asp > (accessed 6 Mar.2003).

105 CMS (2000b).

106 CMS (2003h), *National Coverage Analysis, Positron Emission Tomography (FDG) for Breast Cancer, Decision Memorandum* < www.cms.gov/ncdr/memo.asp?id = 71 > (Accessed 6 Mar. 2004).

107 CMS (2003h).
108 CMS (2003h).
109 MCAC (2001), *Minutes, Diagnostic Imaging Panel, Positron Emission Tomography (FDG) for Breast Cancer, 19 June 2001* < www.cms.gov/mcac/8b1-g6.asp > (accessed 3 Mar. 2004).
110 CMS (2003h).
111 CMS (2003i), *National Coverage Analysis, Positron Emission Tomography (FDG) for Thyroid Cancer, Decision Memorandum* < www.cms.gov/ncdr/memo.asp?id = 70 > (accessed 3 Mar. 2004).
112 CMS (2003i).
113 E. Balk and J. Lau (2002), *Technology Assessment, Systematic Review of Positron Emission Tomography for Follow-up of Treated Thyroid Cancer*. < www.cms.gov/ncdr/tadetails.asp?id = 70 > (accessed 6 Mar. 2004).
114 CMS (2003i).
115 CMS (2003i).
116 Thus the technology industry has successfully lobbied Congress and the executive, and used litigation, over the past decade and a half alternatively to push for or to oppose the promulgation of rules at the national level to establish criteria for coverage decisions, depending on whether they thought a stronger national presence in coverage policy would strengthen or weaken their hand. Foote (2002), pp. 712–20.
117 Foote (2002), pp. 714–15.
118 Foote (2002), pp. 717–19.
119 Foote (2002), pp. 719–20.

10

WHAT CAN WE LEARN FROM OUR COUNTRY STUDIES?

Timothy Stoltzfus Jost

Having now considered the approaches that each of our eight case-study countries have taken to using technology assessment for establishing coverage policy in public health insurance programmes, we turn now to comparative analysis. In this chapter, we will first compare the institutions and procedures used by our case-study countries for coverage determinations. We will then focus on our specific case-study technologies, considering what we can learn from the experience of our countries with these technologies. In the next and final chapter we will reflect more globally on what we can learn from the experience of our countries with the use of HTA for setting coverage policy.

TECHNOLOGY ASSESSMENT FOR SETTING COVERAGE POLICY: INSTITUTIONS AND PROCEDURES

Each of our study countries uses HTA to establish coverage policy, though the institutions and procedures through which it is used vary dramatically from country to country. Some, such as Germany, Switzerland, England, Germany, and the Medicare programme in the US, use HTA for establishing coverage policy for all categories of health care products and services that are covered by their public insurance programme.[1] Others, including Australia and the Netherlands, limit the use of HTA for coverage assessment at the national level to particular categories, such as pharmaceuticals and, in Australia, some medical procedures. Most programmes focus almost exclusively on new products or services, though most, including Germany, the US Medicare program, Switzerland, Ontario, Australia, and England, have also on occasion reviewed coverage of existing services.

In some countries, including Germany (for ambulatory care), and Australia and the Netherlands (for drugs), HTA is mandatory – products or services must first be assessed and approved for coverage before the programme will pay for them. In Switzerland, all new medical services are subject to a screening procedure, and those found to be controversial must undergo an evaluation based on HTA information. In England, assessment is not necessary before a product or service can be covered, but if the National Institute for Clinical Excellence (NICE) recommends NHS coverage of a health intervention, it must 'normally' be made available by a local primary care trust within three months. In the US Medicare programme, products and services may be provided by hospitals (which are paid on a global, per-admission basis) without an explicit coverage decision, and even new professional services or medical equipment, which are supposed to be governed by coverage policies, are sometimes covered without an explicit decision. In Spain, decisions of the regional HTA authorities remain advisory.

In several countries, including the US, England, Spain, and Switzerland, national coverage decisions are supplemented by local or regional decisions, and coverage may vary between different parts of the country. Indeed, in Canada, Spain, and England most binding coverage decisions are made at the provincial, regional, or local level. Finally, in most of our countries, part of the population is covered by private insurance (in Germany, the Netherlands, and the US in particular), or by other public insurance programmes (the US); thus coverage decisions do not necessarily affect the entire population.[2] And in all of our countries, technologies that are not covered by public programmes can be purchased privately if they are otherwise approved for marketing.

The nature and composition of the entities that make coverage policy based on HTA vary significantly among our sample countries. Here, not surprisingly, one major dividing line is between countries that have Beveridge-model national health services and those that have Bismarck-model social insurance programmes. In England, Australia, and Spain, coverage policy is effectively established by independent agencies usually appointed by the government (in Spain by regional governments).[3] In Switzerland and Germany, Bismarck-model social insurance countries, the commissions that establish coverage policy are corporatist institutions, whose members represent interest groups involved in the operation of the social insurance programme. In both countries, the decisions of these bodies are in fact advisory, with final decisions being made by the government, but the decisions of these bodies usually prevail. But divisions among the countries are in fact more complex. In the Netherlands, another social insurance country, decisions are made by the Health Care Insurance Board (CVS) and the Committee for Pharmaceutical Help (CFH), which are both independent bodies appointed by the Ministry, though the members of the CFH represent medical professionals and pharmacists. Coverage determinations in the US Medicare programme are made by government, but local coverage determinations are made by contractors, which are effectively private insurance companies making decisions for the government under contract. Ontario, Canada, which has a tax-financed system, seems in general to prefer having quasi-independent bodies do HTA, with the final say in the government. For example, the decision whether or not to cover a physician service seems to be largely made by a Physician Services Committee (PSC) jointly staffed by the Ontario Medical Association (OMA) and the Ontario Ministry of Health, though the final decision is made by the Ministry of Health.

In most of our countries, expert advisory bodies play a significant role in coverage determination processes. As already mentioned, both the German and Swiss committees are themselves advisory to the Ministry of Health. This is also true of the Australian Pharmaceutical Benefits Advisory Committee (PBAC) and Medical Services Advisory Committee (MSAC). The other countries also have expert advisory committees as well. These may be standing committees or may be constituted for particular assessments. In the United States the Medicare Coverage Advisory Committee (MCAC) is a standing committee of experts to which Center for Medicare and Medicaid Services (CMS) may turn for advice, particularly involving complex cases. In England, the NICE constitutes for each coverage determination, first a committee of 'consultees' composed of experts representing interest groups to help define the scope of an appraisal, and then an expert 'appraisal committee' to formulate an appraisal document, which serves in turn as a recommendation to NICE. In the Netherlands, the CVZ is advised by the CFH, a standing committee of experts, for assessing drugs for coverage. In Australia, the MSAC (again, itself technically an advisory Committee) appoints expert advisory committees on an ad hoc basis to assist it with assessing technologies. In Ontario, the Central Tariff Committee of the OMA provides reports on benefits to the PSC, which in turn advises the Ministry. Similarly, through the Common Drug Review process, the Canadian Coordinating Office for Health Technology Assessment (CCOHTA) will now provide reports on benefits to the various provincial governments on the benefits of pharmaceuticals.

The involvement of expert committees or corporatist institutions in technology assessment presents the problem of conflict of interest. A technology manufacturer should obviously not be represented on a committee that assesses one of its technologies, and neither should the competitor of that manufacturer. Representatives of providers (such as hospitals) who might stand to benefit from the use of new technologies; disease-specific patient groups; and health insurance funds (who must, on the one hand, pay for a new technology, but, on the other, may be able to attract members through expanded coverage) present more complex conflict situations.

Some of our countries take these issues into account. Manufacturers and patients do each have a representative on MCAC assessment panels in the US Medicare programme, but do not have voting rights. Similarly, the ESC advisory panel that advises the Australian PBAC on drug issues includes only a non-voting member from the drug manufacturers association, and advisory committee members refrain from taking part in the consideration when the product of any company, in which they have a financial interest, is discussed. In Germany, the Netherlands, Canada, England, and Switzerland, the expert committees or subcommittees that conduct or review technology appraisals do not include representatives of technology manufacturers. The German and Swiss coverage commissions do, however, include provider and health insurance fund representatives, and the NICE consultees, which establish the scope of NICE assessments, even include manufacturer representatives. The MSAC in Australia is advised by panels of experts who may have a direct or indirect financial interest in technologies under review. In each of our countries, however, it is ultimately the government that makes final coverage decisions, and in several countries experience has shown that the government is amenable to political pressure from manufacturers or patient groups in the one hand, or to budget pressures on the other.

The answer to the question of who has standing to initiate an assessment varies from country to country. In those countries where technology assessment is a necessary prerequisite to coverage, technology manufacturers or other sponsors usually have the opportunity to apply for coverage. This is true in the United States, Switzerland, Australia, and the Netherlands. Indeed, in the Netherlands, only manufactures have standing to request coverage. In Spain, Canada, the US, Australia, and England, requests for appraisals can come from other sources as well, including patients, providers or insurers. Between 1998 and 2000, 40 per cent of the applications received by the Australian MSAC came from industry, 31 per cent from a professional medical organization, and 29 per cent from individuals.

In Germany and Switzerland (and in Ontario, Canada, as to medical procedures) the corporatist institutions serve as gatekeepers to the technology assessment process. In Germany, a new technology cannot be covered out of hospital without a coverage determination, and the determination process can only be initiated by the sickness funds or by the insurance doctor's organizations. In Switzerland, by contrast, a new technology will be covered unless the application for coverage is contested by either the insurance fund or medical association. In Ontario, proposals to list new technologies, or to delist existing ones, are sourced in the Ontario Medical Association, the representative organization for physicians. In England, requests for assessment by NICE are formally initiated by the Department of Health, but the Department is in turn advised by an Advisory Committee on Topic Selection, a 30-member committee which represents the government and other stakeholders.

In most of our countries coverage determinations are usually reactive. Appraisal bodies respond to a request for an assessment. Only in a few places, England, some of the Spanish regions, and to some extent in the US and Switzerland, is 'horizon scanning' conducted proactively to identify new technologies that merit assessment.

The procedures followed by the various appraisal groups vary from highly structured to quite informal. The US Medicare process, for example, is a multi-stage process with time limits (not always strictly observed) at each step. Recent legislation has considerably tightened up these limits. The Australian MSAC and Spanish regional committee processes, by contrast, appear quite flexible. Most countries contemplate a multi-step process that usually involves a screening process to make sure the application is complete, review of the application by commission staff, review and recommendation by an expert committee, and preliminary and final coverage determinations. The process also sometimes involves the commissioning or acquisition of an external technology assessment. Provision may be made during the process for comments by the technology sponsor, or, in a few instances, as in the US or England, by the public.

The Dutch process, for example, involves initial screening by the Ministry to assure that the application is complete, the development of a concept paper by CFH expert staff (which is reviewed by the Ministry and applicant for comments), review by the CFH expert committee, which may submit questions to the applicant, and finally a recommendation from the CFH/CVZ to the Ministry. The Ministry makes the final decision, following further comment from the applicant and perhaps other stakeholders. MSAC review in Australia begins with consideration of an application within the Ministry of Health and Ageing. If the Ministry decides to refer the application to the MSAC for assessment, the MSAC next commissions an independent evidence-based HTA, and then appoints a specialist Advisory Panel to review the application and HTA. The MSAC then formulates a recommendation with respect to whether the technology should be funded or not (or funded only on an interim basis), which is forwarded to the Ministry accompanied by policy recommendations from the department.

The procedure that has been followed by the German Federal Committee begins with a decision to assess a technology and solicitation of comments from external experts. The technology is then reviewed by an expert subcommittee, which formulates a formal Health Technology Assessment report. This report is submitted to the Federal Committee, which publishes a final report that serves as a recommendation on coverage to the Ministry. Finally, the NICE process begins with proposals for topics to study by an Advisory Committee on Topic Selection, then is 'scoped' for assessment by NICE, which receives evidence by interested parties, 'consultees' or other invited 'commentators'. Then assesses the technology through an expert 'appraisal committee', which first proposes an appraisal consultation document. Then, after the appraisal committee receives comments from consultees and commentators, it produces a final appraisal document, which NICE reviews, after further opportunity for comment, and relies on to formulate guidance.

Coverage processes in general seem to be investigational as opposed to adversarial in nature. An attempt is made to assess scientifically the proposed technology without a predisposition toward coverage or non-coverage, rather than requiring the proponent of a technology to meet a particular burden of proof in the face of opposition from a party contesting coverage. In some countries, notably Australia, the procedure is viewed as somewhat more adversarial, though the process is described in our Australian chapter as really more a process of bargaining. Opportunities for appeal vary from country to country. The United States is most generous, offering several paths for appeal, and allowing challenges to the substance of coverage decisions, and not just to the procedures through which they were formulated. In Germany appeals to the Ministry are only available for procedural errors, while in the Netherlands an appeal can only be brought if there is new information with respect to the therapeutic value of the drug. Appeals in England are available only if NICE failed to act fairly or in accordance with its own procedures, the decision is perverse, or NICE exceeded its powers. Patients who are denied services in Ontario, or who face extraordinarily long waits, can appeal to an independent tribunal, the Health Services Appeal and Review Board.

In most countries coverage denials can be contested in court. In some countries these challenges can be brought by the applicant denied coverage, but in most countries a patient who needs a product or service has the right to appeal a coverage denial as well. In Germany and Switzerland, cases involving coverage are quite common, though in Switzerland they rarely involve new technologies. In Australia and the Netherlands such litigation is apparently unusual and rarely successful. In the US Medicare system, appeals of individual technology coverage decisions are very common, but there are many layers of administrative review through which an appeal must wend its way before judicial review becomes available, and thus judicial review is quite uncommon. There is no appellate review of the decisions of the Spanish regional technology assessment bodies. Even when formal judicial processes for appeal are not available, however, technology sponsors may still find a way to challenge a decision in court, as is demonstrated in the Canadian situation where Bristol-Myers Squibb sued (unsuccessfully) to block release of a report from the Canadian Coordinating Office for Health Technology Assessment arguing 'negligent misstatement'.

On the whole, the processes reviewed here are not very transparent. The most transparent is the American system, where assessment processes are tracked at each stage on the web, and opportunities for public comment are offered at several stages. England also seems to be moving toward a more transparent process, though comments are only accepted from invited participants in the process, who are often interested parties, such as technology sponsors, providers, or patient groups. By contrast, the German, Dutch, and Swiss processes take place largely behind closed doors. Reports are published, and comments are accepted at points in the process, but the decision-making processes are not visible to the public. If anyone has access to information regarding an assessment process, it is usually the proponent. In Australia, the proponent of a technology, and only the proponent, has the right to comment on draft assessment papers. Similarly in Switzerland, only the applicant receives a written summary of the reasons supporting the Federal Department of Home Affairs coverage decision.

Concerns of commercial confidentiality have also stood in the way of transparency, particularly where drugs are concerned. Submissions to the Australian Pharmaceutical Benefits Advisory Committee, commentaries on the submissions, and even, until recently, the identity of drugs being considered, have been kept confidential. Only since 1999 has the PBAC published the reasons supporting its agreement to list a drug, and since 2003 its decisions not to list a drug. Confidentiality concerns have also limited the information that can be disclosed by CMS in the US.

Most countries base coverage decisions on the criteria of efficacy, effectiveness, and medical necessity. These terms may be defined comparatively – a product or service may only be approved for coverage if it is as or more effective than existing technologies. In several countries there is a conscious effort to avoid the appearance of rationing, however, and all effective technologies will be covered. The authors of our German report, for example, report the findings of their own research which demonstrates that only effectiveness, and not cost, is considered in the German process. The United States has also been reluctant to embrace cost as a concern in coverage policy, though more expensive technologies get closer attention than less expensive technologies.

In some countries, however, there is more openness to consideration of economic concerns. This is clearly true in Australia, and will soon be true in the Netherlands. Even in Australia, however, imatinib (also called Glivec® or Gleevac®), has been covered despite its high cost per case and a comparatively high cost-effectiveness ratio because it was the only drug available for treating CML for some patients, as is discussed more fully below. NICE in England also takes cost per quality adjusted life year (QALY) into account in making coverage policy, though the experience of imatinib in England also demonstrates that cost is far from the only consideration taken into account in approving technologies for coverage. The purpose of a drug and distributional concerns are also important. The Ontario Drug Quality and Therapeutics Committee requires drug manufacturers to submit information as to a product's cost effectiveness, but seems to base its decisions primarily on considerations of efficacy. Similarly, the Cancer Care Ontario Policy Advisory Committee seems to take cost into consideration in combination with other considerations in making recommendations as to which services to cover.

HOW COVERAGE DETERMINATION WORKS IN PRACTICE: THE CASE-STUDY TECHNOLOGIES

While it is useful to consider how coverage determination institutions and procedures vary from country to country, we can also learn from seeing how they deal with particular technologies in actual practice. The case-study technologies that we chose for this book each highlight different issues raised by the use of technology assessment for coverage policy.

PET scanning illustrates several problems. First, a PET scan is an expensive medical device. Indeed, historically PET scanning has required two medical devices, since the radiopharmaceuticals used for scanning were usually produced on site using a cyclotron. PET scanning thus necessitates a considerable capital investment up front, as well as ongoing expenditures for operations. Though PET scanning can increasingly be made available with a lower capital investment than was formerly required because of mobile scans, modified SPECT scans, and the regional production of radiopharmaceuticals (which obviates the need for an on-site cyclotron), it is still an expensive technology. Second, it is a diagnostic technology. As such, two questions must be asked before coverage can be approved: (a) does it in fact produce accurate (adequately specific and sensitive) diagnostic information; and, (b) is this information of any use in managing the condition diagnosed? If knowing more about a condition makes no difference in the management of a condition, perhaps because there is no known intervention that will alter its course, then it is difficult to justify large public expenditures to acquire the information. Third, like most imaging technologies, PET scanning is not limited to one medical condition. In fact, its use has been proposed for diagnosing a variety of oncological, cardiological, and neurologic conditions. Coverage is not, therefore, a yes or no question, but rather a question of which uses will be covered for what kind of patients under what circumstances. Fourth, as is true with many technologies, PET is one among several alternatives. While PET is not completely fungible with MRI, CT scans, or even conventional x-rays, a technology assessment must consider whether it is more effective than alternative diagnostic approaches for particular conditions, and may consider whether any added value for a particular condition is justified by added cost.

Because PET technology is expensive both to acquire and to operate, and because its advantages over less expensive scanning technologies are not well established, PET has been explicitly evaluated by most countries that conduct technology assessments of medical devices to establish coverage policy. Six countries in our study group – Australia, Canada, Germany, Spain, Switzerland, and the United States – have considered coverage of PET scans under their public insurance system. All cover it in some contexts for some indications, none cover it for all possible indications. Several lessons emerge from our reviews of PET scan coverage.

First, approval of coverage for technologies with multiple uses tends to expand over time. PET has been continually under review since 1994 in Switzerland, with new indications being periodically added, most recently in 2004. PET was approved for five indications in Australia in 2000, with three more added in 2001. PET is currently covered for 12 indications in the US arising out of eight national coverage determinations, with several more under review. While this incremental process results in steady expansion, it also slows coverage expansion while effectiveness research goes forward.

Second, coverage of PET is expanding, even though the evidence does not unequivocally support expansion. The German Federal Committee decided against coverage of PET in ambulatory care when it found that PET was no more effective than existing technologies already covered by social health insurance for five indications. At the same time, the Swiss, Australian, and US agencies expanded coverage, while some Canadian provinces cover it and others do not. Australia has taken an intermediate approach, only funding PET on an interim basis and for limited purposes, citing current lack of sufficient evidence on clinical and cost effectiveness to warrant unrestricted funding. The US Medicare programme initially approved funding for six indications, despite technology assessments that found significant limitations in studies of PET for the indications considered. It then extended coverage to PET scans for monitoring breast cancer tumour response during therapy, despite a HTA and MCAC report concluding that there was insufficient evidence to support coverage for this purpose. Finally, the US Medicare programme decided to extend coverage for some purposes for diagnosing thyroid cancer despite a HTA concluding that studies with respect to the use of PET for thyroid cancer were small and of poor quality.

Third, participants in processes that are available to review expansion have uniformly favoured expansion. All expert statements in the German process – from oncology, cardiology, neurology and nuclear medicine and radiology professional groups – favoured expanded coverage. All of those who testified at the MCAC meeting considering PET for breast cancer diagnosis testified in favour of coverage, including representatives of professional and patient groups, the physician president of a technology company, and a professor of nuclear medicine.

Fourth, availability in research hospitals and in the private sector seems to drive public coverage. In most of our study countries, PET was initially available in research institutions. This availability seems to have raised the question of whether PET scans would then be covered by payment from public insurance programmes for clinical use. This has clearly been the case in Spain. In Canada, on the other hand, availability of PET scans in the private sector presented the question of whether PET was 'medically necessary', and thus should be covered publicly. By contrast, however, extensive availability in Germany in the private sector did not result in a positive coverage decision by the Federal Committee.

Fifth, in federal or sector-specific systems, coverage may be inconsistent. PET may be covered in some Canadian provinces but not in others. In Spain, coverage also varies among autonomous regions. PET is covered in the hospital sector in Germany, which is governed by the Hospital Committee, but not in the ambulatory sector, which is governed by a separate Committee. It might make sense to limit availability of technologies to certain settings, like hospitals, but it is in general hard to believe that a technology may be 'medically necessary' in some parts of a country, but not in others (though if the concept of 'medical necessity' involves an evaluation of cost, it might be understandable that coverage might vary among regions if they vary in wealth and resources). Finally, coverage can be used to drive research and quality control. Several countries – Spain, Australia, Switzerland, and Canada – recognizing the lack of evidence supporting the effectiveness of PET, have covered PET on the condition that ongoing registries be kept of patients who receive PET, tracking issues like therapeutic impact, changes in treatment attributable to PET, measurement of health outcomes, and resource use or cost effectiveness. Thus coverage is used as a tool to encourage evaluation of the technology, which might in turn form the basis for further or more permanent coverage decisions. Switzerland and Australia have also required that PET be provided in facilities that meet accreditation standards, thus using coverage as a lever for influencing quality of care as well.

Our second case study involved hyperbaric oxygen (HBOT) therapy. HBOT was chosen because it is a therapeutic medical device that has been evaluated by all of our countries that have a programme for assessing medical devices for coverage policy. As is true with PET, the advocates of HBOT promote it for multiple uses. On the other hand, the cost implications of HBOT are not as great as those of PET, so it has not received as much attention.

Several lessons seem to emerge from our HBOT case studies. First, in several of our countries, the use of HBOT therapy seems to have come into wide use without explicit evaluation and approval. This was the case in Australia, and, according to an Office of Inspector General's report, seems to have been true in the United States as well. It seems to be more difficult to cut back on existing use of a technology than to hold the line on expansion of new uses, as is demonstrated by the fact that in the 2002–2003 HBOT assessment in the US, CMS did not restrict existing coverage, even though the HTA it commissioned failed to find support for four of the ten indications then covered for HBOT.

Second, again as with PET, coverage tends to expand over time. Switzerland covered HBOT for two indications in 1988, and added another in 1994. Coverage in the US has been expanded several times, most recently in 2003, and now extends to 15 indications.

Third, as was true with PET, scientific evidence supporting coverage for many indications is quite weak, but different countries respond to this fact in different ways. The German ambulatory-care

Federal Committee, after a two year review process, simply refused to cover HBOT for any of the 36 indications for which coverage was considered, citing a lack of medical necessity, effectiveness, or cost effectiveness. The US Medicare programme, on the other hand, currently covers HBOT for 15 indications, though for some it is covered only as an adjunct to conventional therapy or if the disease is refractory to other forms of treatment. The US Medicare programme has recently extended coverage for diabetic wounds, and has continued coverage for ten other wound-care indications despite an HTA questioning scientific support for at least four of these indications. Australia has approved coverage for HBOT for several wound-care situations, recognizing the lack of evidence supporting effectiveness, but also the widespread use of HBOT and the ethical and practical constraints on conducting effectiveness studies. Other considerations influencing the Australian determination included the fact that HBOT is used for life-threatening conditions for which there are limited therapeutic alternatives, and that further limiting indications would threaten the financial viability of HBOT.

Finally, where we have information about involvement of outside parties in the coverage assessment processes it uniformly supported extension of coverage. In the US, requests for expansion of coverage came from provider groups. HCFA met twice with the requester groups during the coverage assessment process, and all responses to a request for public comment were from physicians supporting the requesters. In Australia the MSAC recommendation to continue coverage also came after a meeting with HBOT provider groups.

Imatinib (or Glivec® or Gleevac®) is our primary drug case study. Imatinib represents a technology with promise for treating a rare but life-threatening condition (chronic myeloid leukemia) for which other treatment options are very limited, or for some patients, nonexistent. It has been assessed by four of our study countries, Australia, England, Switzerland, and the Netherlands. All four have approved the use of imatinib under some circumstances despite the fact that evidence supporting the effectiveness of imatinib is as yet quite thin. The three countries, however, have taken quite different approaches.

As was noted above, imatinib was approved by the FDA, EMEA, and the Swiss marketing approval agency in 2001 as an orphan drug for chronic myeloid leukaemia on the basis of phase II open-label, non-randomized trials that showed significant haematologic and cytogenetic response rates to therapy despite the lack of long-term studies showing clear clinical benefit or increased survival. In the following year, marketing approval in Switzerland was extended also for treatment of gastrointestinal stroma tumours (GIST). In Switzerland, reimbursement was approved, and reimbursable indications immediately extended, after marketing approval. The Dutch CFH approved imatinib for list 1b coverage through an unusually rapid approval process, with only one meeting, because of its orphan drug, breakthrough status, and because of the lack of existing therapeutic alternatives.

NICE took a different approach, attempting to evaluate imatinib in terms of cost per QALY. Its evaluation suggested that the cost of imatinib therapy per QALY varied considerably between the chronic, accelerated, and blast phase, with therapy being most cost effective during the accelerated phase. At the preliminary, ACD stage, therefore, NICE proposed recommending imatinib only for the accelerated phase. In the end, however, NICE, considering evidence from CML patient groups and clinical experts, decided to approve for patients in the blast and chronic stage of CML as well, based on evidence of cytogenic and haematological response. Clearly the absence of alternative therapies for a deadly disease influenced NICE in approving therapy, despite its estimates that imatinib therapy could cost up to £64,750 per QALY for treatment in the blast phase.

Finally, the Australian PBAC initially approved imatinib only for the accelerated and blast phase of CML based on high, but acceptable, cost-effectiveness ratios. In 2002 it approved a second application to extend imatinib coverage to the chronic phase, but only if interferon alpha treatment had failed, the patient achieved a major cytogenetic response within 18 months, and the response was maintained as demonstrated by annual testing. In 2003, coverage was extended to imatinib as a first-line treatment, but only for patients between 18 and 70, the group represented in the imatinib clinical trials. Finally in 2003, imatinib coverage was extended to all patients, irrespective of age, and to certain patients with GIST, again with continuing review requirements. A consideration in the extension was that even patients with partial responses may experience quality of life improvements justifying coverage.

Although each country has responded differently to imatinib coverage, each was willing to extend public coverage to imatinib for the treatment of CML based on evidence that only demonstrated hematologic and cytogenetic response, rather than actual long-term increases in survival rates, and despite very high costs per QALY. When a new treatment shows promise for addressing otherwise untreatable life-threatening conditions, cost does not seem to be a determinative factor. On the other hand, the Australian approach of requiring evidence of response to treatment on a continuing basis has great promise as a way of dealing with unproven technologies. Public funding is essentially used to support ongoing clinical evaluation of the technology, leading, it is hoped, to more definitive evidence of effectiveness as time goes on. This is, of course, the approach that several countries mentioned above have taken to PET coverage.

Finally, the NICE experience with zanamivir presents a cautionary tale as to the hazards attending the approval process. NICE first disapproved zamavir for treatment of influenza in 1999 due to the absence of cost-effectiveness information, but reversed itself and approved it the following year. Many believed at the time that the approval was in response to pressure from the drug manufacturer on the government, and pressure exerted in turn by the government on NICE. A further review by NICE of zanamivir in 2002, which reaffirmed approval for zanamivir for influenza epidemics, but limited approval for oseltamivir and rejected approval for amantadine, led to an appeal, that on the whole affirmed the conclusions of NICE, though it remanded the evaluation of oseltamivir for further consideration.

The Dutch CVS reviewed zanamivir also, concluding that there was insufficient evidence to support coverage for influenza B or for high-risk groups. It further concluded that the benefits of zanamivir did not justify its costs when it was used on a symptomatic basis, but that first to establish influenza clinically through serological/virological tests would increase the expense of treatment and delay it. Despite its knowledge of the NICE approval process, the CVS decided not to cover zanamivir. Indeed, the initial NICE decision, disapproving zanamivir, had a strong influence on the Dutch decision. Switzerland also does not cover zanamavir.

The NICE experience demonstrates the obvious: that the coverage process is potentially open to political influence, and that the credibility of assessment organizations can be damaged if political influence is suspected. Comparing the Dutch and English experience illustrates that different countries can reach different judgements as to the cost effectiveness of a drug, even though they start with the same scientific evidence.

LESSONS TO BE LEARNED

When we look for overall lessons that can be drawn from our comparative study of institutions and procedures, and of how they have dealt with specific technologies, several emerge. First, despite widespread fears that technology assessment will lead to rationing, most countries still focus primarily on questions of effectiveness rather than on cost considerations. Only in Australia and England does cost seem to play a major and explicit role in making coverage determinations.[4] Moreover, in England, NICE only has authority to require coverage, its jurisdiction with respect to non-coverage decisions is strictly advisory, thus primary care trusts may be required to cover cost-effective technologies, but are not barred from covering technologies that are not cost-effective. The drug approval process in the Netherlands is moving toward consideration of cost-effectiveness data, but it is not there yet, as the imatinib approval process demonstrates. Coverage evaluation in other countries focuses on effectiveness, or at most, on effectiveness in comparison to existing technologies.

Moreover, coverage assessment organizations seem quite willing to approve coverage for life-threatening, or even serious non-life-threatening, conditions, when there is some evidence of effectiveness of a breakthrough technology and no other technology adequate to treating the condition is otherwise available, as our case studies of imatinib and HBOT demonstrate. The 'rule of rescue' still plays a major role in technology approval. Finally, political considerations independent of science can play a role in coverage processes, as is demonstrated by the Swiss experience with in vitro fertilization.

Second, each of the technologies that were the subjects of our case studies are approved only for limited, specific indications. In some programmes, as in the US, technologies are also explicitly not covered for other specific indications. In other countries, technologies are implicitly not covered for indications for which they are not explicitly covered. However, because technologies are only covered for particular indications, and sometimes when provided in particular settings by particular providers, coverage determination based on HTA, which was supposed to result in macro-rationing, has in fact become micro-rationing. Coverage policy decisions often takes the form of cost-effectiveness guidelines that resemble practice guidelines, rather than up or down determinations of what a public insurer will pay for.[5]

Third, partial coverage tends to expand over time. Technology proponents tend to return with applications for coverage of additional indications, and thus coverage tends to expand to new indications. This is probably an inevitable process, as accumulated experience with a technology may lead to the discovery of new applications or provide additional evidence supporting coverage for applications for which coverage was earlier denied. Overall, however, the process has the effect that denials of coverage are rarely final. Moreover, in several of our countries, coverage expansion can take place de facto, without explicit approval, through doctors prescribing outside of approved indications, or through the use of existing codes to cover new technologies, albeit at a reduced price. In the end coverage assessment often has the effect of delaying rather than ultimately denying coverage.

Fourth, lack of hard scientific evidence does not necessarily block coverage expansion (but different countries reach different results). As to each of the four technologies on which our primary case studies has focused, technology assessments commissioned, conducted, or reviewed by at least some of the coverage assessment organizations either failed to find hard evidence of effectiveness (imatinib), of cost effectiveness (zanamivir), or of effectiveness for some proposed uses (PET and HBOT). Indeed, on the whole, the results of the technology assessments from the various countries were quite consistent. The responses of the coverage assessment organizations, however, were not. In some cases, notably in Germany with respect to ambulatory care and in the Netherlands with respect to zanamivir, lack of proof of effectiveness or cost effectiveness was sufficient to result in a coverage denial. In the US Medicare programme, on the other hand, technologies were in several instances finally approved for coverage despite adverse technology assessments, or even adverse recommendations from the MCAC. In several countries, notably Australia and Spain (with respect to PET), technologies were approved in the absence of hard evidence for coverage with the understanding that assessment would continue post-coverage. The fact that different countries reach different conclusions based on the same evidence suggests, of course, that the process is not wholly driven by scientific evidence, or, at least, that where evidence is open to varying interpretations, different countries place different weight of various aspects of that evidence reflecting different values.

Of course, in each of our countries coverage has also continued for existing technologies despite lack of hard scientific evidence supporting effectiveness. It is always easier to block expansion of coverage to new technologies than to remove existing technologies from coverage, a phenomena referred to by our Canadian authors as the 'stickiness' of coverage.

Fifth, where agency procedures afford opportunity for public participation in the process, participants uniformly press for coverage. Where outsiders are permitted to apply for coverage, applications usually come from technology manufacturers, groups of providers or professionals who offer a new technology in their institutions or practices, or patient groups. When public hearings are held or public comments are solicited regarding technologies under consideration for coverage, these are also the groups that testify and comment. To the extent that processes are transparent, these are the groups that follow the technology approval process, and intervene when necessary. Indeed, in some of our countries, only the technology sponsor will know what a determination concludes, or even that it exists. In others (NICE in England), participants must be invited to participate, and the prime participants (consultees) are usually interested in promoting the product. Interested groups also call upon political representatives to intervene on their behalf where this is possible, and sometimes this intervention is quite effective. Product sponsors also mount major marketing or publicity campaigns for their products prior to consideration by assessment agencies. Examples include Celebrex, certain AIDS drugs, and cancer drugs such as Tamoxifen and Herceptin. This creates public expectation of availability, and creates pressure on agencies for coverage.

It is rare, on the other hand, that pressure is brought directly to bear on assessment agencies opposing coverage of any particular technology. Cost is, of course, a major consideration affecting all public insurance systems, and coverage organizations cannot help but be aware of it. Also, competitors may on occasion show up to contest exclusive coverage of one product to the exclusion of their products, as happened with oseltamivir and amantadine in the zanamivir proceedings in England. There have also been examples of this in Australia, for example naltrexone and acamproate. But except in rare instances, pressure is rarely directed at any particular product.[6] Even managers of social insurance funds, who would seem to have a strong incentive to limit coverage, may under certain circumstances, as in the German case, favour expansion of coverage for certain services if it could provide a means of attracting new members. And the opacity of health care coverage processes in most countries makes it likely that only the most motivated, usually technology proponents, will even attempt to participate. There are situations, however, where pressure might appear in opposition to expansion of coverage. In both Germany and Ontario, for example, access to the coverage determination process is controlled in part by the physicians' union. In both contexts also (though more clearly in Germany), the system is budget limited, and doctors realize that extension of coverage to new procedures might diminish payments for existing technologies. In both Germany and Ontario this structure seems somewhat to limit coverage expansion. There are also situations like those seen in the Dutch pharmaceutical coverage process – where the stakes may be low enough because the market is small, or because the coverage determination is not an all-or-nothing decision – in which technology proponents may have little incentive to get involved, and the decision-maker may be able to go about its task without undue outside pressure.

Sixth, coverage in the private sector or for research coverage tends to drive expansion, as does coverage in some regions of federal systems. High-cost technologies are often acquired by research institutions well before they become standard practice. Once research institutions begin providing these services, however, pressure builds to obtain payment for the services from public programmes. Similarly, when products or services are covered by private insurance, or simply by private payment, public insurers will be pressured to cover the service also.

Seventh, coverage can be made contingent on actual effectiveness. Public insurance programmes are increasingly approving coverage of technologies conditional on the technology actually achieving favourable health outcomes. Payment for imatinib in Australia, for example, is contingent on it actually resulting in a partial response. Coverage of PET in Spain depends on maintenance of treatment registries showing outcomes. Similarly, several recent coverage decisions in the United States have essentially funded ongoing clinical trials to determine whether in fact continued payment is advisable. Thus coverage can be used to drive research, which in turn can support more accurate coverage determinations.

Finally, coverage can also be used as a tool to assure quality review. Payment for PET scans in Switzerland and in Spain is dependent on accreditation. Accreditation standards can, in turn, be designed to make sure that equipment is adequately maintained and calibrated, that staff are adequately trained, or that ancillary services are available as necessary to complement technologies. Coverage review can, therefore, improve quality of care as well as to increase diagnosis and treatment options.

References

1 This means, of course, that these countries do not make coverage determinations for products and services that they do not cover, as, for example, is the case currently with respect to outpatient prescription drugs in the US Medicare programme.

2 Public coverage decision-making processes, however, do not need to be limited to coverage by public programmes. Coverage decisions in the Netherlands define the basic benefits package for both public and private insurers.

3 Except for Catalonia, where the technology assessment agency, the CAHTA, is a non-profit public company.

4 In other countries, such as the United States and Canada, cost may play an implicit role in decision-making, driven by the internal dynamics of the system. Higher priced technologies, for example, may receive more extensive scrutiny.

5 Moreover, in Australia, National Health and Medical Research Council guidelines on writing clinical guidelines include a section on cost effectiveness, blurring the distinction even more.

6 One exception, for example, was Viagra. See R. Klein and H. Strum (2002), 'Viagra: A Success Story for Rationing?' *Health Affairs*, 21(6): 177–87.

11

CONCLUSION

Our eight-nation study began with two hypotheses: 1. nations were using and could use coverage policy based on technology assessment to address the problem of rising health care costs, but 2. their ability to do so through participatory processes would be tempered because participants in those processes would overwhelmingly represent technology advocates. What evidence have we found, then, that addresses these hypotheses, and to what conclusions does this evidence lead us?

All of our nations are using health care technology to set coverage policy for their public insurance programmes in at least some sectors and with respect to some technologies. In none, however, does this seem to have led to rationing in the strictest sense, where cost–benefit or cost-effectiveness ratios are the primary consideration driving coverage policy. Only in one of our countries, Australia, has cost-effectiveness become a major consideration in setting coverage policy, though the Netherlands will soon consider cost effectiveness in its drug coverage approval process, and other countries consider cost implicitly. Even in Australia, Switzerland, and the Netherlands, however, imatinib (Glivac® or Gleevac®) was quite rapidly approved for coverage for chronic myloid leukemia (and in Australia for GIST), despite lack of definitive evidence of its effectiveness, much less cost-effectiveness, based on a 'rule of rescue' principle because there was no other treatment available for some who suffered from the condition. England's NICE evaluates new products in terms of cost per quality adjusted life year, and can advise against adoption of a new technology with too high a cost per QALY, but its advice is only binding on purchasers if it favours coverage, negative evaluations are only advisory. Moreover, NICE also approved Glivac® for indications for which its per QALY cost greatly exceeds NICE guidelines because, again, it was the only treatment available for some CML patients. The purpose of a technology, therefore, is at least as important as its cost effectiveness – a cost-effective drug for treating toenail fungus may not be covered as readily as a less cost-effective drug for treating a fatal and otherwise untreatable condition. The focus of technology assessment in our case-study countries is rather on effectiveness. The primary focus of technology assessment is whether the technology in fact works, or, in some countries, whether it is more effective than existing technologies available to the same patients. For many technologies, including all of our case study technologies, this analysis is indication-specific – the question addressed is whether the technology is effective for certain purposes, and perhaps even under certain conditions. The cost of the technology is generally not a deciding factor in ruling on coverage.

On the other hand, the coverage assessment programmes that we have examined will inevitably have an impact on the cost of health care. First, each of the programmes is in fact designed and intended to screen out ineffective technologies. Coverage of technologies that are only identified as ineffective after years of practice cost us a great deal, as has been illustrated in recent years by the examples of hormone replacement therapy or autologous bone-marrow transplantation for breast cancer. Different systems in fact reach different judgements as to effectiveness. The German Federal Committee has rejected coverage for both HBOT and PET scans in ambulatory care based on HTAs showing that effectiveness was not proven, while the CMS in the US approved both for some indications despite this lack of evidence. Regardless, all coverage determination systems attempt to screen out ineffective technologies, and doing so prospectively could spare health care systems considerable expense.

Second, technology coverage determinations often, as we have already noted, limit payment for new technologies to certain indications, to patients with certain characteristics, and even to certain facilities. They often, that is, function effectively as practice guidelines. There is overwhelming evidence that there is great variation in the use of many medical procedures. Much of this variation is attributable to the fact that physicians vary greatly in their use of high-cost technologies, particularly for chronic conditions and at the end of life.[1] Better focused use of technology is, therefore, likely to save money for health care systems.[2]

Third, coverage assessment agencies do make judgements as to whether technologies are as effective or more effective than existing technologies. This was one reason, for example, why the Dutch did not approve coverage for zanamivir for influenza, or why PET scans have not been approved for indications where CT or MRI are as or more effective in some countries. Public health insurers can obviously conserve their budgets better if they do not have to pay additional money to cover new technologies for indications for which existing, less expensive, technologies are equally effective.

Fourth, technology assessment can be used in tandem with other features of payment systems to help control costs. In the Netherlands, for example, the role of technology assessment is often not to determine whether or not a drug will be covered, but rather whether it will make the 1b list and thus be paid at a higher price. Coverage determinations need not be all or nothing, but can determine whether a technology is sufficiently 'breakthrough' in nature to deserve separate payment, or whether it can be grouped with other technologies and be paid at a lower price.

Finally, the simple fact of delay of coverage during the time that assessment and determination processes are pursued may save public insurers money. Coverage determinations take time, and while they are in process a health care system is not burdened with the cost of the new technology. If, of course, the technology turns out to be less expensive, or significantly more effective than existing technologies, delay may result in a net loss to patients, or even to the public health care programme. But, if it turns out that the technology is not an improvement, not only will the public health insurer be spared the cost of paying for the technology in the interim, it will also be saved from an ineffective technology becoming standard practice before it is thoroughly assessed, as it is always more difficult to withdraw than to withhold coverage.[3] Moreover, the process that our case study countries often seem to follow, approving technologies like PET scans or HBOT on a step-by-step basis as more information regarding effectiveness becomes available, avoids rapid across-the-board adoption of the technology for a wide variety of indications, including indications for which a technology turns out to be ineffective.

Counterbalanced with these cost-saving considerations is the fact that technology assessment can also result in broader use and more rapid dissemination of expensive, but effective, technologies. Again NICE, whose positive recommendations as to medical interventions are binding on primary care trust purchasers, could in fact increase the costs of the total system, or, to the extent the system is budget limited, redirect resources from other parts of the health service to new technologies. To the extent that determinations of coverage bodies are widely publicized, they may encourage rapid adoption of new technologies that would otherwise diffuse slowly, thus driving up health care costs. Of course, to the extent that the new technologies are more effective than existing technologies, patient care will be improved. Indeed, if new technologies are more cost-effective than old, total health care system costs may drop, though public insurers may not be the payers that realize the savings.

On balance, however, it would seem that the use of technology assessment for making coverage determinations has the potential for reducing the growth in health care costs, and, more importantly, for better directing the application of health system resources. It is unlikely, on the other hand, to result in the near term in rationing decisions driven solely, or even primarily, by costs, as it remains focused on questions of effectiveness.

Our second hypothesis was that outside influences on coverage determination processes would be heavily weighted in favour of coverage adoption, and that this would make it difficult for countries to hold the line on coverage of new technologies. Drawing on public choice economics, we predicted that technology manufacturers and sponsors, providers and professionals and their associations, and patient advocacy groups would all put their weight behind technology adoption, while those who pay for public health care programmes – taxpayers, employers, and employees – and those patients or professionals who stand to face service cutbacks in budget-limited programmes if new technologies are covered at the expense of existing services, will rarely have a direct voice in coverage procedures.

We found some evidence to support this hypothesis and little evidence to reject it. In each of our case study countries (except for Germany and Canada for some technologies), technology sponsors – manufactures or providers – can and usually do initiate coverage determinations. In most of the countries technology sponsors provide data supporting coverage with their applications, and in some countries (for example, Switzerland) this data becomes the primary source of information on the basis of which evaluations are conducted. To the extent that proceedings are transparent and participatory, sponsor and provider organizations are overwhelmingly the most frequent participants. The only outside persons to offer public comments or attend hearings in the US Medicare HBOT and PET proceedings were coverage proponents, including manufacturers, provider groups, and patient advocacy groups. In Switzerland, the only persons entitled to information about the otherwise opaque proceedings are coverage sponsors. In systems like the US Medicare system where political pressure is possible, it is usually exercised in favour of coverage determinations. There is a widespread belief that political pressure was also brought to bear on NICE in the zanamivir proceedings described in the UK chapter. Only when competing products simultaneously seek coverage does active opposition to coverage of a product or service become a possibility, though this does not seem to happen often.[4]

On the other hand, the way in which agencies and processes are structured can and does to some extent counterbalance this pressure toward coverage. In Germany, for example, the only entities empowered to initiate coverage proceedings are the sickness funds and the sickness fund doctor's organization, both of whom have incentives under some circumstances to restrict coverage. Technology manufacturers, moreover, are not represented in the organizations represented in the federal councils in Germany. These factors may help explain why Germany does not cover PET or HBOT for ambulatory care, while our other cases study countries do. Similarly, in Ontario the medical association plays a significant role in controlling access to coverage for new medical services, and seems to exert a conservative influence, since any new services must be covered by a fixed budget and there are strong political and legal forces that make it much more difficult to delist existing services as opposed to restricting listing new services. In Australia, on the other hand, the technology assessment agencies are sufficiently independent and free from political influence, both internally and externally, that they can make decisions largely based on the evidence.

It would also seem that less transparent and participatory processes afford fewer openings for technology sponsors to exert pressure toward coverage, and thus are less driven by supporters of technology coverage. The Dutch, German, Swiss, and Australian procedures, for example, offer few toeholds for technology advocates to get involved because they are largely non-participatory and non-transparent. On the other hand, the most transparent and participatory process, the US Medicare system, seems also to be the one that is most open to pressure from technology proponents. Thus, perversely, increasing participation and transparency, two of the key elements of the Daniels and Sabin criteria for evaluating the fairness of coverage processes, may lead simply to more pressure for technology adoption.

Appeals and judicial review proceedings are (almost) inevitably brought by proponents of technologies or, more commonly in some systems, patients denied access to technologies. This may even involve, as in the Canadian situation, indirect judicial challenges where direct appeals are not possible. Even the possibility of judicial challenges, moreover, seems to have had in some countries a deterrent effect on rigorous coverage review. Further, free-trade agreements are now being used to force open doors for technology proponents, as the Australian experience shows, while recent court decisions interpreting the European Charter may afford new opportunities for technology sponsors to challenge coverage decisions by particular Euopean countries.[5] By contrast, we identified no examples of favourable technology coverage determinations being appealed. Thus, again, the Daniels and Sabin criteria of contestability uniformly favours coverage.

On the other hand, the influence of technology advocates seems to be to some extent tempered by the institutional culture of the approving agency. The Australian agencies, for example, seems to be particularly focused on cost effectiveness and well insulated from outside pressure. Correspondingly, Australia seems to be more careful in extending coverage, though in some of our case studies it extended coverage even though cost-effectiveness ratios were quite high (imatinib), or where other countries (Germany) had denied coverage (PET and HBOT). NICE also seems to be increasingly focused on cost per QALY as an assessment criteria, and, though it still approves virtually all technologies that it considers, has limited the use of some technologies. The Netherlands drug approval process also does not seem to be disproportionately affected by technology advocates.

Finally, the larger health care environment within which the approval process functions also undoubtedly influences coverage determinations. In Germany, for example, the Federal Commission that approves coverage for ambulatory services has greater freedom to reject coverage because the technologies it refuses to cover are often available in hospitals, which are governed by a different commission and different presumptions as to coverage. In Canada, technologies not covered in the public sector often remain available in the private sector. It may be easier to resist pressure for coverage when the technology may still be available, just in different places or under different payment conditions.

In sum, the picture seems more complex than the simple model suggested by public choice economics, yet it also seems to be true that economic and political pressure in most instances favours adoption of technology coverage, and that coverage determinations institutions are only partially insulated from this pressure. As noted at the outset, this constant pressure toward approval comes with a cost, both in increasing the cost of the entire system and in the redirection of resources away from existing, low-technology products and services, toward newer, higher-tech procedures. This problem raises, of course, the question of what should be done to respond to this pressure. One approach suggested by our case studies would be to limit transparency, participation, and appeal rights. A moment's thought, however, should lead us to reject this alternative. At its heart, the technology assessment process is an information gathering and analysis process, and transparency and participation can play a vital role in assuring that decisions are made with a maximum of information. Appeal rights are also important when coverage determination bodies make unfair or ill-informed decisions.

There are steps that could be taken, however, to balance out the disproportionate influence of technology advocates on the coverage determination process, and thus to produce better decisions. First, care needs to be taken (as it is in our case study countries) to keep technology sponsors from having a seat at the table when decisions are being made. This means not only that technology sponsors should not be members of decision-making bodies, but also that they should not play a decision-making role on expert bodies that advise final decision-making bodies. This should clearly be true for technology manufactures, but also for providers who will profit directly from providing technologies once they are approved.

Second, care should be taken more broadly to avoid conflicts of interest for decision-making bodies. Persons directly involved in making coverage decisions (including members of expert advisory groups) should not be allowed to receive research grants or consultant contracts from technology sponsors whose technologies they are evaluating. Though we saw no evidence of this happening in our case study countries, such conflicts of interest have become common with respect to health care research, and should not be allowed to develop in this area.[6]

Third, somewhere in the process there needs to be a devil's advocate. Someone needs to counterbalance the overwhelming pressure from technology sponsors toward coverage approval. In the Australian PBAC process, this role is played to some extent by the PES secretariat. In other systems the formal HTA partially fills this role. In each process there should be some participant to make the case against coverage, and this participant should have appeal rights in cases where positive coverage decisions are issued inappropriately. This is important not just to save money for payers, but also to make sure that adequate funds are available for covering all of the other products and services that a public insurance system must cover.

Finally, appellate tribunals and reviewing courts should in general give considerable deference to the expert bodies that make coverage determinations. Review processes, and in particular judicial review, provides a ready weapon that can be used by disappointed technology advocates to pressure determination bodies into doing their bidding. Review of technology coverage decisions is necessary, but should in general be restrained. On the other hand, to the extent that assessment bodies are themselves subject to conflicts of interest, review should be quite searching. Appellate bodies or courts may even need to bring in independent expert evidence to assure accurate review. In combination, these measures could balance out the disproportionate influence that technology advocates play in current decision-making processes.

A final important contribution of our case studies has been to reveal a third characteristic of contemporary health technology coverage determinations not addressed by our initial hypotheses – the potential use of technology assessment to improve our knowledge of technology, to direct the targeting of technology toward situations where it is most effective, and to improve the conditions under which new technologies are applied. Our study revealed that in most instances complex technologies are not approved across the board, but rather only for certain types of patients with certain conditions, and perhaps only for certain treatment settings. In several instances, moreover, treatments were approved only upon the condition of the maintenance of treatment registries and outcome tracking. In some situations, the use of technologies was approved for use only after less expensive technologies have failed, or only conditional on the technology actually making a sustained difference in outcomes. Finally, some technologies have been approved only for use in accredited institutions where certain quality standards are maintained. Thus technology coverage determinations are increasingly being used effectively as practice guidelines, which in turn have the potential to improve the delivery of health care generally. Moreover, public insurance coverage is increasingly being used to fund research in new technologies –

through the conditional or indication-specific coverage approvals – thus improving our knowledge of new technologies, as well as outcomes from their use.

In the end, therefore, our case studies lend cautious support for the use of technology assessment coverage processes in public insurance systems. These processes do offer some potential for controlling the cost of public insurance. This potential is tempered by the fact that these processes will be largely driven and dominated by technology proponents. To the extent that the processes are participatory, transparent, and offer appeal rights, they are probably even more dominated by proponents. On the other hand, if an institution develops an institutional culture oriented also toward protecting the public purse and providing equitable access to existing low-technology products and services as well as innovative high-technology products and services, it can to some extent resist this pressure and produce reasoned decisions. Additional steps can also be taken to further counterbalance this pressure toward coverage. Finally, coverage processes offer an exciting potential to improve the quality of health care generally, a potential that is only beginning to be realized in our case study countries.

References

1 J.E. Wennberg, E.S. Fisher, and J.S. Skinner (2002), 'Geography and the Debate over Medicare Reform', *Health Affairs Web Exclusive*, < content.healthaffairs.org/cgi/reprint/hlthaff.w2.96v1.pdf > (accessed 20 Apr. 2004).

2 Though we must be careful that the transaction costs of controlling the use of technology do not exceed the cost-savings such controls afford.

3 There is, however, the danger that a technology that is not initially covered by a public programme will spread rapidly in the private sector, without guidance or control. If it is later brought within the coverage of public programmes, it may be difficult to control the use of the technology. Standard practice within the private sector may become by default standard practice in the public sector, regardless of its wisdom or evidence base.

4 There is some evidence that it may be happening more often in the US Medicare programme. The NICE proceedings involving zanamivir, oseseltamvir, and amantadine also seem to have involved competitors vying for coverage of their products.

5 ECJ (European Court of Justice), 2000. Case C–157/99. Judgement of 12 July 2001, *Smits and Peerbooms*.

6 See, e.g., J. Bekelman, Y. Li, and C.P. Gross (2003), 'Scope and Impact of Financial Conflicts of Interest in Biomedical Research: A Systematic Review', *Journal of the American Medical Association*, 289: 454–65.

INDEX

Please note. Because this book is a collection of country-specific case studies, most topics, including in particular descriptions of national institutions, their role and procedures, are indexed by country. When topics are treated on an international comparative basis (particularly in the first chapter and last two chapters), they are indexed separately. Specific technologies are also indexed separately, as are criteria used in coverage determination processes.

Related books from Open University Press
Purchase from www.openup.co.uk or order through your
local bookseller

CULTURES FOR PERFORMANCE IN HEALTH CARE

Russell Mannion, Huw T.O. Davies and Martin N. Marshall

- What is organizational culture?
- Do organizational cultures influence the performance of health care organizations?
- Are organizational cultures capable of being managed to beneficial effect?

Recent legislation in the United Kingdom has led to significant reforms within the health care system. Clinical quality, safety and performance have been the focus for improvement alongside systematic changes involving decision-making power being devolved to patients and frontline staff. However, as this book shows, improvements in performance are intrinsically linked to cultural changes within health care settings.

Using theories from a wide range of disciplines including economics, management and organization studies, policy studies and the health sciences, this book sets out definitions of cultures and performance, in particular the specific characteristics that help or hinder performance. Case studies of high and low performing hospital trusts and primary care trusts are used to explore the links between culture and performance. These studies provide examples of strategies to create beneficial, high-performance cultures that may be used by other managers. Moreover, implications for future policies and research are outlined.

Cultures for Performance in Health Care is essential reading for those with an interest in health care management and health policy including students, researchers, policy makers and health care professionals.

Contents

256pp   0 335 21553 X (Paperback)   0 335 21554 8 (Hardback)

THE EUROPEAN PATIENT OF THE FUTURE

Angela Coulter and Helen Magee (Eds.)

Health care is changing fast and patients' experiences and expectations are also changing. Developments in information technology and biotechnology are already having a profound influence on the way health services are delivered and the organization of health care is under reform in most countries. Patients no longer see themselves as passive recipients of care: increasingly they expect to be involved in all decisions that affect them.

This book reports the results of a major study carried out in eight different European countries to look at health policy dilemmas through the eyes of the patient. Drawing on literature reviews, focus groups and a survey of 1,000 people in each of the eight countries, the book addresses the following questions:

- Why might the patients of the future be different?
- What will patients and citizens expect from health systems?
- Will the public be willing to pay more for better health care?
- What kind of value trade-offs are people prepared to make, for example between prompt access and continuity of care, or between choice and equity?
- How will patients access information, advice and treatment?
- How should policy-makers and providers react to patients' desire for greater autonomy?
- How can public confidence in health systems be maintained in the future?

The European Patient of the Future is a clear, jargon-free text which will be a key resource for all health service professionals, health policy analysts and patient advocates.

Contents

224pp   0 335 21187 9 (Paperback)   0 335 21188 7 (Hardback)